PAGAN
Every Day
Finding the Extraordinary in Our Ordinary Lives

PAGAN
Every Day

Finding the Extraordinary in Our Ordinary Lives

. . .

BARBARA ARDINGER, PH.D.

Barbara Ardinger

WEISER BOOKS
San Francisco, CA / Newburyport, MA

First published in 2006 by
Red Wheel/Weiser, LLC
With offices at:
500 Third Street, Suite 230
San Francisco, CA 94107
www.redwheelweiser.com

Grateful acknowledgment is made to the following for permission to publish: Ruth
Barrett for the original chant *Every Woman Born*; Donna Henes for the excerpt from
Streams of Conscience: Chants for peace*chance for peace; Norma Gentile for the translation
of Hildegard of Bingen.

ISBN-10: 1-57863-332-X
ISBN-13: 978-1-57863-332-6

Library of Congress Cataloging-in-Publication Data
Ardinger, Barbara
 Pagan every day : finding the extraordinary in our ordinary lives /
Barbara Ardinger.
 p. cm.
 Includes bibliographical references.
 ISBN 1-57863-332-X (alk. paper)
1. Neopaganism. 2. Spirituality. I. Title.
BP605.N46A73 2006
299'.94--dc22
2006006737

Design by Kristine Brogno
Typeset in Bliss, Pablo and Weiss
Printed in Canada
TCP

10 9 8 7 6 5 4 3 2 1

Dedications

As always, to my son and daughter-in-law, Charles and Phish Ardinger, because of the joy they bring to every single day of my life.

To Denise Dumars, Lori Nyx, and Dan Hooker for keeping my spirits up when things all fell down.

To all my friends whose names I've been listing in my books for over a decade. You've given me support and inspiration and reminded me to keep my feet on the ground. You know who you are.

Finally, to the extraordinarily patient authors whose books I was editing while I wrote and edited my own book. I edited in the morning, wrote in the afternoon, and did my research at night. You know who you are, too. Thanks again for understanding my priorities.

. . . CONTENTS . . .

365+ Pagan Days

> The Pagan resurgence . . . seems to be part of a general process
> of putting humanity, long seen by both the monotheistic religions
> and by secular materialism in abstraction from its surroundings,
> back into a more general context.
> —Prudence Jones and Nigel Pennick, *A History of Pagan Europe*

Yes, we're pagans. We meet a god or a goddess and, like Dorothy in the cyclone, we're lifted out of our humdrum, black-and-white lives, twirled around, and set down in a Technicolor paradise where we have glorious adventures and discover the true meaning of life, the universe, and everything. We're special.

Don't you believe it.

As pagans in the twenty-first century, we may see the world in a horizontal paradigm, whereas the standard-brand religions see it vertically, but we still live in the same world as everybody else. Like everybody else, we have house payments, car payments, and credit-card payments. We work at jobs we maybe don't like so much, we help our kids with their homework, we deal with cranky computers and noisy neighbors.

As our Zen friends say, "Chop wood, carry water. Meet the Buddha. Chop wood, carry water." Just like everybody else, we pagans live ordinary lives.

But think about it—the ordinary can be extraordinary! Because we understand that the sacred—call it Goddess, God, Spirit, or Creator— manifests through us, in us, and *as us*, our ordinary lives are as luminous as the life-giving breath of the Goddess. When we remember who we *really* are and where we *really* live, we know with a heart-thumping certainty that the ordinary is as sacred as anything any sage ever set apart as holy or divine.

Sometimes pagans who live in houses full of altars and attend a ritual every time the moon hits a new phase still need to be reminded to pay attention to the fact that every day of the year (plus the extra day that gives us "a year and a day") is ordinary and luminous at the same time. This is a "remindery" book to help us remain aware of that fact.

Reader, you can read this book in any order. You can march straight through the year from January 1 to December 31 and follow every suggestion. You can open it at random every morning and find a possible augury. You can start at the end of December and work backwards if you want to.

Because our lives get so jammed up with family and work and rituals and sabbats and crafts and e-mail and spam and the Eyewitless News and . . . and . . . and . . . it's useful to have just one page to read in the morning. Maybe one page is all you have time for. Maybe, having read one page, you'll have something to think about, off and on, during the day. You can read a page at lunch and write your thoughts about it in your journal. You can read the page at night and have something to dream about. You can even read a page or two when you're planning a ritual and perhaps find an idea for an invocation or meditation.

HOW THIS BOOK IS ORGANIZED

When I was asked to write this book, my first thought was, "Three hundred and sixty-six separate essays? Good grief! How will I ever find so many topics and come up with so many ideas?"

As you probably do, I work best with deadlines, even if I have to set them myself. So I set milestones for myself. Buy some lined paper. Write down ideas as they come. Get on the Web, do some Googling, and find out who celebrates what and when. I looked at my own bookshelves and found books of days when gods, goddesses, festivals, and feasts are celebrated. I filled in as many days as I could. I promised myself that on Sunday I would start committing this puppy to paper (well, to electronics).

After a little while, I said to myself, "Three hundred and sixty-six pages isn't really that much."

One of my early decisions was not to divide the year by the usual sabbats. My intention is to stretch our minds and find fresh things—like historical contexts and what the words we use all the time *really* mean—for us to think about. I want to give pagans new things to do.

Next I decided that I wanted to acknowledge the work of other pagans, especially organizations, temples, magazines, and Web sites. So I sent e-mails to priestesses, priests, editors, Web crafters, and others. I asked when they founded their organization, purchased their land, or went online. I sent e-mails to people I know well, to people I know slightly, to people I met twenty years ago, to people whose reputations I know, to people with whom I have mutual friends, to people on lists I found out about, to perfect strangers whose Web sites I Googled to. I asked questions about gods, goddesses, magazines, Web sites, temples, festivals, moveable feasts, traditions, and dates (or best guesses).

Like Blanche DuBois, I depended on the kindness of strangers. Kind people answered my questions and helped me straighten out my year. They are in no way responsible, however, for how I used their information.

I put the moveable and lunar feasts on the closest appropriate dates in our Western calendar. But even after I'd filled in the festivals of classical Greece and Rome, the moveable feasts, saints' days that are germane to pagans, significant days in other religions, and the founding dates of our magazines and temples, there were still blank days.

That's when it occurred to me to give each month a general topic. If it's not a designated holy day, I said to myself, then I can write about something I think other pagans might want to know. Some topics logically follow from the preceding months (as when I came to the four elements), whereas others just sleeted through my imagination. Here's how it came out:

- January — Home and community
- February — Light and darkness
- March — Women and (I gotta admit it) feminism
- April — *Veriditas*
- May — Gardening
- June — Animals and birds
- July — Water
- August — Fire
- September — Earth
- October — Air
- November — Silence
- December — Divination

I also wanted to note the progress of the sun signs through the year. Because I'm not an astrologer, I asked my friend, Lilith Mageborn, a professional astrologer for thirty years, to tell me how she interprets each sun sign. She is not, however, responsible for any metamorphosis of her information as it passed through my imagination. There are numerous books of complete astrological information; this isn't one of them. Please note that sometimes I found a festival or other event on the day a sun sign opens, so I put off describing the sign for a day or two. This is why one month can say "Sun *enters* Aries" and other times it's "Sun *in* Capricorn."

Having generally arranged the book, I considered the individual pages—the "dailies," which constitute the "juice" of the day. Most books use the term "meditations"; I say "conversations," because as I write, I'm talking not only to myself but also to you.

Reader, I want this to be an interactive book. I want you to talk back. Talk out loud. Talk to your friends. Write notes in the margins. Send me an e-mail. The purpose of the daily conversations in this book is to engage you, to elicit reactions from you, to make you look at your ordinary life with fresh eyes.

Sometimes you'll already know about a god or goddess, though I hope to present some fresh information (like differences between Greek and Roman pantheons). Sometimes you'll learn what I learned (the lessons of history or the history of agriculture or the Crusades).

Sometimes you'll probably think I'm nuts. Miss Piggy and Barbie as goddesses? *Dirty Dancing* as a spiritual experience? Please just keep reading. And consider this: *the spiritual is embedded and embodied in the material*. Spirit turns up in unexpected places, even on *The Muppet Show*.

• • •

Also note that if I mention a book or an artist, an author or a Web site, you can find more information on it in the lists of sources at the end of the book. Visit these books and sites and find out what people are doing.

And if I suggest an activity, a meditation, or a ritual, why not give it a try?

• • •

Each day we live upon the earth can be a blessing. Every day, we can do something to help our mother planet. We can give something we were about to throw away to someone who doesn't have one and might want it. We can keep in mind the irrefutable fact that we are all descended from the same "mitochondrial Eve." This means we're all related. Regardless of skin color, there are no "races." The only race is the *human race*. That's *us*. Every day, we can be mindful of our kin, the four-footed, feathered, finny, leafy, and crystalline children of Gaia.

Every day is new. We can mull over a fresh idea or a new way of look-ing at something (a god's biography, a familiar pagan festival) we think we know all about. We can get in touch with people who share our philoso-phy. We can seek the spiritual and find it where we're not even looking.

Every day, when we are kind to just one person, when we express our gratitude for just one small thing in our lives, we are adding to the collec-tive consciousness of the planet. We can celebrate every ordinary day by being aware that, as Dame Julian of Norwich said, "All will be well, and all will be well, and all manner of things will be well."

Starting a New Year Together

Usually, we invoke Janus on this first day of the year. He was the Roman two-faced god of the doorway (*ianus*), the transition point between the safe indoors and the outside world, where anything could happen. Romans weren't alone in believing that this opening needed to be protected. The *mezuzah*, which holds verses from Deuteronomy, is affixed to doors of Jewish houses. The façade around the doorway of a medieval cathedral is as elaborate the altar inside, and nearly every pagan is taught to cut a "doorway" in the energy of a circle. As the doorway stands between inside and outside, so does the turning year stand between an old year and a new year we don't yet know.

Janus gave his name to January, and the Romans honored him all month. Before he came to the city, however, he was Dianus, an Italian oak god whose consort was the woodland goddess Diana. Let's honor Janus, then, and let him be.

Let's turn to Cardea, the Roman goddess who represents the hinges on the door. As the hinge goddess, Cardea supervises our comings and goings. Every time we go through that door, there she is, the hinge of our busy life. Sometimes she squeaks. Sometimes she sticks. Could these be auguries? Almost always, Cardea permits us to move at will. She knows that we will be coming home again.

Reader, in your mind's eye see Cardea at your door. Expand your vision and see her balancing on the hinges of your life. Where will you go this year? She'll be with you.

Just so we have it by heart, let us repeat with Dame Julian of Norwich, "All will be well, and all will be well, and all manner of things will be well."

New Year's Resolutions, Inanna

Oh, dreadful, dreadful thought! How long will I be able to stick to my new year's resolutions? Will I do better than I did last year? Probably not.

The problem with most resolutions is that they're too grandiose. They require too much sturdy resolve. When I worked as a secretary for five psychologists, I learned a handy phrase: "impoverishment of behavioral response repertoire." That means that when we're faced with a huge, impossible task, it's easier to keep doing what we have been doing.

But I also learned that we can make minimal changes. We can take baby steps. We can try one new thing instead of a dozen.

Reader, today's a good day to commit yourself to one small change. Think about one thing you can do this year and write it down.

I'm not talking about a major life change, but something as modest as reconciling your checkbook as soon as you receive your bank statement, washing dishes every day instead of letting them pile up, or scooping out the cat box every night. Some small positive thing that will make your life better. Promise yourself you can do this.

Today is Inanna's birthday. When this Sumerian goddess-queen decided to visit her sister, Ereshkigal, in the underworld, she had to give up a piece of her royal regalia at each of the seven doors on the way. We're not going into the underworld; we're moving into a new year. In addition to making one resolution, how about also giving up one small thing, the giving up of which will improve your life this year? Give up the morning doughnut at work. Give up gossiping (too much) about your friends. Give up talking on your cell phone while you're driving or walking down the street. Write down what you promise to give up to make your year better.

Home

My friend Beth Johnson, a Unitarian Universalist minister and witch, once preached a sermon on "home." She said that when she first moved to California, she'd say, "I'm going *home* to Chicago." Before getting on the plane to return to California, she'd say, "I'm going *back there*." Home, she explained, was "where they knew me when."

I started out in a blue-collar, Republican, Calvinist family in the village of Dellwood, five miles north of St. Louis. Five miles was a long distance in the 1940s, and Dellwood was rural. Remember those sentimental old movies about small-town life in which Hollywood producers like Louis B. Mayer invented our so-called traditional family values? That's where I started.

I was the first girl in my family to go to college, the only one to earn advanced degrees, the first to get divorced, the first to move out of state. I'm the only pagan in my family. I wouldn't move back to Dellwood if you paid me. That's *back there*.

Reader, where's your *back there*? Where did you start from? Who "knew you when"? How far away—in miles, in time, in emotional space—are you now from *back there*? I changed when I left Dellwood and went to college. What first changed you? Do you ever go *back there*? How do the people there react to you now? When you "came out" as a pagan, what did they say *back there*?

If your *back there* and your *home here and now* are as divergent as mine are, how do we reconcile the differences and still keep the love of our families? Think about your family today. In what ways are you still their baby? In what ways are you an autonomous adult? What part of *back there* will you always carry with you, no matter where you go?

Hestia

As Roman historian Diodorus Siculus tells us, the goddess of the hearth protects all who come to her for tutelage, at home or in public places. The Greeks considered her iconic fire to be so sacred that if it went out, it could only be rekindled with a sanctified fire wheel. One of the Homeric hymns tells us that Hestia, alone of all the Olympians, never took part in wars. For this, even Zeus paid her the greatest honor and reverence.

Hestia is primarily a domestic goddess, the spirit of the hearth before which the head of the household made regular ritual offerings. She's the goddess of the ritual meal, the best part of which goes to her. We see an echo of this custom when we save a bite of our ritual "cakes and ale" to return to the Goddess.

If you have a figure of Hestia, it's probably not her. Her only true image was glowing charcoal covered by white ashes, which was how Greek housekeepers kept the hearthfire overnight. Unlike Vesta, her Roman counterpart, Hestia never appeared in human form. In later days, she was represented by a flame.

The popular World War I song, "Keep the Home Fires Burning," wasn't about Hestia, but its sentiment captures the idea of the goddess. She is everything homely we fight to protect. She's the one we come home to every night. Home protects us; Hestia protects our home.

Reader, how do you honor Hestia? One way to do so is to light a white candle and set it near the center of your home. Invoke the goddess, give thanks that you *have a home*, and ask for her blessing. Another way to honor her is to clean house. Not just the fireplace (if you have one), but the whole house.

Home as Process

Moving into a house or apartment does not automatically render us "at home." We need to build our home, not with boards and bricks but with intention.

When I move into a new place, even before I unpack the kitchen, I have to hang my walls. My art collection—mostly original pieces, but not by anyone famous—does more than hide the landlord's white paint. It adds personality to my space. My familiar paintings and photographs are old friends in a new neighborhood.

The next thing I do—I'm still not cooking—is to mount my floor-to-ceiling bookshelves and unpack my books. Sometimes I alphabetize them. Then I change my mind and experiment with topical shelving. Next (still not cooking), I get out my collections of witches and goddesses. I'll place "the girls," stare at them, and then move one an inch or across the room. But I swear that as soon as I've got them properly arranged, *they move.* When I count them, I never get the same number twice. When I'm making my house a home, the word *obsessive* is inadequate to describe my process.

Just as we grow in our relationships, so do we grow our house into a home. We're inhabiting our home, creating sanctuary, establishing headquarters, setting up a covenstead. And home is never finished. By bringing in new goodies or recycling old stuff, we're creating good vibes.

Reader, what were your priorities when you moved into your home? There is often one thing that, when you take it out of the box or bring it home from the store, shows you that you're home. What is that thing for you?

Freya and Elvis

The Saxons of northern Europe called the first Monday after January 6 Plough Day and on that day honored Freya, "the Venus of the North." As a goddess who engages in indiscriminate sex, Freya is the spirit of the earth's fertility. Like Persephone, she is in the underworld during the winter, but early in January we already see hints that she might be rising. We'll soon set our ploughs into the earth and plant our crops.

In cold climates, Earth's wilder children are said to be sleeping through the winter. What everything looks like is *dead*. Trees and plants are bare, the sky is gray. Some wild animals are hibernating; those that aren't have to break through the snow and ice to find wisps of food to eat, or they'll die. January can be a hard month.

Freya is the leader of the Valkyries, warrior maidens who gather fallen heroes and carry them to Valhalla. Persephone is queen of the dead. Honor Freya and Persephone. Make love to someone you love. Have a feast. But don't be greedy. If you live where there are birds or squirrels or other critters, set something out for them, too. Take a winter nap and ponder how similar sleep and death are.

Reader, have you ever had a near-death experience? I once had an asthma attack that lasted all day (I was too busy to slow down and just kind of hoped it would go away) until two friends took me to the emergency room. I remember seeing the glass doors of the ER. The next thing I remember is floating around the ceiling and watching the hands of the clock moving very, very slowly. I'm told I was "gone" for twenty minutes.

Today is Elvis Presley's birthday—is the King up and singing again?

The Year's First Sabbath

Sabbath is a loaded word. What does it signify to you? A day of enforced worship and endless sermons? Suffering through Sunday school? Borrrring. All that awful stuff we abandoned when we became pagans!

Whoa, there, Reader. Slow down. The sabbath is the seventh day of the week. The word is the end of a trail of Middle English, Old English, Old French, Latin, Greek, and Hebrew words that all, basically, mean "rest." What can be wrong with a little rest?

The Jewish *Shabbat* is the period from twilight on Friday to Saturday evening. The state of rest we strive to achieve during this time is called *menuhah*. It's not simply not working, however; it's refraining from *melakhah*, which *The Jewish Catalog* defines as the work needed to build a sanctuary in the wilderness. Thirty-nine acts of work are forbidden on the sabbath, including writing and erasing. The idea of keeping the sabbath is to stop struggling to survive and to rest instead.

We live in an overworked world. We're on call "24/7." The companies where we work are forever downsizing, outsourcing, or committing reductions in force (RIFs). Our jobs are always in peril. If we survive the latest RIF, we end up doing the jobs of five RIF'd people. Because we're afraid we'll be fired if we don't work the required (but often unpaid) overtime, we work harder for less. If we're self-employed, we know that if we're not up and at 'em every day, someone else will be. We're exhausted.

Let us keep the sabbath. Take a day of rest. Turn off your beeper, hide your cell phone, close your laptop. Read a novel. Take a nap. You've earned it.

The Spirit of Our Home

We know two dozen goddesses and half a dozen gods of the home. More familiar from folklore and fairy tales are the humbler home spirits— brownies, elves, nixies, and others.

Every Roman house had *lares* and *penates*, which came in pairs and had neither names nor personalities. Originally, the *lares* were enshrined in border stones, but in the first century B.C.E., they moved indoors. Each family had a *lar familaris*, which was kept in a niche by the hearth and watched over the house. Is this where the witch's *familiar* comes from? One historian says that little figures of Jesus and saints are a continuation of this Roman custom. Other indoor spirits, the *penates*, ruled the household's cupboard, *penus*, and contributed to the family's survival.

Reader, who lives in your house? Ask your animal companions or watch to see if they're carrying on silent conversations with invisible beings under the stove. If you're not psychic, ask a friend who is to come and look. If you keep missing spoons, crystals, or earrings, you may be hosting a greedy fairy. If you want its blessing, count the lost items as gifts.

To talk with your spirit, light a fat red candle and sit as close as possible in the center of your home. Close your eyes and take several deep, easy breaths. Visualize two chairs facing each other. Sit in one chair and invite the spirit of your home to sit in the other. When the spirit appears, greet it with great courtesy. Ask its name and what kind of being it is. Ask how you can make it more comfortable. Ask if there are any dangers in the house. (Our house spirits notice things like frayed wires and leaking pipes. Sometimes they know why our houseplants are drooping and pindling.) Finally, ask your house spirit for advice and blessing.

Sacred Home

In earlier days, farmers often hauled stones from ancient circles and built their houses with them. What might it be like to live in a house built of materials that were once part of a sacred circle? What might it feel like to be surrounded by hijacked holiness?

Would we be able to feel the original vibrations of the stones? Would we feel their contentment to live placidly as the bones of Mother Earth? Would we feel the communal life of these constituent parts of the landscape? Would we feel the reverence paid to these stones, which they've absorbed over thousands of years of worship? Or would we feel their outrage at being plundered from a sacred site?

Perhaps—because they are longer-lived than we are—stones are more philosophical. Perhaps they understand that change is a natural part of life.

Reader, consider the construction of your home. When was it built and from what materials?

Many buildings today are framed with wood and rebar, and others have elements of concrete, stucco, or bricks. See if you can find a real, live stone—perhaps a cornerstone—somewhere your building. Is there a real cornerstone? If you can find a stone, and if you're feeling psychic, see what you can learn from it. If this doesn't work, you can bring stones to your building. I like the tumbled river pebbles we can buy at building supply stores. Depending on your neighborhood, you can arrange some pebbles on your doorstep, set some in a tray and put a potted plant on them, or even put some in an iron cauldron and use it as a doorstop.

This January day, set your imagination along a stony path. What do the stones from the old circles say to you in your meditation or your dreams?

Temples, Chapels, Altars, Shrines, and Tchotchkes

For her book *Holy Personal*, Laura Chester traveled across the United States and found "small private places of worship" that people have built, including Greek Orthodox and Roman Catholic chapels and shrines, a chapel in a garage, and a "flaming stupa." The only Goddess altar she describes is in San Francisco.

I think it's safe to say that every pagan lives in something like a temple. We collect gods and goddesses and divine tchotchkes. We are so fond of our "stuff" that I once found a shopping goddess and named her Tante Tchotchke. Pagans go to flea markets and yard sales with her.

Though we tend to use the words *altar* and *shrine* interchangeably, strictly speaking, they're different. An altar is a place where we do our magical work. The word comes from Latin and originally meant a high place closer to the gods. We reconstruct or redecorate our altar for rituals and spellwork. A shrine is permanent. The word comes from Old English, *scrín*, and Latin, *scrinium*, which means a chest for books or papers.

For example, I have an *altar* to Fortuna. I invoke her and ask her to turn her wheel for my friends and me. I have several working charms on the altar. I have a *shrine* to Lakshmi and chocolate—to me, they're luxury and wealth. It's full of as many kinds of chocolate as I can find, plus magical red, gold, and silver things (Chinese New Year envelopes, red ribbons, bells, a cinnabar pen). I also have two Tara shrines; the Green Tara shrine is filled with photos of family and friends, the White Tara shrine holds other mementoes.

Reader, do you live in a temple? Which are your shrines and which are your altars? Where do you do your best magical work? What is holy and wholly precious to you?

Housecleaning

Feng shui is today's popular decorating trend. We use the principles of feng shui to encourage the flow of *chi* (beneficial life energy) in our homes and discourage the flow of harmful *sha*, but Reader, do you know what the most important feng shui principle is? It's not hanging bamboo flutes in your hallway and romantic paintings in your bedroom. It's not installing goldfish or octagonal mirrors.

The most important principle is *cleaning your house*. Getting rid of the clutter. Getting the boxes out from under your bed. Neatening up your collections. Dusting more often. Changing your vacuum cleaner bag and sweeping up the pet hair. Straightening up those piles of paper, throwing away the useless stuff, filing the good stuff. Giving the books you aren't reading to Goodwill. Holding a yard sale and letting your friends recycle your extra candle holders, tambourines, ribbons, beads, and those little oddiments you keep saving.

In my house, I have little witches everywhere. They're on tables and on shelves above my bed (when I look up at night, I see feet). When a feng shui practitioner came, she just shook her head. Then she looked again. "I can feel the energy," she said. "It's really good."

Reader, I'm trying to imagine what pagan feng shui might be. The feng shui *bagua* map sets forth seven areas around the center of a house and each room: knowledge and self-cultivation, family, prosperity, reputation, love and marriage, creativity and children, helpful people, and career. Find a good feng shui book or Web site and see where the areas are in your home. Look at your collection of gods and goddesses. Who goes where?

You don't have to wait to start your spring cleaning. When your home is clean and the chi is flowing nicely, you'll know where to redistribute your shrines and altars and deities.

St. Distaff

We have two spinning words that describe women. *Spinster* wasn't originally an unmarried woman, but one who did the family's spinning. *Distaff*
describes the female side of the family, the women's domain. But in the
ecclesiastical calendar of apocryphal saints or Christianized gods and goddesses, there's no St. Distaff. This day is named for the women's spinning
tool that holds the flax, tow, or wool being spun. In England and northern
Europe, women went back to their spinning on St. Distaff's Day after Yule
and/or Christmas celebrations.

Women's work made this day sacred to Frigg, wife and sister to Odin.
There are numerous similarities, including a story about a famous necklace
and sex with dwarves, between Frigg and Freya. Frigg is a domestic goddess of womanhood. Her mother is the earth goddess, Fyorgyn; her sisters
include Saga and Fulla. Like Hera and Juno, Frigg is the protector of marriage. She is sometimes shown nude, riding her distaff, which makes her
look like a witch riding a broomstick.

Reader, what is "women's work"? Cooking and housekeeping? Then
why are so many great chefs male? Childcare? Teaching in elementary
schools? Nursing? Then why do the salaries in these professions rise when
men enter them? Modern women are doing "men's work" in construction
and heavy industry. Think again about gender labels and who can do
what work.

I have friends who do magical spinning and weaving. One friend,
Tom, sits in meetings and knits. I'm sure his peaceful knitting energy pre-
vents arguments. He once brought his spinning wheel to a ritual to spin
thread that he later used to create something useful for the group. During
another meeting of a group that was horrifically divisive, a woman brought
her drop spindle and stood in the corner and spun amity into the group.

Leaving Home, Midvintersblót

Like life itself, our individual lives move in cycles. We leave our mother's womb and emerge into a larger world. We leave our family circle for school. We leave childhood to go to college or work. We leave our earthly lives and enter the universe.

Sometimes when we leave, it's voluntary. Like the nautilus, we move into a new chamber because we've grown too big for the old one. Sometimes we have to be kicked out of the nest. Reader, when you've moved, what has motivated you?

Do you remember Beth's sermon from January 3? It took only a couple of years before she was telling her family in Chicago she was going "back home" to California. She left her childhood home to return to her adult home, where her friends who make up her chosen family live.

I think "leaving home" means we're outward bound. We're facing a new stage of life. We've outgrown our old home, our "in here." We don't fit anymore—our philosophy or thealogy has changed, our lifestyle has become incompatible with the old ways. The egg has cracked. It's time to see what's "out there."

Heraclitus wrote that we can't step into the same river twice—it's an ever-flowing, continuously new river. Thomas Wolfe wrote, "You can't go home again." We leave home. We go "back there" to visit. But nothing is the same now as it was then.

In the Norse calendar, today is Midvintersblót, when offerings were made to Tiw (also called Tyr, Ziu, and Tiuz), who was a law-giving god who became a war god identified with Mars. Tyr's rune looks like a sword or upward-pointing arrow. Another of his Germanic names is Thing, which refers to councils and meetings. If we're outward bound, let's set out not to war but in peace.

Carmentalia, Juturnalia

The Carmentalia is a five-day festival honoring the Roman goddess Carmenta, also called Car, Carya, or Car the Wise. To the Greeks, Carmenta was Metis, the Titaness whose name means "Prudent Counsel." Metis was the first wife of Zeus and mother of Athena.

The Roman Carmenta was the mother of Evander, who appears in the *Aeneid* as the king of the Arcadians. He lived in Latium in central Italy, where Rome would be founded. Evander displayed great hospitality to Aeneas, one of the legendary founders of the city. When Carmenta first arrived in Latium, she climbed to the top of the Capitoline Hill and began prophesying. After she invented the fifteen-letter Latin alphabet, the earliest Latins made her a deity. The Romans erected a temple to her, the right arch of which came to be called the *porta scelerata*, or "portal of guilt." This was because during one of the Roman Republic's numerous civil wars a large army passed under the arch and was slaughtered on the battlefield.

Another festival celebrated by the Romans on this day is the Juturnalia. Juturna (or Diuturna) was a wife of Janus and the goddess of fountains, rivers, and still waters. She was venerated by the Fontani, the artisans who designed the famous Roman aqueducts, some of which are still standing more than two thousand years after they were built.

The Romans invented concrete and used it to build their city on the seven hills. In addition to the Coliseum and the aquaducts, other famous concrete structures are the Circus Maximus, where chariot races were held; Trajan's Forum, a marketplace with food courts on five levels (our malls are nothing new); the Roman road system, which took the armies and merchants across the continent; and Caracalla's Baths, which used two million gallons of water heated in hypocausts.

...JANUARY 15...
The Neighborhood

The minute we step outside our door we face our local community. Who are our neighbors? *The American Heritage Dictionary* gives the expected definition of *neighbor*—"one who lives near or next to another"—and its etymology. It comes from the Old English (before 1066 C.E.) *neahgebur*, which comes from *neah*, "near," and *gebur*, "dweller." These two words arose from Indo-European roots. What does this tell us? That people have been neighbors for thousands of years.

Reader, do you know your neighbors? Do you ever actually stop and talk to them, or is everyone too busy commuting? If you live in the city as I do, do you know the other people in your apartment building?

Given today's conservative political climate, how out as a pagan are you in your neighborhood? I have attended open rituals in a dozen cities in people's back yards. Without exception, these back yards were highly protected by tall wooden palisades or thick bougainvillea. The idea was that the neighbors should not be able to see what was going on, although I suspect they could certainly hear the drumming. And they'd no doubt watched us drive up and walk to the front door in our ritual garb with our athames and potluck dishes. I can just imagine what they thought. *There go those crazy people again. What on earth are they doing over there?*

In one ritual, our intention was to do magic to make changes in our lives. I can still hear the words of one woman as she stood before the fire and sprinkled her handful of incense on it: "Let the day come when we can do our rituals in our *front* yard." So mote it be!

Make today the day you meet your neighbors. Say hello to them. Keep saying hello until they recognize you and say hello back.

Concordia, Neighborhood Magic

When sociologist Jane Jacobs wrote *The Death and Life of Great American Cities* in 1960, city planners like New York's Robert Moses were destroying old neighborhoods by declaring them slums, using eminent domain to seize them, and building freeways where homes had stood for a hundred years. Six lanes of speeding traffic separated families who had been neighbors for generations.

What is the lesson here for pagans? Some of us might exclaim, "Get outta there! Cities are evil. Buy a farm!"

But, Reader, is this a realistic option? Most of us live, work, and circle in metropolitan areas. How would our lives change if we moved to the country? How many of us have day jobs that let us telecommute?

The Romans honored Concordia, a goddess of civic and communal harmony, on several days of the year. We can honor her and do some practical good at the same time. We can do magic. First, find out what your neighborhood needs. It might be something as basic as picking up the trash on the sidewalks or it might be something more complex, like safer schools. We can't solve all problems, but we can make our intention the survival and prosperity of our neighborhood.

Here's a modest example. One tenant in my building began playing loud hip-hop radio at 1 A.M. and not answering the door when the police knocked. I did a binding spell to turn off that radio. Remembering that we also need to work on the mundane level, I complained to the landlord, too.

Let's do neighborhood magic and work to protect our neighbors. Gather your circle or coven and create magical space. Speak your intention, build your cone to hover over your neighborhood, and, as James Taylor sang, "shower the people with love."

Pagan Feasts and Festivals

The Architectural Engineering Graduate Students Association (AEGSA) at Pennsylvania State University has created a spectacular Web site dedicated to all things Roman. The Roman calendar part of the site explains the system of *calends* (the first day of the month), *nones* (the fifth or seventh day), and *ides* (usually the fifteenth day). The days weren't numbered but identified by a series of letters and names that identified the day for purposes of religious observance or legal business.

AEGSA's entry for January 17 has two Roman illustrations and includes the following information:

> This day was set aside to honor Felicitas, the goddess who personified Good Fortune, happiness, or felicity. One temple in Rome was dedicated to this goddess . . . . On this day in 395 A.D. the emperor Theodosius died and left the empire to his two sons . . . . The Romans had numerous temples to Janus. Whenever war was declared, the chief magistrate would lead a ceremony in which the doors of the main temple of Janus were opened. In time of peace they were normally shut.

Our pagan ancestors had numerous feast and festival days to honor gods and goddesses. The custom carried over into medieval Christianity with its numerous saints' days and liturgical holidays, many of which were adaptations of the old pagan holidays. The peasants and townspeople couldn't abandon their fields and shops for every holiday, but the calendars were full of holidays so people got lots of days off.

In our secular American culture, what festivals do we have? These are maybe six civic holidays a year, most of which create three-day weekends. If someone who works for a large corporation wants to take a personal day (to, say, celebrate a sabbat), that day is usually taken off without pay.

Theogamia of Hera, Paradise in the Neighborhood

In Greece, the Theogamia of Hera, or Gamelia, celebrated the sacred marriage of Hera, whose name means "Lady," to Zeus. The oldest story of their wedding says that it took place in the Garden of the Hesperides on the rim of the western ocean, where Gaia had planted a tree of life bearing golden apples.

I once had a friend who loved to garden more than anything else in the world. Every time I'd visit her, she'd be knee-deep in lavender, or fennel, or something else that smelled good. When she used up all the land around her house, she claimed a strip of the city's community garden, where she grew melons, sweet peas, and five kinds of lavender. She established her own paradise. Another friend had a small front yard. In one corner grew a Mexican sage so big that all of her friends got bouquets of purple flowers. In another corner, she piled rocks and grew succulents. Another paradise. People walking by always stopped to admire her plantings. They often got sage bouquets.

Where I live, in southern California, we have a Mediterranean climate, so even in January I see urban gardens. There are geraniums and petunias in front of one building. Rosemary lines the front of another. One morning, a man was trimming it, and the scent followed me down the block. Along Lime Street, someone has planted a garden between the sidewalk and the street. There are red and yellow roses, scarlet bougainvillea, orange impatiens, a bright green creeping charlie, blue hydrangeas, white callas, and heavenly bamboo, plus other plants I don't recognize.

We make our gardens grow with our labor and devotion. We're rewarded with flowers and heavenly scents.

Homelessness

We realize that homelessness is an enormous social problem and wish we could help people who have to sleep in doorways and depend on charity to eat. Let's support worthy organizations. Let's also bring the topic down to a personal level.

In 1998, when the people who owned the condo I was renting let it go into foreclosure and a bank bought it, I was evicted. I'd had time to plan ahead, but couldn't find a place I liked that would take two cats, so I put everything I owned into storage. I ended up sleeping for a week in a friend's spare bedroom. Then I spent a month in a shabby transient hotel. Besides the two cats, I had five shopping bags to hold some clothes and my washcloth, towel, soap, and shampoo. I was luckier than most homeless people because I had a good job and a good car. I persisted in apartment-hunting during this awful period, and the Goddess led me to a new home.

My son worked in telemarketing after he graduated from high school; when I asked why, he replied, "Well, it's better than sleeping outdoors." I can't think of much that's worse than being homeless.

With my own ears, I once heard a homeowner—a woman whose house had a dozen bedrooms and bathrooms—say that homeless people clutter up our cities and should be put away where people can't see them. She was complaining about people who carried all their earthly goods in a shopping cart or five shopping bags.

Reader, look at your earthly goods. Pagans are collectors—books, candles, altar accessories, jewelry. Imagine that you've just lost your home. All you can have is five shopping bags. What would you put in those bags?

The Eve of St. Agnes

> St. Agnes' Eve—Ah, bitter chill it was!
> The owl, for all its feathers, was a-cold.
> The hare limp'd trembling through the frozen grass,
> And silent was the flock in woolly fold.
> —John Keats, *The Eve of St. Agnes*

Like his fellow Romantic poets of the early nineteenth century, Keats was attracted to tales set in a faux Middle Age. Romantic poetry is lush and crowded with description of beautiful women, beautiful scenery, beautiful melancholy.

Keats (1795–1821) knew that St. Agnes Eve was traditionally the night when unmarried girls indulged in dream divination. If a girl dreamed of a boy, he would become her husband. In Keats's poem, the "fair Madeline" dreams on the casement of her room. A man appears. Is he real? Is he a manifestation of her dreams?

> Beyond a mortal man impassion'd far
> At these voluptuous accents, he arose,
> Ethereal, flush'd and like a throbbing star
> Seen mid the sapphire heaven's deep repose;
> Into her dream he melted . . . .

If you want the whole story, read the poem. Can you just see that dream lover, rising "flushed and like a throbbing star"? (When's the last time you saw a throbbing star?)

Tonight use whatever technique works best for you to incubate your dreams. Tomorrow morning write down your dreams. I wish you sweet, romantic ones.

> And they are gone: aye, ages long ago
> These lovers fled away into the storm.

Sun Enters Aquarius

People sometimes look at astrology as planets, both good and bad, doing their song and dance in your life and making you the way you are. Maybe, maybe not. We can just as easily find literary quotations that say the opposite. In Shakespeare's *Julius Caesar*, Cassius tells Brutus that "the fault . . . is not in our stars, but in ourselves."

Some people object to astrology and find it foolish and unscientific. Maybe these are people with control issues? Skeptics and materialists who believe only what they can measure or hold? People who have never had—and might not let themselves have—a spiritual or psychic experience? I'm not sure I understand astrology, but I keep an open mind. If ideas have been current for two millennia and haven't led to wars or genocide, maybe there's something useful in them.

I'm fortunate to have friends who are astrologers. When I asked my friend Lilith for a general idea of Aquarius, she said, "Think Data, in *Star Trek: Next Generation*." Aquarians, she said, would rather analyze their feelings that just feel them. Because of this, they are "irresistibly drawn to emotionally expressive people."

Though we were good friends, the last Aquarian man I knew thought I was just way too uppity, which makes me wonder if analytical people and emotional people ever understand each other. This is the stuff of which drama is made. There's attraction, expression, conflict, resolution. There are people having their emotions, big-time, and other people watching them, perhaps wishing they could be more emotional or perhaps being thankful that they're not overly emotional. I'm glad we're not all alike.

Reader, this is (obviously) not a book on astrology, but each month I'll tell you what Lilith has to say and invite you to consider the influence of the stars in your life.

Chinese New Year

The lunar Chinese calendar is said to have been established in 2397 B.C.E. That makes it older than the Roman, Hindu, Muslim, and Gregorian calendars, but newer than the Jewish calendar. Each year in the Chinese calendar is named according to a schematic of celestial signs.

We're familiar with the wondrous dragons that lead Chinese New Year parades. To the monotheistic religions, the dragon, or "loathly worm," symbolizes chaos and evil. Think of Smaug in *The Hobbit*. We're also familiar with the stories of heroes like St. George, who slay dragons, rescue maidens, and save the countryside from draconian depredations. Hans Biedermann's *Dictionary of Symbolism* says that the slaying of dragons represents "the intellectually superior human overcoming the untamed natural world" and is a test of the hero's mettle. In some cultures, crocodiles and snakes were seen as descendants of ancient dragons, which were identified with dinosaurs.

Like the Chinese, we modern pagans know the true nature of the dragon. It represents benevolent heavenly power and the *lung mei* (ley lines) of terrestrial fertility. Four dragon-kings live in the clouds and shower rain down upon the earth. Local dragon-kings preside over every river, stream, and well. Also associated with fire and creativity, dragons can produce the potion of immortality.

Reader, let us not slay any dragons. Instead, let's capitalize on their symbolic fertility and celebrate the beginning of another year. Find some little red Chinese good-fortune envelopes, which often have golden dragons on them. Thirteen is a sacred number, so select thirteen friends and gather them together for a Chinese New Year's party. Put a tiny treasure—a Chinese coin, a fortune-cookie fortune—into each envelope. Give red envelopes and good fortune to your friends. Celebrate another year of friendship.

Community

The Oxford English Dictionary tells us that the word *community* was first used in English around 1570, when it meant "social intercourse." By 1652, it meant "the social state," and in 1727 it was used to mean "a body of people organized into a political, municipal, or social unity" or "a body of persons living together and practicing community of goods." This was also when *community* came to mean "neighborhood."

Roget's Thesaurus gives the following synonyms for community: society, commonwealth, commonality, nation, state; common ownership, partnership, copartnership; semblance, affinity, kinship. Other related words are communication, communion, communism, and commute. The Latin root, *communis*, meaning "common," led to the French root, *commun*, which also means "common" and from which we get "commune."

We like to talk about "the pagan community." We're a community of crones and sages, of businessmen and career women, of mothers and fathers, of boys and girls. We're a community of ordinary people who know what magic is and how to use it. We are communities of tarot readers and herbalists and scholars. We grow Web sites and gardens. Some of us read history and know that when we don't learn its lessons it will repeat itself. Many of us understand that what is local becomes global. We take political action.

Like any other community of human beings, we are diverse and united at the same time. Sometimes we agree and other times we fight among ourselves. Whatever variety there is in the human race, we find it mirrored in our community, for we know that what is above really is also below.

What sets the pagan community apart is that we are aware that the "old gods" and the Goddess are still sparking in us. Our community exists and operates on more than one level of reality.

Sementivae and Paganalia

These two festivals were farmers' rites for sowing seed and harvesting the prosperity the seed symbolized. The goddesses honored were earth goddesses, Tellus Mater and Ceres.

Ovid (Publius Ovidius Naso, 43 B.C.E.–18 C.E.) is best known for his *Metamorphoses*, a collection of the most famous myths of the classical world. In the *Fasti*, Ovid writes about the historical, astronomical, and religious significance of each day of the Roman calendar. Frances Bernstein translates Ovid's comment on the Sementivae:

> Let the community keep festival . . . and offer cakes on community hearths. Propitiate Earth and Ceres, the mothers of grain, with cakes of their own grain.[1]

Seed is related through Latin cognates to *semen*. The Greeks and Romans considered a woman's womb a seedbed in which the man's seed—life's active agent—grew to produce boy children. From the word *semen*, linguistics also gives us *disseminate*, which means to spread about or broadcast, as when we disseminate an office memo; *seminary*, which was originally a "seed plot" of scholarship where *seminars* were held; and *seminal*, which means having the possibility of future development, as in seminal exploration or knowledge. Given that these words all derive from semen, perhaps it's not surprising that throughout history, it was boys, not girls, who were educated. Usually in seminaries.

It's time to make some changes in our language. I have a friend who attended classes in a seminary and was taught by a retired rabbi on feminist spirituality and the Goddess. She and I took to calling the seminary the *ovulary*. *Seminal* learning became *ovular*. Reader, let us sow our Goddess seeds across lands that hunger for the pagan paradigm. Let's keep reminding the world that the egg is as productive as the seed.

The Disir:
Guarding Our Larger Community

Living in a major metropolitan area and watching the Eyewitless News every evening sometimes makes me depressed. Public school students can't read, write, or make change because their parents' neighbors refuse to pay the taxes that support schools and teachers. Reader, what's happening in our formerly "great society"? I want to find a nest of pagans and pull it around me and feel cherished and protected.

Among the Norse, January 25 was the *Disting*, or feast of the Disir, a group of guardian goddesses. The Disir were undifferentiated spirits of fate and protection. I want to call them to come right where I live. I want them to make it all better.

Some years ago, at the first local AIDS walk I attended, a group of rude men came with rude signs to harass us marchers. A month later, this same group of rude men appeared at the Long Beach WomanSpirit solstice fair. The minute they stepped on the lawn, waving their same signs, a witch named Emily (who is a large woman and could well be a Valkyrie) gathered up her coven. They and some other women formed a circle around the bigots and chanted the Ma chant: *Maaaaaaaaa*. That's all they did—louder and louder—until the men slunk away. Here were the Disir at work in our modern world.

We who see the world in a non-standard paradigm and love the old gods and goddesses still live in a Muggle society. But we witches and heathens and mainstream metaphysicals and ceremonial magicians are still part of the society we're trying to change. We still need the Disir. I like to imagine them standing beside us, but not using their swords except in dire emergency. I can still hear them chanting.

Our Cybercommunity

I'm about as much of a computer UNgeek as anyone can be. It took me four days and three phone calls to get signed up for PayPal, and Yahoo Groups still totally eludes me. But I love e-mail. I'm on a couple of lists, I get editing clients via e-mail, and I've built a cybercommunity of people from all over the world.

Many people with whom I have circled insist that energy's not "real" unless you're standing right there, holding hands, in the same room. I've heard people say, "If it's not the way Gerald (or Stewart or Alex or _____) did it, then it's just not right. And they didn't have computers." Maybe not. But those wise men who did much to invent our religion knew energy when they saw or felt it. They knew that energy has no physical boundaries, that time is always now and space is always here. I'm certain they would recognize cyberenergy.

I know some very traditional, conservative high priests and priestesses who run lists, teach on-line, create blogs, and use e-mail to keep in touch with people around the world. Without cyberenergy, we might still be isolated and ignorant. With it, we are able to announce our public rituals and classes and new books. Using cyberenergy, we are able to mobilize the community to take action, whether it's sending healing energy or supporting a political candidate or not buying gasoline on a certain day.

Reader, we are raising cyberenergy and using it with intention. We're standing in a worldwide circle and holding electronic hands.

> Grandmother Spider,
> did you weave the World Wide Web?
> Wise Father Odin,
> do you cast electronic runes?

Wolfgang Amadeus Mozart

Today is Mozart's birthday. If you've seen the movie *Amadeus*, you've seen an approximation of his life. Reader, can you hum the first few bars of Mozart's *Eine Kleine Nachtmusik*? In the movie, even the priest visiting Salieri in the madhouse immediately recognizes the tune.

As we know, Mozart (1756–1791) was a musical prodigy. He was writing symphonies before he could write sentences. In the movie, he's shown composing on the billiard table, absently rolling the balls around as he commits to paper music he's already heard and perfected in his head. He may have been improvident and foolish, but he was nevertheless a true genius. If you made me go to an opera, I'd pick *The Magic Flute*, which is about (among other things) ceremonial magic.

The word *genius* comes from the Latin and means "strongly marked capacity or aptitude." Anyone who can pass Mensa's test can be called a genius, but there is—obviously—more to being smart than just intellectual power and the ability to reason. We know artistic geniuses who cannot make change and people who comprehend the equations of quantum physics but are inarticulate in ordinary conversation.

We're said to have four bodies, physical, emotional, mental, and spiritual. Surely there are elements of physical, emotional, and spiritual genius. Think of great athletes, astonishing actors, shining stars of holiness. Do we all have a spark of genius in us? Reader, what is *your* spark of genius?

Charlemagne

Charles the Great, or Charlemagne (747–825), was king of the Franks (their name means "free") and the first Holy Roman Emperor. In 732, his grandfather, Charles Martel, had defeated a Muslim army at Poitiers and forestalled their conquest of Europe.

The Roman Empire dates from 31 B.C.E. to 476 C.E. At its collapse, which began the Dark Ages, the Christian church took control, and the barbarian tribes started moving around, claiming lands, and eventually creating the Europe that lasted until World War I. Charlemagne's coronation by Pope Leo III on Christmas, 800, made his Frankish empire Holy and Roman—the official, legitimate, and Catholic successor to the Western Roman Empire.

In German, the Holy Roman Empire was the *Heiliges Römisches Reich*. The first Reich was said to be the Roman Empire, the second, the Holy Roman Empire, making Hitler's would-be empire the Third Reich. Only the Holy Roman Empire lasted a thousand years (ca. 800 to ca. 1800).

Why are we interested in Charlemagne? First, his family supplanted the Merovingians, the Frankish dynasty that claimed genetic descent from Jesus through Mary Magdalen. Second, Charlelmagne's reign, which is called the Carolingian Renaissance, helped break Europe out of the Dark Ages. His court sponsored a flowering of art, scholarship, literature, and architecture five hundred years before the more famous Italian Renaissance. Third, the men who worked for Charlemagne came from all over Europe, and it's possible to trace the idea of today's European Community back to Charlemagne. On a less positive note for pagans, Charlemagne had the great sacred tree, the Irminsûl, chopped down, which helped to solidify Christianity in Europe.

Community Magic

Back in the days when I was beginning to learn about metaphysics and magic, a teacher said to me, "Trust the Goddess and do your own homework." At the time, I was trying to get a better job. Silly me—I was lighting green candles and talking to them, but those candles alone couldn't get me a job.

Reader, I can hear you now. "Update your resume," you say. "Get out there and meet people who need a writer." That's good advice.

Here's what we need to know: *our magic manifests through us, in us, and as us*. We can do the spiffiest spell on earth, but if we don't get out and do the work, nothing will happen. The magic won't have a conduit to work in. We are that conduit.

If we want to do magic for our community, spellwork is a good beginning. So is meditation. Close your eyes and enter your alpha state. With the eyes of your imagination see your community being the best place it can be. See harmony in diversity. We know that energy is both powerful and invisible. See the work your community needs to do or receive. Send energy to this work and see it being done.

After we set the spell or do the meditation, we need to put our energy into the physical work. There are many levels of community activism. You can carry a trash bag when you walk and pick up some trash. You can help someone learn to read or spend an hour every week as a teacher's aide. You can teach classes in magic or meditation. You can make sure your front lawn or garden is beautiful every day of the year. Today is a good day to start. Don't wait until tomorrow. Find your comfort level and get to work.

Pax

Pax, "peace," is a minor Roman goddess. We don't know much about her beyond her name, but one thing we do know about Roman deities is that most of them represented civic virtues the Romans cherished. Abundance. Boundaries. Discipline. Doorways. Fidelity. Fortune. Generosity. Liberty. Medicine. Truth. These are civilized goddesses, goddesses of the *civitas*, the great city. The Romans were not religious, which is why it didn't bother them to adopt any god or goddess that came along. Like our modern national holidays, their feast days were civic affairs.

So we're not going to find any great statues of Pax, although another goddess of peace, Concordia, is shown as a mature matron holding a cornucopia in one hand and an olive branch in the other hand. If you want to build an altar to Pax, therefore, maybe a collage using images from a magazine or art book will personify this elusive virtue.

Baruch Spinoza, the seventeenth-century Dutch philosopher, said that peace is not an absence of war. It's "a disposition for benevolence, confidence, justice." When was the last time there was a disposition for benevolence on our planet? When was the last time Gaia's children were at peace with each other? Not in our lifetimes.

If we can't create world peace, can we build personal peace? Personal peace can be as elusive as world peace, but that's one reason we're pagans. We have gods and goddesses to work with us. Set time aside to spend with Pax, however you envision her, and engage in some self-examination. What can you change in yourself or your environment to attract her? Pick one small thing to start with and ask Pax for help. If you want to make other changes, appeal to appropriate goddesses or gods. But remember to work for peace every day.

February Eve

In some calendars, a day begins at sunset and runs until the next sunset. This is why we celebrate holiday eves. Tonight, the eve of the year's first fire festival, we're getting ready for the feast of Brigid, Celtic goddess and saint.

When Ireland adopted Christianity, the goddess Brigid became St. Brigid. She established an abbey near a sacred oak at Cill Dara in County Kildare. There she lit a sacred fire. Her nuns kept the fire lit for nineteen nights, and Brigid tended it on the twentieth night. The flame is said to have burned from the fifth century until about 1000, when Henry de Londres, the ferociously anti-Irish archbishop of Dublin, put it out. The flame relit itself. Brigid's fire then burned for another five hundred years until about 1530, when Henry VIII split from the Roman Catholic Church and extinguished it forever.

"Forever" lasted until Imbolc (*Lá Féile Bríde*), 1993, when the sacred fire was lit again by the Brigidine Sisters of Kildare. The Sisters now maintain a shrine that Patricia Monaghan describes in *The Red-Haired Girl from the Bog*. In a plain room with straw Brigid crosses on the walls, a square metal lantern stands on a little table. In that lantern "a fat candle blazed merrily. . . . I stood before a simple candle," Pat writes, "and, like many another pilgrim before and since, I sank down before Brigit's sacred flame and wept."[2]

Let's celebrate February Eve by lighting a candle. Whether you have one lit from Brigid's fire or one from the grocery store, sing or meditate in the darkness. When the night can get no darker, light your candle. How much light does one candle give? Meditate on small beginnings and know that thousands of other people are likewise holding the sacred light of Brigid in their hands and hearts.

Brigid

Because the candles in medieval Christian churches were relit on this day, Brigid's holiday is called Candlemas as well as Imbolc. Just as Samhain (Christianized as Hallowmas) is the holiday that marks the advancing darkness, so does this holiday mark the advancing light that we first glimpsed at the winter solstice when the sun was reborn. Light will be our primary theme this month.

Brigid, whose name means "bright one," is a triple goddess. First, she is goddess of the sun and fire, from which comes her rulership of smithcraft. Because they were able to take raw earth (ore) and use fire to transform it into things both useful and beautiful, blacksmiths were believed to have magical powers. Brigid's second aspect rules poetry and inspiration; from the early days she has been celebrated in poetry and song. Her third aspect is as a goddess and saint of healing and medicine. It's said that the straw left over from making Brigid's crosses and other charms has healing powers.

The *Catholic Encyclopedia* tells us that St. Brigid was born in 451 or 452 of "princely ancestry," although her mother was a slave. "Refusing many good offers of marriage," Brigid became a nun. With seven other virgins, she settled under that oak tree at Cill Dara (Kildare) and subsequently founded her convent and two other centers of learning, one for men, one for women, as well as a school of art. Brigid's hand has been preserved in a shrine in Lisbon, Portugal, since 1587, and another relic rests in Cologne. "Viewing the biography of St. Brigid from a critical standpoint," the encyclopedia concludes, "we must allow a large margin for the Celtic imagination and the glosses of medieval writers." Presumably, this means we know more about our goddess than they do about their saint.

Groundhog Day

Although the calendars tell us that spring officially begins with the spring equinox, our intuition proclaims that spring is starting *now*. By early February it's obvious that the days are getting longer. I remember crocuses popping up through the snow in the back yard of the house where I grew up. When I saw them, I knew that spring was coming. It seems to me that the equinoxes and solstices do not begin the seasons but are really their midpoints, their hinges.

But how on earth did we get a groundhog as a prognosticator of the beginning of spring? It has to do with weather divination. No matter where we live, we want to know when things will start growing again. In Europe, they consulted the hedgehog, which Pliny described as "shrewd" because it stored food. We don't have hedgehogs in America, so we ask a native rodent, the woodchuck, or groundhog, to look at this shadow. For more information on this furry fellow, log on to the Voice of the Witch and at the bottom of the front page, search for a splendid article by Peg Aloi called "You Call It Groundhog Day, We Call It Imbolc."

Do you remember the movie, *Groundhog Day*? A surly weatherman played by Bill Murray goes to Punxsutawney, Pennsylvania, to film the groundhog's weather report. But something happens. . . . He keeps reliving the day, time after time after time, making changes in his attitude and his life until he gets it right.

Every time I think about this movie, I wonder if it's about karma. Is Murray's character living through simultaneous reincarnations so he can learn his soul's lessons? Reader, today is a good day to contemplate what you would do and how you would change if you had to relive one day— any day—of your life until you got it right.

Buddy Holly

Charles Hardin Holley—Buddy Holly—was a shining star of rock and roll back when it was just being invented. A native of Lubbock, Texas, he was a teen-age guitarist whose country band, the Crickets, opened for Elvis Presley and Bill Haley and the Comets. After hearing Elvis, Buddy jumped headfirst into rock and roll, and the rest, as they say, is history.

In February, 1959, Buddy went on tour with Ritchie Valens and J. P. Richardson, "The Big Bopper." After a concert on February 3 in Clear Lake, Iowa, he chartered a plane to take them to the next town. The plane crashed shortly after takeoff, killing everyone on board. That was the day the light went out of rock and roll. It was, as Don McLean sang in "American Pie," "the day the music died." Even though his records have sold something like forty million copies since 1959, a lot of people will tell you that rock has never been the same since Buddy died.

It's interesting to look back at the early days of rock and roll. Elvis was young and sexy. Chuck Berry was strutting across the stage and inventing guitar licks. Jerry Lee Lewis and Little Richard were givin' it all they had at the piano. We look back at those days before sex and drugs and tabloid sensationalism and think, "How innocent they were. No one had OD'd yet. Back in those days, we hadn't been blinded by the too-bright lights of fame and cynicism.

Reader, today's a good day to rent *The Buddy Holly Story* and think about your own childhood. Do you remember how brand new everything seemed? How sunny your days were? Even if your childhood wasn't innocent, just for today pretend that every day was a happy day.

Apollo

They keep telling us that the sun has always belonged to gods and the moon to goddesses. That gold is masculine and silver is feminine, and everybody knows that gold is worth more than silver. That yang is active and yin is passive.

Oh, yeah? You know what I think? I think this mythology is based on the mechanics of sex—the thrusting, projective male on top of the yielding, receptive female. Lighten up, big boy.

According to Pelasgian (early Greek) myth, Sunday—the sun's day—was originally ruled by Theia, "the bright one" and mother of Helios, and her consort, Hyperion, the first sun god. Theia and Hyperion were Titans, pre-Olympic deities who ruled the days of the week. Helios is older than Apollo, who other sources say was originally Hittite, Lycian, or Arabian. Because he visits the Hyperboreans in the winter, it is even possible that he was born in northern lands.

As the best-known solar god, Apollo became the god of fertility, light, truth, medicine, music, poetry, and all fine arts. (One author says that he "absorbed several formerly goddess functions.") But this golden paragon's original name was *Apollo Smintheus;* he was *the god of mice.* Apollo's solar divinity, Patricia Monaghan writes, "came so late that not a single monument shows him as the sun." The solar connection may have arisen from two early coins that show him tossing his hair in a solar aura. Apollo's name may mean "destroyer," which is how he's portrayed in the *Iliad.* In the sixth century B.C.E., the Athenian dramatist Aeschylus mentioned that there was an affinity between Apollo and the sun.[3] Other Greek poets took up the conceit, and a few centuries later the Orphics imagined a solar realm with nothing female in it, only a crowd of gods.

Fortuna

The wheel of fortune isn't just a TV show or a gambling device.
Fortuna is another of those early Roman civic goddesses. Her statues show
her holding an overflowing cornucopia in one hand and a ship's rudder in
the other. Beside her stands her wheel, a multivalent symbol that we see
in mandalas, the wheel of the year, the zodiac, and the rose windows of
Gothic cathedrals. Although Fortuna is sometimes blindfolded, she's not
just "Lady Luck." Her name originally meant "She Who Brings," and what
she brings is what happens in our lives. She steers our fate with her rudder,
and her cornucopia shows that she can bring us wealth. What she brings
in early spring is fertility—to crops, animals, and humans. The Greeks
called her Tyche, the Anglo-Saxons called her Wyrd, and in the medieval
Christian church she was known as St. Agatha.

Tarot Card X is the Wheel of Fortune. When this card comes up in a
reading, I interpret it as a change of fortune, either up or down, depending
on what the querent wants out of life. Fortuna's wheel is always turning.
It's a common theme in medieval and renaissance literature that anyone
who stands on the top of the wheel will inevitably fall, just as anyone who
clings to the bottom will inevitably rise. Thus we have the tragedies of
kings and the comedies of ambitious commoners.

Reader, today is a good day for divination. Get a tarot reading. Toss a
coin (another wheel) and see what Fortuna has in store for you during the
first quarter of this year. As spring begins, do you find yourself at the top
or the bottom of Fortune's wheel? It's likely that your life will change before
the end of spring. That's how wheels work: they're always turning.

Enlightenment

"You light up my life." A charismatic person "lights up the room." When we become aware of something, the "lights go on" or we suddenly "see the light." In cartoons, a light bulb turns on over the head of the guy who has an idea. Conversely, we call someone who isn't enlightened "a dim bulb," or maybe we say, "The lights are on but nobody's home."

Light—especially the famous "white light"—is a major metaphysical symbol. Light has traditionally been equated with spirit. It's the manifestation of intellect, virtue, and morality. Because light is born in the east, when the European Occult Revival occurred in the late nineteenth century, it was ancient Eastern Wisdom that flowed across the planet like healing light to illuminate us benighted Westerners. (I know people who fervently believe that the only true wisdom comes from the Ancient Masters of the East—those guys who are apparently still hiding out in Shangri-La or Shambhala.)

My point is not to argue the relative merits of Eastern and Western wisdom. What I'm wondering is, *what does it mean to be enlightened?* What happens to us when we're illuminated? Physiologists know that MRIs show that parts of the brain do light up when we're thinking. Is this literal or metaphorical light?

Does enlightenment give us a laser-like focus? When we become enlightened, is it a one-time occurrence, or does it last for the rest of our lives? Do ordinary people like you and me get enlightened, or is this state reserved for great, wise, and holy people? Were they common before they got enlightened, and that's why they became great, wise, and holy? Finally, can we fall out of our state of enlightenment and go back to being dim bulbs? How do we tell the difference?

Endarkenment

Yeah, some people say we should never, ever leave the light. We should endeavor to be "light workers" who fill every shadow with light and eliminate all darkness. We should surround ourselves with white light at all times and, like Lady Bountiful, bestow our white light on darker people.

This is an exceedingly naïve attitude. If the light's on all the time, how on earth do we get any sleep? Do we ever get to close our eyes? If all there is, is light, and there aren't any shadows, how do we keep from going blind and bumping into things? How do we distinguish one thing from another?

Nearly every standard reference work I looked at says that darkness signifies gloom and "primigenial chaos." Pagans understand that as much as we crave enlightenment—learning, knowledge, holiness—just that much do we also require endarkenment. The New Age just doesn't seem to have caught on yet. We pagans can help others see that without the darkness we cannot recognize the light. We need literal shadows—and psychological and metaphysical ones—to tell us what's out there.

During the month of February, we witness change. We see the movement from darkness and long nights to light and longer days. Fortuna's wheel turns, the wheel of the year turns, and things change. It's that simple.

Maybe it's also that scary. When we seek endarkenment, we set out to explore dark places, and some of those dark places are in our minds. Readers, it's useful to know that we have dark places. It's useful to be aware of our shadows and know that we're not always kind and good and pure. When we own our shadows, then we can be more tolerant of other people's shadows. When we're endarkened, we are capable of change.

The Light at the End of the Tunnel

What does that light really signify? Is something leaving you behind? Is something heading for you? Yikes!

Let's slow down and think about that tunnel. The tunnel goes under a mountain because it's too hard to build tracks over the mountain. But digging a tunnel is arduous and dangerous work. What if people start digging from both ends but don't meet in the middle? What if that whole mountain falls in on you while you're in there? If it's a long tunnel, where do you get air to breathe and light to see by? No wonder that tunnel has come to be a metaphor for a dark and dangerous time in our lives when it's hard to find inspiration.

I've been in a few of those tunnels myself. I went to graduate school and survived, and if you don't think earning a terminal degree is dark and dangerous work, then you've never tried it. I've raised a very bright and creative child, and some days I wondered if I'd ever see the end of that tunnel. I've almost died, I've been bankrupt, I've been homeless, and I've had a cancer diagnosis. So far, I've dodged those oncoming trains and survived all of my journeys through the tunnel. I've also stumbled in the darkness and hit the wall a few times, but I'm still here.

Reader, how about your tunnels? Consider two or three really dark times in your life. Think about how dark it was while you were under that mountain of troubles. Were you all alone down there in that tunnel? How did you manage to keep walking . . . or crawling? When you finally glimpsed the light at the end of the tunnel, was it sunlight or was it that awful oncoming train?

Apollo (Again)

Let's do a bit of solar magic in Apollo's honor today. We've just been pondering enlightenment and endarkenment and we've found some of our personal shadows. While shadows are not always bad, they're not useful if we want to live peacefully in the world. Maybe we found a bit of jealousy buried deep down or a seed of prejudice or self-pity. Let's heal ourselves with sunshine.

Begin by considering solar correspondences. Gold. Sunflowers and other sun-loving plants. Animals with golden fur and high-flying birds with bright plumage. Amber and honey. You can find more correspondences in the usual books.

Decide what specific solar energies you want to bring into your life to heal the shadows you don't need. Perhaps what you need is to be "brighter," that is, smarter and/or more cheerful. Let's say you want to draw cheerfulness into your personality to balance the gloom you've been feeling all winter.

Select a piece of gold jewelry. Cast your circle and invoke solar gods and/or goddesses. Standing in the center, hold the jewelry in your left (receptive) hand and invoke the bright, beneficial energies of the sun into it. After you've opened your circle, wear the jewelry on your receptive side. Focus your mind on optimism. Be cheerful when you'd normally be grumpy. Bring objects that symbolize cheeriness into your life, maybe something silly that makes you laugh every time you see it. Hang yellow curtains at your window, use a yellow washcloth for your morning shower, wear yellow clothing. Set a little solar bird or animal or a chunk of amber in your workstation. Finally, remembering that Apollo is also a god of music, sing sunny songs to yourself. Start with "You Are My Sunshine," then go on to "Oh, What a Beautiful Morning."

Anahita

Anahita, one of the earliest of the Great Mothers and whose titles include Golden Mother and Immaculate One, originated in Babylon, traveled throughout Asia Minor, Egypt, and India, and finally became the pre-eminent mother goddess of the Persians, who identified her with the planet Venus. During the reign of Artaxerxes (436–358 B.C.E.), Persians built numerous temples in her honor. She was so popular that it is said that Ahura Mazda himself worshipped her, though Zoroaster generally ignores her. She was also said to be the mother (or consort) of Mithra.

In a part of the world where water is scarce and a spring can mean the difference between life and death, this goddess of fresh water deserves great honor. Another of her names is Ardvi Sura Anahita, which means "humid, strong, immaculate one." As Nahid (a modern name), she is associated, like Aphrodite and Ishtar, with love and music. As the ruler of water, semen, and milk, all of which flow and fertilize, Anahita also rules human propagation, which is why "sacred prostitution" was practiced in her many temples. An Iranian scholar says, "After the occupation of Iran by Moslem Arabs, the ritual of respecting women and mother and the sanctity of Nahid . . . became a secret creed."[4] If any rituals to Anahita/Nahid remain in the Islamic Republic today, they must be conducted in extremely remote locations by people who are careful not to be found out.

To celebrate Anahita, remember that Imbolc is when ewes were milked for the first time in the spring. Drink a glass of milk today. Consider the connections between milk and fertility and praise this ever-flowing goddess. As you drink, ask Anahita for good health, good sex, increase (of herds and/or wealth), and safe childbirth.

Solar Visits to Japan, France, and Hollywood

☯

After Amaterasu defeated her brother, Susanowo, and came out of the cave, she was weary. Declining to rule on the earth any longer, she gave her power to her grandson, Ninigi no Mikoto, whom she sent to some unnamed islands near Asia. Ninigi married a local princess, and their great grandson grew up to be Emperor Jimmu, traditional founder of Japan. To this day Japan's royal house claims descent from Jimmu and, through him, from Amaterasu. While history cannot locate Jimmu, mythology places him in the seventh century B.C.E. In 1872, the Meiji government proclaimed February 11, 660, as the date Japan was founded, and the holiday was celebrated until 1948. When the post-World War II occupation of Japan ended, the holiday became Kenkoku Kinen-bi, or National Foundation Day. The Great Shrine of Ise still shelters Amaterasu's mirror, which is the most precious object in Japan (though no one has seen it in a long time).

In 1858, the Blessed Virgin Mary appeared to a fourteen-year-old French girl named Bernadette Soubirous. A statue of the Madonna of Lourdes was erected at the site in 1864, a tourist center was built, and Bernadette was canonized in 1933. The spring water from the Grotto of Lourdes is believed to possess healing properties; it is, of course, a Christian version of a magical pagan spring.

If you've seen the 1943 movie *Song of Bernadette*, starring Jennifer Jones and based on a maudlin novel by Franz Werfel, you'll notice that the actress who played the BVM is not credited. The actress was Linda Darnell, who had posed nude for some photographs and was pregnant when she made the movie. She was photographed, thoroughly draped, in a bright light to represent "the woman clothed in the sun."

Artemis and the Amazons

☯

The Larousse Encyclopedia of Mythology tells us that the archaic Artemis is "probably a replica of Apollo Nomius," an aspect of Apollo as an Arcadian shepherd-god. Perhaps Artemis and Apollo were one deity that split into two.

Although Artemis was first an agricultural deity, she soon became goddess of forests and may have been confused with Callisto, the she-bear who later became her companion. As Phoebe and Selene, she was associated with the moon, an echo of Apollo's solar association. Greek coins show her holding a torch in her hand.

The Greeks said she was the daughter of Zeus and Demeter or Persephone, or perhaps of Dionysus and Isis, though tradition finally decided she was the daughter of Leto. She preferred the wild places, where Oceanids and nymphs accompanied her. She was not a gentle goddess. Because of her murders of Acteon, Orion, Aloadae, Chione, Niobe, Admetus, and others, Robert Graves calls her "dark and vindictive."

Artemis of Ephesus shares none of the characteristics of the Hellenic Artemis. The Ephesian goddess is a fertility figure said to have first been worshipped by the Amazons of the Caucasus Mountain region of Cappadocia and other lands around the Black Sea.

The myth that Amazons each cut off one breast so they could hold their bows more efficiently has no basis in factual etymology or art. Their most famous queens were Antiope, who was kidnapped by Theseus; Hippolyta, who was killed by Hercules; and Penthesileia, who was killed at Troy by Achilles. Graves suggests that "by their warlike habits and their horror of men the Amazons offer some resemblance to the Greek Artemis, which is doubtless the reason why their great goddess was given the same name."[5]

Goddess Light

I've read somewhere that part of the alchemical process of transmutation involves breathing light into the physical body. In this exercise, which is said to go back to two early (and probably apocryphal) female alchemists, Isis the Prophetess and Mary the Jewess, the alchemist is directed to begin with seven days of meditation and fasting. As is typical with alchemical writing, we're not told whether we're breathing in ordinary daylight or some elevated mystical light, though my money's on the latter.

If you need some energy on a gloomy February day, here are a couple of techniques for bringing light into your body.

Kundalini yoga teaches pranic breathing. Prana is energy, which we see as light. Close your eyes, relax, take a deep, easy breath, and in your mind's eye see Brigid standing before you in her aura of sunlight. Ask the goddess for healing or inspiration, then ask her to breathe with you. (Don't worry—you're not going to inhale a goddess.) Inhale deeply and feel the aura of goddess light flowing into your nose, your throat, your lungs. This is, literally, *inspiration*, breathing in. Send the goddess light flowing throughout your body and feel it settling into your stomach, your arms and legs, wherever it needs to be.

In color breathing, we fill our lungs with a healing color, which we send to parts of our body for healing. When you're feeling disspirited or uninspired, breathe in golden light. Pull it in through your nose and hold it for a moment in your head. Now exhale slowly and gently. Don't force the light to move. As you exhale, allow it to flow down your neck, shoulders, arms, and fingers. Let the golden light flow through your torso, touch your lower chakras, and flow down your legs to your toes.

Valentine's Day

Although February was named after Februus, an Etruscan god of the underworld, in the Middle Ages people began celebrating life and love. In Chaucer's *Parlement of Foules* (ca. 1380), a council of birds comes together on St. Valentine's Day "upon an hil of floures" near a temple of Venus, where "ther sat a queene/That, as of lyght the somer sonne shene. . . . She fayrer was than any creature." This "noble goddesse Nature" assigned today as the day when birds would choose their mates.

Reader, let's leave the hearts and flowers to regular people and get into some Valentine's Day mischief.

First buy two or three boxes of little kids' valentines. You know the ones I mean—the ones with pictures of Kermit the Frog or Spiderman or SpongeBob SquarePants, the valentines that fourth graders take to school and hand out. Using gold ink and maybe a calligraphic pen, sign each valentine. But don't use your own name! Sign them with the names of characters in Shakespeare's plays. Or superheroes. Or sports or rock stars.

Here's the fun part. Being very sneaky, put a valentine in every mailbox in your building, at every workstation or cubicle at work, in every locker at the gym. Leave two or three at the ATM or on the counter at the post office among the priority mail labels. Then lurk and watch people's reactions as they get a valentine from Hamlet or Wonder Woman or Brett Favre or Roger Daltrey.

There's some legitimate magic in this valentine silliness. You're spreading positive energy: love, affection, friendship, good cheer. Some people never receive valentines; you're the mysterious friend who makes them smile on an otherwise lonely and gloomy day. Your silence makes the positive energy more finely focused. It makes your intention more powerful.

Lupercalia

This Roman festival, said by Roman poet-historian Cicero to be so ancient that it began before civilization existed, commemorates the she-wolf, *lupa*, who lived in the Lupercal grotto under the Palatine Hill in the center of Rome.

When Mars raped the vestal virgin Rhea Silvia, she gave birth to twins, Romulus and Remus. Like other riverine heroes (including Moses), the twins were placed by their mother in a basket and cast into a river, in this story, the Tiber. The river overflowed and deposited the basket under a handy fig tree in the grotto. Like other orphans (Tarzan, Mowgli), they were cared for by a compassionate wild animal, the she-wolf. Later, they were adopted by the shepherd Faustulus and his wife, Acca Larentia, "Lady Mother," an Etruscan goddess.

One day in 753 B.C.E., the twins decided to found a city. They sought an omen in the flight of birds. Remus spotted six vultures in the sky. Romulus saw twelve, which made him the winner. He began ploughing a furrow to mark the boundaries of the city, which he named after himself. When Remus jumped over the furrow, Romulus murdered him, then made the Capitol an asylum for homicides and runaway slaves.

But no woman would marry a criminal, so the lonesome Roman men kidnapped the Sabine Women. (Stephen Vincent Benet told this story in verse. It's also retold in the movie *Seven Brides for Seven Brothers*.) Later, Romulus and the Sabine king, Titus Tatius, ruled Rome together . . . until Titus mysteriously died. Romulus thereafter ruled alone until, it is said, Mars carried him into heaven in a fiery chariot.

During the Lupercalia, young men called *Lupercai* ran naked (except for animal skins in strategic places) around Rome, making a magic circle around the Palatine Hill to ward off evil spirits.

Time for a Feast

Back in the really olden days, by mid-February people could see that the season really was turning and the days really were getting longer. That was good. It meant they could start planting soon. They'd been eating through their food stores since the final harvest. Supplies were probably running out by now, and much of the food was probably spoiled. As anyone who's ever been on a diet knows, when food is scarce, that's what fills our dreams.

To celebrate the waxing of the year (plus the fact that now we have refrigerators) let's have a little feast today. Not a big, fancy, fattening feast. A modest indulgence. Reader, what's your secret pleasure? During the Great Depression and World War II, people endured shortages and rationing of everything except what they could grow in their own gardens. We've just passed the "depression" of winter. What do you crave at half-past February? What rare and special comestible would delight your taste buds? I can remember when you never saw strawberries or fresh fish this time of year. Nowadays, with worldwide shipping, we can find any delicacy at any time. Strawberries in February are no longer worth their weight in gold.

Planning is half the fun of a feast. Start daydreaming. Open your recipe books. Find the scraps of paper with recipes your friends have given you. Get out your mother's old recipes. Begin by selecting the appetizer for your feast. In my old copy of *The Joy of Cooking*, I find recipes that send me straight to gustatory heaven. Perhaps I'm not going to actually make a roast beef and Yorkshire pudding or a strawberry trifle, but, oh, the dreaming is delicious. Reader, keep dreaming. Select one dish that pleases you. Indulge yourself. Just this once . . . eat whatever calls to you.

Fornacalia

Romans, whose diet was largely vegetarian, ate a lot of bread. The Fornacalia honors Fornax, the goddess of ovens. Yesterday we had a feast; today let's eat more simply. Go to your local bakery and buy their finest loaf of bread. Buy a baguette or Italian bread or dark German rye bread. Buy the yummiest, sweetest butter you can find, the sublimest honey or jam. While the bread is still warm from the oven, hurry home, get out your good bread knife to slice the loaf and a little knife to spread the butter, and make yourself comfortable. Just for today, damn the cholesterol. Have a *real* feast.

We know the symbolism of bread. It's the staff of life, our basic necessity. It's a sacramental food, food of the body (as wine is food of the spirit) and a symbol of masculine energy (as the wine is feminine). We have evidence of bread from the Paleolithic era. When Jesus of Nazareth prayed, "Give us this day our daily bread," he was asking his god to provide the day's necessities and to provide them *every single day*.

Breaking and eating bread together can symbolize friendship and a truce between enemies. It can also commemorate the sacrifice of a god.

Reader, what is your daily bread? It's not just the food you eat to keep your body alive. Your daily bread is the authentic energy of your life, the sustenance of your soul. It's what makes you sing in the wilderness. My daily bread is words. If I weren't reading and writing, I'd wither away. What sustains you, body and soul, and makes you what you are in the world? Eat good bread today and give thanks to the god or goddess you invoke most often for your true daily bread.

Tacita

Tacita, the Silent One, mother of every taciturn person and tacit agreement, is another of those practical Roman civic goddesses. Her job was to bind unfriendly speech; as I read history, however, it seems to me that she wasn't very good at it. Like us, the Romans were a litigious, noisy lot, forever giving speeches in the senate and on street corners.

Binding magic is an issue that creates a great deal of noise in the pagan community. If we're supposed to harm none, are we harming someone when we do a binding spell? What if we're binding someone who has caused real harm? It's conundrums like binding, plus defensiveness about "black" and "white" magic, that lead some pagans to swear off "manipulative magic." *Any* magic, however, manipulates something, if only energy. I'm not sure that binding a criminal with New Age white light is actually going to stop him. Yes, sometimes we need efficient binding magic.

If you're thinking of binding someone, first consider consequences, both intended and unintended. Think about what binding magic will do to your target. Consider what your proposed binding magic can do to you. Ask yourself what this binding may do to the world.

Here's a visualization that works but causes little harm. See the person who needs to be bound as small but unharmed. Now see a big envelope. Let the envelope be an appropriate color and big enough so that the person fits comfortably inside it. Put the person inside the envelope. Seal the envelope. If necessary, wrap duct tape around it. Several times. Then fling the envelope over your left shoulder and let it sail into space. You don't need to know where it lands. It's best to do this visualization at dawn and dusk for nine days in a row.

Sun Enters Pisces

My friend Lilith, the astrologer, tells me that people whose sun sign is Pisces are overwhelmed by feelings. They're the folks who make mountains out of molehills. Feelings, she says, "are great, sprawling, nebulous, messy, and almost uncontrollable creatures." When you let your feelings take over, any scenario is possible. When we let our feelings run our lives, things can become way too interesting. What are we in addition to our feelings?

Although it was somehow decided in the twentieth century that people are all basically alike (Freud said we were all driven by sex; Adler, by power; Sullivan, by social solidarity; the existentialists, by a seeking after the true self), that's a false democracy. The evidence for variety is strong and goes back at least to the Greeks. Hippocrates described the four temperaments (sanguine, choleric, phlegmatic, and melancholic), the "four humours" were well known in the Renaissance, and Jung's description of four "function types" is well known.

Thirty years ago, building on the work of Jung and others, David Keirsey and Marilyn Bates created sixteen temperament types. More recently, Dawna Markova characterized people as auditory, visual, or kinesthetic. These typologies may not be perfect, but they're worth considering. Reader, find copies of books by these authors and take their tests. Find out how you're classified and see if it agrees with your own idea of yourself. If you find any surprises, see if you can understand why you're not quite who you think you are.

The Pisces fish swim up and down. What are your ups and downs? Where are your head and your heart? Is there balance in your life? We may be idealistic pagans, but we also have to work and live in the world as it is. Let's aim for equilibrium in every part of our lives.

The Stone Pages, Archaeo News

☯

After sixteen years of touring European archaeological sites, Italian photojournalists Paola Arosio and Diego Meozzi began posting information and photos on the Web. The Stone Pages (*www.stonepages.com*), which went online on February 20, 1996, was the first online guide to megalithic sites and other ancient monuments. Over the years, the site has grown to 2,500 pages.

Arosio and Meozzi also publish *Archaeo News*, a weekly e-zine with up-to-date information about ancient sites on every continent. Here are abbreviated excerpts:

- Northern Ireland's historical monuments are to come under the spotlight in a new survey. Northern Ireland has 15,000 monuments, relics of a cultural heritage stretching back over 9,000 years.

- Investigators for the Israel Antiquities Authority have been informed that a precious ivory pomegranate, on display at the Israel Museum since 1988, is a fake. On the basis of an inscription, it had been dated from the period of the First Temple, tenth century B.C.E. However, information on the origin of the inscription has raised doubts about the authenticity of the item.

- A 7,400-year-old pottery jar stamped with the design of two flying phoenixes was excavated recently in central China's Hunan Province, helping archaeologists unveil the secret of the "birth" of the sacred bird.

- The accepted theory of prehistory in the Americas says that the first humans crossed a land bridge from Asia at the end of the last ice age, about 13,500 years ago. But a site found on the banks of the Potomac River may date to 14,000 B.C.E. Maybe people have been in the New World—and, Goddess help us, around Washington, D.C.—longer than we thought.

Atargatis

This Syrian or Aramaic goddess was originally a spirit of fertilizing moisture who descended from heaven in an egg and emerged as a beautiful mermaid. After giving birth to the goddess Semiramis, she threw herself into a lake and became the all-powerful fish mother who also tempted men to pleasure and pain. A thousand years later, her believers were lured into a temple in Jerusalem by Judas Maccabaeus and slaughtered. In Rome, Atargatis was worshipped by madly dancing eunuch priests.

We've always felt the lure of mermaids. Archaeologists have found 3,000-year-old pieces of bronze in the Middle East that are women with tails. Other images have appeared in areas as far apart as Chile and China. Goethe, Tennyson, and others have written mer poems. Two of the most famous mer stories are Hans Christian Andersen's "The Little Mermaid" and the movie *Splash*, at the end of which the mermaid, Darryl Hannah, takes Tom Hanks to her wondrous city under the sea.

We call these creatures nymphs and undines, nereids and sirens, selkies and Lorelei. Nereids often acted as guides to seafarers and helped the Argonauts pass between the Wandering Rocks on their way to Colchis. But other sea maidens, gazing into their magical mirrors and combing their untamed hair, were less friendly. The sirens—their name means "entangler"—sang so sweetly that, of all the men on earth, only Odysseus and Orpheus heard them sing and lived. Like the call of the sea itself, sirens sing to sailors and lure them to watery deaths. Plato calls their siren song the "music of the spheres."

Mermaids continued to be popular during the Middle Ages, when the church used them as symbols of licentiousness. Christopher Columbus recorded seeing sirens near Hispaniola in 1493. He said they weren't as beautiful as he'd expected.

Concordia

Concordia, the personification of community harmony, had at least two temples in Rome, a city that certainly needed her blessings. The Romans acknowledged her by holding a feast called the Charistia, where people met to reconcile their differences and settle their disputes.

Reader, it sometimes happens in a tradition, coven, or circle that fragmenting issues arise. Fault lines of power and control appear. Eris, goddess of discord, starts whispering in our ears. Words are said that were better left unsaid. Actions are taken that cannot be taken back. Let's bring Concordia into our circle.

Here's a ritual to keep Concordia present. First, get a big ball of rainbow-colored yarn. Next, everyone sit on the floor in a circle. Sit so close that you're all touching, shoulder to shoulder, thigh to thigh. Now, holding the end of the yarn in one hand, the first person tosses the ball so it flies like a comet with a rainbow tail to someone across the circle. As you toss the yarn, speak the words that Concordia whispers in your ear. "I honor the way you tell the truth" or "I respect your right to want to do things differently." The person who catches the yarn touches it to his or her heart, then tosses it to someone else with another affirmation of harmony.

Keep tossing the ball around the circle and speaking words of harmony until you've used up all the yarn. What you'll have now is a great big knot, an untidy web. (Well, concord is seldom tidy.) You also have a cone of harmonious community energy hovering above you. Ground the energy into yourselves and work together to figure out a way to preserve that great big knot as a symbol of your determination to preserve the harmony of your community.

Terminalia

The Roman god Terminus, ruler of borders and boundaries, was portrayed as a pillar with a human head. He watched over property. When we hear echoes of his name in English words, we know we've come to the end of the line.

It's useful to set boundaries, both physical and psychic. If there's a picket fence or a brick wall, we know we're looking at someone else's territory. Perhaps it's better not to trespass.

When I was an AIDS emotional-support volunteer, my job was to be a professional friend to whom a person living with AIDS could talk openly. Because the agency gave me some of their most troublesome clients, I learned real fast to set boundaries. "No," I told one buddy, "you cannot call me twelve times a day." This was the man who pulled the IV out of his arm to get attention. (It worked.) Another buddy told me about his sex life. In graphic detail. I was blushing on the phone. "Stop," I told him. "I'll listen when you tell me how angry you are at the doctors who can't make you better, but I'm not interested in these details."

When I was feeling overwhelmed, I couldn't focus on service. I still had my own life to live, so I set boundaries to protect myself. My buddies could phone me between noon and seven. I would happily visit them once or twice a week, but I wouldn't stay for more than an hour. We could go to an occasional movie or concert, but I would not go to bars with them.

Reader, are there people in your life who are trying to take over? Setting boundaries is not being unloving, rude, or cruel. It's making a space where you can meet another person heart to heart.

Carnival

Carnival, which occurs six weeks before the moveable feast of Easter, is the occasion for magnificent parades and parties. Sometimes called Mardi Gras, or "Fat Tuesday," it is the day before Ash Wednesday, the first day of the Lenten fast. The word *carnival* may come from the Latin *carne vale*—"good-bye to meat." Some historians, however, see Carnival as a festival that, like Saturnalia and Lupercalia, reverses a society's "natural" order of things. If this is true, the etymology may be *car navale*, or "ship cart," which is a reference to the floats that make up a parade. It is also said that the trumps of the tarot represent the medieval "triumphs," or floats, in parades through the streets of Venice or Florence. When we lay the cards out for a reading, we can think of them as forming a sort of procession that carries the querent from the past into a potential future.

Reader, if you can't get to New Orleans or Rio de Janeiro, how about making your own parade? If it's still cold outside, gather your coven, circle, or local community and have a party. Make it as fancy and energetic as you want to. Come in costume. Bring props. You can put gods and goddesses in your kids' little red wagons, then add flowers and greens, and every possible symbol and correspondence. Parade around the room. Dance a winding spiral dance until everyone collapses on the floor.

If you're a solitary, make your own parade. Do a tarot reading for yourself. Make fantasy floats or miniature ship carts out of balsa wood or cardboard and add wheels. String them all together with bright ribbons and pull them along in a parade. This will entertain the household cats and dogs, who will surely want to join in.

A Day to Fast

If yesterday was Carnival, today is the first day of Lent, and we have to give up everything we enjoy. But wait—we're pagans. We've abandoned that puritanical, penitential custom. We don't have to give up our favorite things. So there!

Reader, you're right. If we give up meat—*carne vale*—we do it in allegiance to moral principles. It's not theology, it's ethics.

Let's consider a different meaning for *fast*. I have a friend who took a five-year fast from driving. She sold her car. If she went out, she walked, took the bus, or called a friend to get a ride. Her fast from driving gave her a new view of our modern urban society, where our cars are major ego symbols. During her fast, my friend found out that she was not her car. She also discovered no one believed her—"You did *what?* How do you get around?" She learned that some people were generous with their time when she really needed to go somewhere. She learned the difference between needing to go somewhere and wanting to go out. She learned that she could just as well stay home.

Reader, the true meaning of fasting is not martyrdom. It's setting something aside to gain an invisible benefit. It's understanding priorities and being contented without something that we thought was integral to our existence. Think about the valuable lessons my friend learned while she was fasting from driving. What could you give up and be content without? Your fast is not punishment, not a bribe to any god or goddess, not earning brownie points in heaven or on Mt. Olympus or in Valhalla. What fast would you engage in to change your life or your consciousness? Are you willing to fast for a day or a week or a month?

Mut

Mut, a Nubian vulture goddess whose name means "mother," came into
Upper Egypt very early in history. Her winged headdress represents the
opening of the third eye and the expansion of the mind.

In our imagination, let's put on Mut's vulture headdress and light up
our brain. I like to imagine little lights twinkling as brain cells fire and
synapses close. Because Mut is an archaic goddess, her power first illumi-
nates the oldest area of the brain, the reptilian brain, which is buried deep
inside our gray matter. This part of our brain rules our instincts; perhaps
we can "shed some light" on them. Overlaying the reptilian brain is the
"paleo-mammalian" brain—the limbic system—which generates our basic
emotions. There are "experts" who say aggression is the most basic emotion and talk about "man the hunter." Illuminate your limbic system and
tame that aggression.

Now let's move up to the newer part of the brain, the cerebral neo-
cortex. When we look at drawings of the brain, this is the part that looks
like two halves of a walnut. As we've known for half a century, the two
hemispheres have different functions. The left brain is verbal and logical,
whereas the right brain is visual and holistic. Still wearing Mut's wings,
light up both hemispheres.

Do you remember the stories that tell how the rainbow is a bridge
between heaven and earth? The area of the brain that bridges the two cor-
tical hemispheres is the *corpus callosum*. Light up your *corpus callosum*. See it
strung with twinkling lights in all the colors of the rainbow. Know that
you can be both logical and holistic at the same time. Know that you can
write and speak with grace and intellectual rigor. Know that you can create art and music and dance.

Lighten Up

We water signs—Pisces, Cancer, Scorpio—tend to become too full of our feelings. Like laundry in the dryer, our wet and heavy feelings keep going round and round and round. We have to open the door, let the soggy air out, and let fresh air in. We have to stop the cycle.

If you're in one of those cycles where all you can think about is how you're being neglected by your kids or a member of your coven is starting rumors about you, *stop the cycle*. Begin chanting a chant or singing a song that will fill your mind so there's no room left for that soggy thinking. I always start with the Green Tara mantra: *Om Tare Tutare Ture Soha*. You can sing Deena Metzger's Goddess Chant: "Isis, Astarte, Diana, Hecate, Demeter, Kali, Inanna." Look these goddesses up and read their stories so you know who you're chanting to. You can also sing Starhawk's "She changes everything She touches, and everything She touches, changes."

It's also fun to make up modern stories about gods or goddesses. Give Odin an e-mail address, a cause, and a blog. Write his blog for him. Put Zeus, Hera, Europa, Leda, and all of Zeus's other girlfriends in a daytime drama together. Can you just see them in the sexy costumes the characters in soaps always wear? Shoot a movie about Isis, Osiris, Set, and Horus. Add lots of special effects and explosions and computer-generated desert demons. In another story, put Shango and Oya on a slave ship and set them to work. What would they do to the captain? Precisely how would they rescue the people chained together belowdecks? Park the pantheon of your choice, aged but neither sedate nor sedated, in a modern retirement home. The possibilities for distraction are endless.

The Music of the Night

The dark has much to tell us. Reader, if you wake up at three or four in the morning, try this meditation of extended hearing.

Lie still and listen. Listen to your own breathing. Listen to your heart beating, to the other sounds your body makes, chugging along, keeping you alive.

Now begin extending your hearing. If you sleep with a partner, listen to his or her breathing and other little sleep sounds. Feel the comfort these accustomed sounds bring you. What other sounds can you hear in your bedroom?

Extend your hearing through your home. Listen to the little noises your children make in their sleep, to your dog or cat doing what it does in the nighttime. Listen to the humming of the refrigerator, to the plumbing, to the settling of your foundation. As you listen, be glad for your home and its familiar noises.

Extend your hearing past your walls. Listen to the nighttime animals outside—an owl, a feral cat. Hear an occasional car or truck driving down your street. Who could be driving at three in the morning, and where are they going in the dark? Wish them a safe arrival. Listen to your neighbors. In the building next to mine lives someone whose lights are on twenty-four hours a day and who plays soft classical music all night. I've never seen this person.

Extend your hearing to wider and wider areas. By now, you're not hearing very much with your physical ears. Perhaps you hear a train whistle or an occasional siren racing across town. If you hear a siren, send blessings. Listen with your imagination. Now, in the hours before the dawn, you are hearing the voices of the earth. What are they telling you? What are they singing about?

...FEBRUARY 29...
Leap Year Day

In November, 1937, cartoonist Al Capp introduced a new folk holiday: Sadie Hawkins Day. Every year, Capp's comic strip, *L'il Abner*, showed Sadie, "the homeliest gal in the hills," and her gal friends totin' their shotguns and chasin' hillbilly men through the woods with matrimony in mind.

Sadie Hawkins Day was not an entirely new idea. It's said that the tradition of women proposing to men originated in fifth-century Ireland, when St. Patrick informed St. Brigid that desperate women could pop the question on leap year day. In 1288, it's also said, a law was passed in Scotland to allow women to propose to men on February 29; any man who declined had to pay a fine, which could be a kiss, a pair of gloves, or a silk dress.

Sadie Hawkins Day sounds like Saturnalia to me. When women (and other slaves) took liberties, it signaled the reversal of the "natural" social order. Order was also extremely important in Elizabethan England. Characters in several of Shakespeare's plays defend the established order of things: God, angels, heaven, and man above; women, other lesser creatures, and mud below. In our times, before the uproarious sixties, girls *never* chased boys. (At least not so's anyone would notice.) *He* phoned, *he* drove the car, *he* opened doors, *he* paid for dinner and tickets. Just take another look at any 1950s movie (think Doris Day and Rock Hudson) or TV show. "Chivalry" was alive and well, people stayed in their proper places, and the natural order prevailed. All was well. And boring.

Yeah, women proposing to men reverses some kind of natural order. Uppity women introduce chaos into society. Who knows what that can lead to? It's the first step down a slippery slope. Religious dogmas and political parties have been built on that premise.

The Golden Dawn

♀

During the European Occult Revival of the second half of the nineteenth century, William Wynn Westcott, a London coroner and Freemason, received a cryptic letter from one Fraulein Sprengle, said to be a Rosicrucian adept but whose true identity is unknown to this day. When Fraulein Sprengle authorized the creation of an occult order in England, Westcott asked his friend Samuel Liddell MacGregor Mathers to create an occult rite (which, some say, he stole from the French occultist Eliphas Levi). In 1888 Westcott, Mathers, and W. R. Woodman, another London Rosicrucian, opened the Isis-Urania Temple of the Hermetic Order of the Golden Dawn. During the 1890s the new order attracted Irish poet William Butler Yeats; A. E. Waite, who conceptualized our most popular modern tarot deck; Mary Wilde, wife of playwright Oscar Wilde; Aleister Crowley, occultism's "bad boy"; and Israel Regardie, a chiropractor who was Crowley's secretary for a few weeks and became the world's self-proclaimed expert on the magic and ritual of the Golden Dawn. The order established a system of high magic, but personalities flew higher and the Golden Dawn dissolved around the time of World War I.

I recommend Mary K. Greer's *Women of the Golden Dawn*, which focuses on Maud Gonne, Moina Bergson Mathers, Annie Horniman, and Florence Farr. These four women, rebels and priestesses, can serve in many ways as role models.

Reader, have you ever noticed that although pagans say they're dedicated to gender equality, it's often the men who are still in charge? Who serves at the altar and who serves the potluck? I used to know a high priest who had a new high priestess by his side at every sabbat. Usually, she was half his age and half his intelligence. Guess who's in charge at that temple! How different, really, are pagan organizations from mundane organizations?

...MARCH 2...

Mars and Ares

♀

It's common to think the Greek and Roman pantheons were identical and just had alternate names. This is not true. The Roman gods and goddesses were born among the early Latin tribes and adopted later by Rome, usually for political purposes. As the upstart republic in central Italy conquered Greece during the third and second centuries B.C.E., the Latin tribal deities were swallowed up by the Greeks, who were older and grander. The Roman gods and goddesses personified civic virtues, whereas Greek mythology was largely philosophical.

Mars, after whom March was named, was originally Marspiter, Father Mars. *Mar* may mean "generative force" or "to shine," and *piter* is the same as *pater*. He was an Etruscan and Sabine agricultural god, known to the early Romans as Mars Gradivus, grower, and Silvanus, who oversaw their herds of cattle. The wolf and the horse were also sacred to him. His mother was Juno, his father, a flower. After Mars fathered Romulus and Remus and moved to the city, the Romans built him a temple on the Palatine Hill. Mars became a god of defensive warfare because the Romans needed someone to defend their fields and produce. Like his people, he was a farmer first; he took up arms later.

Ares, on the other hand, was a berserker and a bully. In Homer's *Iliad*, Athena loathes him, and Zeus calls him the "most odious" god who enjoys "nothing but strife, war and battles." His sons, Deimos (Fear) and Phobos (Fright), are horrifyingly destructive. Read the *Iliad* again. I've always rooted for the Trojans. If any war has good guys, the defenders of Troy were the good guys in that war.

We can find honor, virtue, and nobility in Mars, but those who worship Ares must be out of their minds.

Church of All Worlds

♀

In the 1960s, Tim Zell moved to St. Louis, read Robert Heinlein's *Stranger in a Strange Land*, and, with a little help from his friends, founded the Church of All Worlds (CAW). When it was incorporated in 1968 and recognized by the IRS in 1970, CAW became the first pagan church in the United States. Tim changed his name to Otter, then to Oberon; today, as Oberon Zell-Ravenheart he is the headmaster of the new Grey School of Wizardry.

When you visit CAW's official Web site, the first thing you read is its mission, which is "to evolve a network of information, mythology and experience that provides a context and stimulus for re-awakening Gaia, and re-uniting her children through tribal community dedicated to responsible stewardship and evolving consciousness."

In *Stranger in a Strange Land*, protagonist Valentine Michael Smith learns a new way to live and founds a church called the Church of All Worlds. As people read and were inspired by the novel, Zell's little group grew, and soon the members decided to become "water-kin." In their communion ritual, they shared water with each other and recognized the divine being in all people, saying, "Thou art God" or "Thou art Goddess." The phrase, "Never thirst," a page on their site explains, "serves as a reminder of one's conscious connection with living as an experience of Divine being." Individual branches of the church are called nests. Oberon and his wife, Morning Glory, are also famous for breeding unicorns, which looked suspiciously like goats, and recreating the Eleusinian Mysteries.

Reader, if you call yourself a neopagan, it's thanks to Oberon, who coined the term in the 1970s. He also created the Gaia Thesis, which says that our planet is a living, self-regulating organism. This was several years before biologist James Lovelock made the term "Gaia Hypothesis" famous.

Juno Lucina

♀

The Roman Matronalia, or Festival of Women, began on March 1, when the Vestal Virgins entered a sacred grove and hung offerings of their hair on the oldest tree. Some historians say that Roman matrons served their female slaves at this feast. For each baby born in Rome, a coin was deposited in the temple of Juno Lucina (*lucina* means "light") to give thanks to the goddess for a safe birth.

Juno is the guiding light of women of all ages. Let's have our own Matronalia and invite mothers and daughters, grandmothers and grand-daughters, aunts and sisters and girlfriends.

Decorate the room with garlands and sprays and bunches of flowers, and green plants and blooming plants in pots. Because we're honoring Juno Lucina, illuminate the room with masses of beeswax candles or lamps with beautiful silk, beaded shades. Put pale pink bulbs in the lamps. Let's decorate ourselves, too, and wear our most colorful, most fantastic outfits.

This is a feast day. Find out what the girls and women *really* like to eat. If it's pepperoni pizza and chocolate cake and tacos and fried rice and crudités, that's fine. Order take-out food so no one has to cook or wash dishes, but if someone wants to cook, honor her (and help her clean up). Before you eat, give a bite of food to another woman and say, "May you never hunger."

How do we spend our day together? Let's tell stories. Let's talk about the springtime of our lives, when we had invisible friends and thought we could do anything. Grandmother can tell us how she had fun in the days before computers and cell phones, mother can tell stories about the succulent things she's done, and granddaughter can talk about what she wants to be when she grows up.

Isidis Navigium

♀

Enormously popular throughout the Greco-Roman world, Isis was worshipped until the late fourth century, when her temple and other pagan holy places were destroyed by Christian fanatics. Her worship was revived 1976, when the Fellowship of Isis was established.

A major Hellenistic Isian festival occurred in early March, when the rivers around the Mediterranean Sea were reopened to navigation after the winter. This launching of the ships commemorated the goddess's invention of the sail. Celebrants asked her blessings for sailors, fishermen, traders, and all who traveled on the sea. The ritual was marked by an elaborate procession down to the sea and the launch of a ship loaded with offerings and libations. The celebrants watched the ship until it disappeared over the horizon, then returned to the temple to offer prayers for its safety.

In 1998, Karen Tate revived the ritual and added new elements for modern pagans. Her popular ritual attracts participants from all over southern California and has multiple layers of meaning. It's a community event that teaches, entertains, and inspires everyone who attends. Participants launch not only tiny ships, but also their desires for the coming year.

Reader, reconstructing ancient rituals is a popular activity. Though I honor and respect those who do their proper homework and make every attempt to create costumes, altars, and ritual words and music that reflect what they believe the original to have been, I can't figure out how anyone can reconstruct a mystery ritual that only initiates ever witnessed. I've met some people who even try to carry these rituals off in their original (dead) languages. If you were asked to revive an authentic ancient ritual, what steps would you take to (1) preserve its original flavor and (2) make it meaningful for modern pagans?

Household Gods and Goddesses

♀

In an evening's research on domestic deities, I found ten gods and twenty-seven goddesses. I was going to list them and suggest that you pick one and build an altar. You could honor Anna Purna, the "food-giver" of ancient Benares, or Fetket, who was Ra's butler, or Kikimora, who lived behind the oven in Russian houses, or T'u Ti, the Chinese god of place.

It makes more sense to me to find a household deity from our personal or ethnic past. If I want a divine personage to bless and protect my home, I think I want one who knows who I truly am. Our African friends, after all, build altars to their ancestors. Let's find an ancestral deity for our home. Most of my ancestors are German. Although I'm intrigued by Ghar-Jenti, a spirit from India's Assam region that walks around the house at night making little cat noises, I might prefer to honor Hlodyn, a goddess of the Germanic tribes. The name of this protectress of the hearth may be one of Hertha's epithets, or she may be a separate entity.

Reader, think about where you come from. Go back as far as you can, not just to the city your parents are from, but to the land where your many-times-great grandparents lived. Read about the history of that land, about the beliefs of the people. See if you can find a household god or goddess—a food giver, perhaps, or one who protects the hearth or the walls or the pantry, or a giver of hospitality—in your own ethnic back- ground. Set up an altar, which can be a single candle and maybe a doll-size plate on which you place a tiny bit of every meal you prepare. Standing before your altar, cast a circle that encloses your entire home (including the garage and the garden), and ask the blessing of the Beneficent One.

Goddess Temple of Orange County

♀

How do we know the Goddess is alive and magic is afoot? Because new temples and sanctuaries are being established. On March 7, 2004, I was honored to be one of many priestesses who gathered to dedicate a Goddess temple in a business park in Irvine, California. My friend Ava Park, the Temple's spiritual director, started holding weekly "goddess gatherings" in her living room in 2002. In 2003 her gatherings became the Goddess Circle, which outgrew her living room within a year. By 2005 her community had outgrown its first temple and moved to a bigger one.

"The Goddess Temple," Ava says, "is a temple for women of all faiths dedicated to restoring the Sacred Feminine in today's spirituality." Most of the women who attend Sunday morning worship services come from mainstream metaphysical backgrounds. They gather around the central altar, cast the circle, and light altar candles for the healing of women and the world. When I'm a guest priestess, I talk to women who are new to the Goddess about goddesses and sabbats.

Here's the first stanza of the poem I wrote for the Goddess Temple:

> Welcome to the temple, Dearest Sister, Precious Friend.
> No matter where you're coming from,
> Come into the temple.
> Here's a hug, a cup of tea. Relax before our altars, be at peace.
> Yes, come into the temple.

An important issue today is establishing sacred space for women. Many pagan women refuse to admit men to their circles, rituals, and classes. The energy of an all-woman group is different from a mixed group, where men habitually tend to try to take over. (Not all men, but enough to prove the policy.) Many women are working to overthrow the patriarchal paradigm. Reader, where do you stand on these issues?

International Women's Day

♀

So why do we need an international *women's* day? Because men—the *phallocracy*, as author Mary Daly calls 'em—have been wrestling women to the ground for thousands of years. Because during the Age of Pericles, when Athenian men were inventing democracy, married women weren't allowed to leave the house. Because in Victorian England a law said the stick a man beat his wife with could be no bigger around than his thumb. Because the Taliban took away every possible human right from women in Afghanistan. Because in the twenty-first century women's jobs still have lower status and pay than men's jobs.

I'm not writing a feminist rant. We love our husbands and adore our sons, but it's our girlfriends we turn to when we need support.

A Pakistani scholar I knew in graduate school recently found my Web site and sent me a note: did I remember her? But of course! Now we're friends again via e-mail, catching up on thirty years. Thanks to a couple of e-lists that I'm on, I have female friends around the world, including other authors and fans who have become friends. I share concerns and celebrations with these women nearly every day. We support each other's work. In my life, nearly every day is an international women's day.

Reader, imagine a worldwide web of women. In your mind's eye, see the women joining hands. See them rise into the air and dance among the stars. See their blessings shower down upon all the lands and all the people of the earth.

> There is a web of women living lightly in the world.
> As gently as hand upon forehead, checking for fever,
> the web touches the pulse of the planet
> with intention
> to help
> to heal
> to comfort.

Barbie

♀

Like Athena from the head of Zeus, Barbie was born (in 1959) from the mind of Ruth Handler, cofounder of Mattel, Inc., and named after her daughter. Well . . . if you want to know the truth, Barbie is a knock-off of *Bild Lilli*, a lascivious doll from a German tabloid. But our Barbie wasn't a naughty German plaything. Like "Kitten" on *Father Knows Best*, like Mouseketeer Annette, our Barbie was an All-American Girl. She became the most popular doll in America. The author of *Forever Barbie* writes that she "may be the most potent icon of American popular culture in the late twentieth century."[6]

Reader, have you noticed that Protestants don't have goddesses? The faithful of the Roman Catholic and Orthodox churches have Mary Mother of God and gaggles of saints, but the sixteenth-century Reformers re-formed Mary right out of the church. The Puritans further purified the church of beauty and holidays, and in the early Protestant churches everyone could be a saint, but no one could even think about any goddesses.

Today, America worships the goddesses of the silver screen and MTV, but who's the greatest popular goddess? I nominate Barbie as Protestant Goddess, as the Goddess of All Girls. Just as Isis is "She of Ten Thousand Names," so Barbie is "She of Ten Thousand Wardrobe Changes." Behold the apotheosis of the doll.

> Hail, Barbie, full of grace,
> Mattel is with thee.
> Blessed art thou among dolls
> And blessed are thy multitudinous accessories.
> Holy Barbie, girlfriend of Ken,
> Play with us now
> And as long as plastic and fabric will last, amen.

Girlfriends

♀

Back when we were hunters and gatherers, it was the women of the tribe who did the gathering. They gathered the beginnings of civilization and wove them together. Later, they put down the roots that became homes and villages. In my imagination, I see these archaic women gathering and planting grain, domesticating animals, building houses and altars, weaving and cooking, feeding each other's children, supporting each other through bad times. I'm sure they worked closely together. I'm convinced they gossiped the whole time, explaining what they were doing and showing the others how to do it. I believe our ancient mothers were the first girlfriends.

Where would we be without our girlfriends? How would we survive without loyal friends who *pay attention* to us? Who give us wardrobe advice and reality checks. Who go with us to have the cat euthanized. Who help us pack when we move and unpack when we arrive. Who are the mirrors of our souls, our roommates, and our teachers.

Some of us have lifelong friendships. We grow up together, attend each other's weddings (and divorces), babysit each other's children. Because we live in such a rootless society, other friendships may be deep but shorter-lived, though with e-mail and long-distance phone plans, it's easier than it used to be to keep in touch after we've moved away.

Reader, who are your best friends? I hope you have not just one but a whole circle. Make a list of your girlfriends. Next to each name, write down how long you've known her. ("Forever" is an acceptable answer.) Now make notes about experiences you've shared—her surgery, your college graduation, a project you worked on together. Finally, visit or telephone each of your girlfriends and thank her for being in your life.

The Hesperides, Johnny Appleseed

♀

The Hesperides were the three (or four) daughters of Night and Erebus, or Zeus and Themis. They lived in a garden on the western edge of the world, where they protected the golden apples Gaia had given to Hera when she married Zeus. Stealing these apples was the eleventh labor of Hercules. (He later returned them.) It is believed by some scholars that Mount Atlas in Morocco may be the "real" location of the Garden of the Hesperides.

We also know the story of the Irish sea-god Manannan, who used a silver bough to lure mortals into the underworld. Cut from a mystical apple tree, the silver bough bore nine golden apples. Those who shook it heard irresistible music.

Shortly before 1800, a fellow from Massachusetts named John Chapman (1774–1845) set out to explore the western wilderness of a brand-new United States. For forty-nine years, Johnny Appleseed, as he became known, wandered through Pennsylvania, Ohio, Indiana, Illinois, and Kentucky. He slept outdoors, wore sacks for clothes and a pot for a hat, walked barefoot, read the Bible every night, and planted apple trees wherever he stopped. Two hundred years later, some of those apple trees are still bearing fruit. Fort Wayne, Indiana, honors Johnny Appleseed every fall with its Johnny Appleseed Festival. If you go there, you can see Johnny's gravesite in Archer Park.

We're familiar with the pentacle we find inside an apple. The five-pointed star is also the shape of most leaves, as well as starfish and sand dollars. You can even lay a reversed pentacle over your cat's face. (Try it and see.)

Planting seeds is a favorite pagan metaphor. This is a good day to plant seeds either real or metaphorical. Tend them carefully until they grow and bear fruit.

Hypatia

♀

In 312, Constantine "the Great" had a vision that told him to conquer in the sign of the cross. He did so and ruled for thirty years, during which he extended religious toleration to Christians. In 361, Constantine's nephew, Julian "the Apostate," became emperor. He decreed toleration for pagans and reopened pagan temples. If Julian had ruled for thirty years instead of eighteen months, it's possible there would have been no Christian rigorists, no heretics, no schismatics, no martyrs. The papacy might have been spiritual, not militant, and there might have been no Crusades or Inquisition.

Hypatia (370–415), an Egyptian female scholar who was both wise and beautiful, studied the pagan gods and goddesses. She mastered philosophy, mathematics, astronomy, and the natural sciences and rose to become head of the University of Alexandria.

She also earned the enmity of Cyril, Archbishop of Alexandria and nephew of Theodosius I, the emperor who made Christianity Rome's state religion. On March 12, 415, led by Cyril, a gang of fanatical monks burst into the hall where Hypatia was teaching. They dragged her into a nearby churchyard, stripped her naked, scraped the skin off her body with shards of pottery (or clam shells), hacked her body into pieces, put the butchered body parts on display to be a lesson to other pagans and uppity women, and finally tossed her remains into a fire.

Judy Chicago's awe-inspiring book *The Dinner Party* includes a place setting for Hypatia. Embroidered around the place setting, whose symbols "suggest the destruction of female genius," are the names of seventeen other early female scholars, pagan and Christian, who "tried to exercise their intellectual, cultural, and political power."[7]

Today and every day, let us honor Hypatia and all female scholars.

Diotima

♀

Socrates is said to be the greatest of the classical Greek philosophers. In the works of Plato, who was one of his students, we learn the Socratic Method, in which the teacher keeps asking picky questions until the student finally comes up with the right answers. From Plato we also learn of the death of Socrates. He was teaching young Athenian men to think for themselves, something to which old Athenian men objected. They sentenced him to death. He drank a cup of hemlock and kept talking until he expired.

While Plato mentions Xantippe, the shrewish wife of Socrates, what we do not ordinarily hear is that Socrates had a female teacher named Diotima of Mantineia. In the *Symposium*, Socrates tells the all-male dinner party that this prophetess taught him love. Love, a *daimon* or spirit, is "intermediate between the divine and the mortal." This is not physical or romantic love, but the exalted, spiritual love relationship two good— male—souls have for each other. According to Plato, Socrates says:

> And the true order . . . of being led . . . to the things of love, is to begin from the beauties of earth and mount upwards for the sake of that other beauty . . . and from one going on to two, and from two to all fair forms to fair practices, and from fair practices to fair notions . . . until he arrives at the notion of absolute beauty, and at last knows what the essence of beauty is. (*Symposium*, 211).

From love to the Platonic ideal of beauty, and not a tender caress along the way. Reader, do you think Socrates really learned this from a woman? Is true learning gender-driven?

Reader, consider teachers you've had, both in school and out of school, both female and male. Why do you remember them?

Feminie

♀

In case you've been residing in a cave, here's the news. It's not politically correct to be a feminist. The "first wave" of feminism arose from the 1848 women's rights convention in Seneca Falls, New York. The "second wave" began in the 1960s and '70s when Betty Friedan wrote *The Feminine Mystique* (1963), Z. Budapest founded the Susan B. Anthony Coven #1 (1971), Gloria Steinem founded *Ms. Magazine* (1972), Mary Daly started her series of radical feminist books with *Beyond God the Father* (1973), and Merlin Stone wrote *When God Was a Woman* (1976). Today, young women are being discouraged from women's studies or Goddess research, and a backlash has arisen against the work of Marija Gimbutas, mostly by people who don't know the evidence from the field (either the digs or the literature).

The words *feminism* and *feminine* come from the Latin *femina*, "woman," which simply identifies a gender. Whereas *feminism* has taken on a connotation of ferocity and separatism, *feminine* is seen as soft, weak, and generally less admirable than the qualities of the word *masculine*. In grammar, a feminine ending like "-ess" or "-trix" diminishes a noun. A poetess has less status than a poet, an actress is less serious than an actor, and an aviatrix is less brave than an aviator. That's why women today call themselves poets and actors and aviators. Even in poetry, feminine rhyme (two syllables) is less powerful than masculine (one syllable), even though it's harder to write.

I know women who believe that men came from another solar system entirely and should probably go back there. Consider the phrases "divine feminine" and "feminine divine." What's the difference between them? Which describes a more active force? Does anyone say "divine masculine"?

Feminie is a Middle English word that means "women collectively." Should we bring this word into modern usage?

Anna Perenna

♀

Anna Perenna, whose name comes from the Latin *amne perenne*, "eternal stream," is another of those creatrix goddesses who are so old no one knows where they were first worshipped. Her name may also come from the Latin *annis*, "year." When the year began on the spring equinox, she was goddess of the new year. We get *perennial* from her name; perennial plants come back every year. It's believed that she came originally from Sumeria or Carthage, though the best guess of some scholars is that, like many Roman deities, she was originally Etruscan. Ovid identifies her with Minerva and Themis, elder goddesses of wisdom. Wherever she came from, Anna Perenna was honored as a goddess of the fruitful earth and a yearly provider. Promiscuity was let loose at her festival to ensure fruitfulness of all kinds.

Humanity has responded enthusiastically to the command in Genesis: "Be fruitful and multiply, and replenish the earth, and subdue it; and have dominion over . . . every living thing that moveth upon the earth." There are more people living on earth today than lived in all previous generations put together. Southern California is so fruitful that we've multiplied right into the territories of wild animals. We get news reports nearly every day of unfortunate encounters between homeowners and animals.

Reader, might it be time to reconsider fruitfulness? If we keep on being so fruitful, where are we going to live? Where will we grow our food? Where and how will Gaia's other children live and eat? The term "zero population growth" is seldom heard today; is this an idea we should revive?

Instead of feasting or multiplying today, let's consider Anna Perenna's other attribute—wisdom. Consider the principles by which we live. Is it time to find a new way to live? What principles would you suggest?

Greater Dionysia

♀

Dionysus originally came from Thrace (now Romania and Bulgaria), a wild land north of Greece where the citified Athenians said witches lived. Semele, his mortal mother, wanted to see Zeus in all his glory; that fiery glory turned her into a cinder, so Zeus sewed the fetus up in his thigh (or maybe another nearby body part). Being twice-born gave Dionysus his title, *Dithyrambos*. He grew up to be a boisterous fellow who brought viniculture to Greece.

The Dionysian myths are many and complex. In one, he shares the shrine at Delphi with Apollo and is in charge during the three winter months when Apollo's visiting the Hyperboreans. In the ninteenth century, deep thinkers espied a tidy Apollonian-Dionysian dichotomy. Civilized Apollo, they said, ruled the intellect and all things rational, whereas the wilder Dionysus ruled the body and earthy passions. The Victorians said they preferred the Apollonian life, but they put a lot of Dionysian characters in their novels.

Dionysus also invented theater. In the seventh century B.C.E., hymns called *dithyrambs* were sung during the Greater Dionysia. The *dithyrambs* were expanded into the *sacer ludus*, sacred play, which was a kind of pornographic skit based on the adventures of Dionysus. Thespis (from whose name we get *thespian*) introduced dialogue into the *sacer ludus*. Myths were dramatized, and eventually we come to the great Athenian tragedians. Aeschylus dramatized the aftermath of the Trojan War and the life of Orestes. Sophocles gave us Oedipus and Antigone. Euripides, a more "realistic" tragedian, retold the tales of Medea and Hercules. Dionysus appears as a character in some of the comedies of Aristophanes.

Reader, celebrate the Greater Dionysia today. Attend a play. Drink a glass of wine during the intermission.

St. Patrick

Patrick (ca. 373–ca. 463) was born in Scotland to a Christian family and kidnapped by Irish raiders. After six years as a slave, he escaped and went to Europe to study. Then he heard the voices of Ireland calling him to return, so after he was consecrated as bishop, he embarked on his mission to Christianize the heathen Irish.

The *sidhe*, or fairies, have always lived in Ireland. Though they live beyond the veil, they protect the beauty and holiness of the land. Woe is he who, in the name of "progress," destroys a fairy mound. In Ulster, some years ago, an American company selected a field with a fairy tree in it to be the site of their factory. Management could not be dissuaded, the bulldozers went to work, the factory went up, modern capitalism seemed to have won that battle. Reader, I ask you . . . how well is the DeLorean Automobile Company doing today?

In one story, Patrick wrestles with the fairy queen for dominion over Ireland. He wins and banishes the *sidhe*. In another story, all of Ireland's fires are doused one spring night. The druids wait for the relighting of the fire, which symbolizes the turning of the season. Instead of the sacred fire on Tara, there arises another blaze on Slane Hill. When the druids arrive, they find Patrick holding a shamrock. He delivers his famous sermon on the trinity and declares, "In this hour all paganism in Ireland has been destroyed."

Every March, I always buy pots of shamrocks, which were called *seamrog* in the eighteenth century. The shamrock is a variety of oxalis. A famous garden book says it's a weed, but pagans know that it draws wealth, health, fairies, and fortune. The plant was so identified with rebellion that the Irish were told by their English conquerors to wear red and green paper crosses instead.

Maenads

♀

The maenads (pronounced MEE-nads), female acolytes of Dionysus (whose male acolytes were satyrs), gathered in the Arcadian wilderness to drink wine and chew laurel leaves. When they reached a state of ecstasy, they celebrated the presence of their god. Mortal men called them mad-women and stayed away from them.

In his tragedy, *The Bacchae*, Euripides tells how Pentheus, king of Thebes, arrests Dionysus for disorderly conduct. Pentheus, whose mother, Agave, is a maenad, is then stupid enough to follow the maenads to Mount Cithaeron. They tear him into pieces and eat them. When Orpheus, the great poet and musician, refuses to acknowledge the superiority of Dionysus, the maenads attack and behead him. His head falls into a river and, still singing, flows downstream.

These are scary stories! Women, the Greek philosophers opined, were defective men. They were put on the earth to bear sons. They were supposed to stay in the house. They were not to be educated. But these mae-nads were *out of control*. They were probably running with the wolves!

Reader, does any of this sound familiar? I keep wondering if Euripides and Ovid are telling cautionary proto-Freudian tales to show what happens when ecstasy overcomes sobriety. When the women get out, chaos is let loose in the land. Who knows what wild women will do. . . .

Let's think of the maenads as the foremothers of modern wild women: Emma Goldman, who was so unruly she was deported; Edna St. Vincent Millay, who committed free love and blank verse; Annie Sprinkle and every female performance artist damned and banned by squeamish old men (or either sex). Maybe even Courtney Love. These are independent, revolutionary women. They bring chaos into a tidy world and explore the degradation of women in creative, eye-popping ways.

Lesser Panathenaea and Quinquatria

♀

After Rome conquered Greece, the Lesser Panathenaea was moved to coincide with the five-day Quinquatria, which marked the birth of Minerva. The five days featured athletic, musical, and poetic contests, the winners of which were crowned with olive wreaths from the tree of the goddess.

We know Athena well. She was the daughter of Metis ("prudent counsel"), but was born from the head of Zeus. Cunning Odysseus, whom she led home from Troy, was her favorite mortal. In the *Oresteia* of Aeschylus, she was "all for the fathers" and ruled in favor of Orestes when he was tried for killing his mother, Clytemnestra. She was the protector of towns, craftspersons, and *ergane* (working women). What we don't know is how old Athena actually was. Did she originate as Neith in black Africa? Was she originally a domestic goddess in Crete or Mycenae? Was she the daughter of a winged giant named Pallas? What is her true connection with Medusa and with snakes?

We know that Minerva was originally an Etruscan goddess named Menvra. She and Juno were wives of Jupiter, which is why these three divine protectors of Rome had a temple on the Capitoline Hill. Menvra/Minerva was a goddess of domestic crafts, commerce, industry, and education who also became a war goddess; Ovid calls her "goddess of a thousand works." It's easy to see how Athena and Minerva became blended together in the popular mind.

Reader, celebrate the first day of Quinquatria by exercising your body and your mind. After your walk, eat some bread with olive oil. Listen to good classical music. Read a book that will make you ponder new ideas, like process philosophy or quantum physics. If you have an ongoing craft project, spend part of the day working on it.

Spring Equinox

♀

> The trumpet of a prophecy! O Wind,
> if winter comes, can spring be far behind?
> —Percy Bysshe Shelley, *Ode to the West Wind*

Mark the equinox with a collage of light and darkness. Buy a piece of posterboard in your favorite springtime color and cut it into a circle, say, eighteen to twenty-four inches in diameter. Gather magazines and catalogs and look for images that suggest light and darkness. These can be the sun and the moon, the woods in winter and summer, bare or leafy trees, shadowy meadows or sunlit gardens . . . you get the idea. For images of solar and lunar gods and goddesses, go to *SacredSource.com* and ask them to mail you a catalog. Finally, gather stickers (glittery stars and suns and moons and flowers and insects) and anything else you might want.

Cut out your images and lay them on the posterboard. Move them around until the design is satisfactory. You may find yourself creating a collage that looks like the familiar yin-yang symbol, where there is a seed of darkness in the light half and a seed of light in the dark half.

We've had half a year of dark. We can hardly wait for the light. We're yearning for spring to rain on us, for green shoots to rise to our ankles. We're listening for little chirpy birds and looking for the bees and butterflies. This is mid-spring, the season when the Goddess comes back to earth. We can smell her. We can taste her. We can touch her. She is our mother and our daughter, and everything she brings to us is new.

Reader, when you finish your spring collage, bless your work and show it to your friends. Hang it where you will see it every day until fall (at which time you may want to make a new collage). Anytime you feel inspired, add another image, another glittery sticker.

Green Egg

♀

Shortly after the Church of All Worlds (CAW) was founded, the first issue of *Green Egg* appeared. At that time, the "Journal of Gaian Consciousness" was a one-page ditto sheet with a tiny circulation. It grew into a major, influential pagan magazine.

Who can forget *Green Egg?* Cover art that made your jaw drop. The table of contents labeled, *Lurking within.* What was lurking? Art and cartoons, including "Pagan Cowboy Joe." Serious articles on pagan theology, like "We Are the Other People," which Oberon says he wrote about Sunday-morning Jehovah's Witnesses who came to his door; he invited them in and talked to them about the people who were living outside the Garden of Eden. The free-wheeling *Green Egg Forum*, which was more than mere letters to the editor. You could read rants on topics, pagan and political, that went on for way too long and "discussions" that occasionally became *ad hominem* arguments that crawled and spiraled through half a dozen issues. Sometimes a famous pagan would decide he had to explain his philosophy to the world, and *Green Egg* gave him the space to do it. "Freedom of speech" wasn't just a principle to Oberon; it was the life force of the magazine.

I was published in *Green Egg* a few times. One of my articles was a parody of literary criticism called "Popeye as Deity." "I yam what I yam," said the burning bush to the prophet. (You can read the article on my Web site.)

Oberon's role at *Green Egg* ended in September, 1996, when he was retired by the CAW board of directors. After more than thirty years of making us think and wonder, *Green Egg* succumbed to financial distress and ceased publication with Volume 32, No. 136 (Nov.–Dec., 2000).

Fellowship of Isis

♀

The Fellowship of Isis (FOI) is a "multi-religious, multi-racial, and multi-cultural" global community. FOI honors not just "one goddess or one path," its Web site tells us, but the Goddess in Her many forms, the "religions of *all* the Goddesses and pantheons throughout the planet." Gods are not left out, though FOI teaches that the Goddess is "Deity, the Divine Mother of all beings" and says, "However expressed, all members acknowledge the divine attributes of the Goddess: Love, Beauty and Truth."

FOI was founded on the 1976 spring equinox by Lady Olivia Robertson, a tiny, charismatic woman who travels around the world speaking to anyone interested in learning more about the Goddess, and her brother and sister-in-law, Lawrence and Pamela Durdin-Robertson.

Membership in FOI is free. There are thousands of solitary members from many esoteric traditions, and members can choose to have much or little contact with the Foundation Center, which is at Clonegal Castle, Ireland. Members seeking priesthood training can join an Iseum or a Lyceum. An Iseum is "a hearth of the goddess," a group of friends dedicated to any god or goddess. A Lyceum is a kind of noncentralized department in the College of Isis, which has a structured program of study, the Magi Degree System. There is no structured curriculum, however, and Hierophants who are inspired by various gods and goddesses can develop their own courses of training. The courses can be taken in person or by correspondence. To join FOI, learn more about the training, and see photos of the gorgeous altars at Clonegal, go to the Web site.

I joined FOI in 1976 and have participated in numerous rituals and classes. I have friends in the Iseum of Isis Pelagia (Isis of the Sea) and the Iseum of Isis Paedusis (Isis the Scholar).

Sun in Aries

♀

Aries people, says Lilith the astrologer, are driven to blaze new trails. They're good starters but lousy finishers. They're often accused of riding roughshod over other people's feelings when they're rushing to be first.

She can't be talking about me. I'm a soggy double Cancer, but . . . well, my Mars is in Aries. I was competitive and ambitious in graduate school. When I'm in edit mode, I become impatient with illogical thinking and sloppy scholarship . . . whoa! What I'm writing now will be edited. Thus does Mars in Aries learn to be less aggressive and more compassionate. When you get hurt, you learn not to be hurtful.

Which leads me to the teachings of Jesus of Nazareth, as given in the Sermon on the Mount: "Blessed are the merciful, for they shall obtain mercy."

The Golden Rule appears in most religious and ethical teachings.

- "Return love for hatred," says the Taoist. "In feeling, make the heart deep."

- "A soft answer turneth away wrath," says the author of Proverbs.

- "He harms himself who does harm to another," says Hesiod.

- "What you do not want done to yourself, do not do to others," says Confucius.

- "For hatred . . . ceases by love—this is the eternal law," says the Pali Canon of Theravada Buddhism.

No matter who says it, it's good advice.

We quote what we think is the law of karma—what we send out comes back threefold. If what we send out has teeth, it'll come back and bite our tail off. If we send out kindness, kindness will come back to us.

Reader, what are you better at than anyone you know? What are you proud of, quick to defend? What makes you aggressive? Where can you be more compassionate?

Heimdall

♀

Heimdall is the Bifrost Guardian who watches beside the rainbow bridge between earth and Asgard. The son of Odin and nine priestesses, this Norse warrior wears silver armor and a horned helmet. (Vikings in horned helmets probably first appeared in Richard Wagner's operas.) Heimdall hears the grass growing and sees for a hundred miles, day or night. That's why the Aesir set him to guarding the bridge: his duty is to blow his magic horn when the Frost Giants try to invade Asgard. The blast of his Gjallarhorn will signal the beginning of Ragnarok, which will be the battle of the destruction of the gods and the end of everything. Like Janus and the Indian Vayu, Heimdall is a god of beginnings and endings. He stands at the threshold between men and gods, between the old time and a new age.

The sound of Heimdall's horn will be heard in every one of the nine worlds. As we are told in the Old Norse *Voluspá*, the Fenrir wolf will eat the sun, causing a three-year Fimbulwinter of total desolation. There will be earthquakes, and the stars will fall. The Frost Giants will invade Asgard. Everyone will die. People who live in war zones live through Ragnarok every day.

And yet . . . there is hope. A new earth will emerge from the raging seas, a new sun will be born, new deities will appear. Baldur will replace Odin as the king of the gods. Human beings, who took refuge inside Yggdrasil and survived the war by drinking the morning dew, will come out into the new world and repopulate it.

Reader, what can pagans do to assist in the birth of a new world (or a new age)? Will the new people be smarter? More careful than we've been so far?

Mati Syra Zemlja

♀

[A]ncient agriculturalists must have recognized the analogy between grain seeds germinating in the field and
new life growing in the womb . . . . Hundreds of pregnant goddess figurines have been unearthed from Old
European settlement excavations.
—Marija Gimbutas, *The Living Goddesses*

Mati, the Moist Mother Earth of Eastern Europe, has been the source
of power to her people from time out of mind. Among the Slavs, just it
was forbidden to strike a pregnant woman so was it a sin to plow the earth
before March 25. When people swore oaths, they did so upon her body
by eating a pinch of earth. If they broke the oath, Mother Earth would
punish them. Among the Russians, Mati was a prophetess. If you wanted
to know the future, you dug a small hole and put your ear to it and
Mother Earth would speak to you. Like every oracle, her words were
ambiguous.

Reader, in my imagination, I see Mati as the many-times great-
grandmother of Marija Gimbutas, who was born in Lithuania in 1921.
During Gimbutas's childhood, the old goddesses still lived on the land.
She fled her homeland to escape invading armies, but the land and its
goddesses must have called to her because she became an archaeologist.
She worked throughout Eastern Europe and the Balkan countries, un-
earthing evidence that Paleolithic and Neolithic people worshipped the
Goddess in her many forms. It is from Gimbutas, professor of European
Archaeology at the University of California, Los Angeles, that we get
the phrase "Civilization of the Goddess." I was honored to meet her
several times and to be present at an exquisite healing ritual held for her.
She often led women's groups to Goddess sites in Europe before she died
in 1994.

Demeter and Persephone

♀

We know the story. Hades, king of the underworld, lusts after Kore and kidnaps her while she's picking flowers in a sunny meadow. Refusing to let anything grow until she gets her daughter back, Demeter, the grain mother, makes a deal with Hades that allows Kore—now called Persephone, "She Who Destroys the Light"— to return to the upper world. The story is allegorical. Vegetation dies for a season. The Eleusinian Mysteries perhaps revealed the mysteries of life and death contained in a seed.

In *Lost Goddesses of Early Greece*, Charlene Spretnak retells an earlier version of the story, without the rape. Humankind lives in a happy land of perpetual spring. Grain and flowers are ever growing, ever blooming, and no one has a care in the world. One day Persephone hears whispering in the meadow. It seems to be coming from beneath the roots of the flowers and grass. She investigates and discovers that she's hearing the whispers of the dead, who exist in a half-life in a shadowy place under the earth. She feels sorry for them and, taking three poppies and three sheaves of wheat, she descends under the earth. She tells the dead souls that she has come to be their comforter and their queen. After she paints their foreheads with the juice of the poppy to initiate them into new life, they are ready for rebirth.

Reader, instead of seeing pale Persephone on her dark throne, let's build a new picture in our minds. Let's see young Persephone sitting among the shades of the dead. She's telling them stories and singing to them. She's holding their hands, caressing their cheeks, reminding them of the joys and sorrows of life. When they're ready, she sends them back up to the land of the living.

Cybele

♀

The greatest of all the archaic great mothers, Cybele (pronounced either see-BELL-eh or CHIH-bell-leh, but *not* sye-bell) personified earth in its primitive state. Because she was worshipped on the tops of mountains in Phrygia, in Asia Minor, she became the Mountain Mother and the first Queen Bee. She married Gordius, the king of Phrygia, who devised the famous Gordian knot; their son was Midas, of the golden touch and the ass's ears.

In 204 B.C.E., when Rome was being threatened by the Carthaginian general, Hannibal, the senate consulted the Sibylline Books and learned that if they brought the sacred black stone of Cybele to Rome, the city would be saved. When the goddess arrived, she was temporarily housed in the temple of Victory. Cybele's temple was built on the Palatine Hill; the first basilica of the Vatican was later built on that same hill. The stones of her temple still lie beneath St. Peter's bones.

One Roman statue of Cybele is now at the Getty Museum. Last time I was there, I noticed that the statue stood a couple feet from the wall. I looked behind it. She was hollow! There was an opening in the goddess's mouth. I was able to speak through the goddess. (I said nothing, alas, of any significance.)

A more famous statue, from Çatalhüyük, in Turkey, shows Cybele enthroned between two lions and holding a frame drum. Wherever she went, she was celebrated with drumming and music. The tambourine was her sacred instrument.

Reader, gather your friends and celebrate the festival of Cybele. Wear your most spectacular clothes. Tie ribbons on your drums and rattles. Get in the groove. Make your most joyful music, not only for the Magna Mater but also to commemorate the opening of Sun Records in 1952.

A New Year

♀

The divine ones we acknowledge during the two weeks around the spring equinox—Cybele, Inanna, Ishtar, Isis, Aphrodite, Minerva, Athena, Demeter, Persephone, Dionysus, St. Patrick, Heimdall—are connected with death and rebirth. Before Julius Caesar made January the first month of the year, the new year arrived with the spring equinox, so we have story after story of death and a stay in the underworld, story after story of resurrection. The Aramaic word for resurrection means "to get up again." I like the simplicity of that. We get up again. After death we get up again, just like we get up every morning. It's not such a big deal. We throw back the covers and get out of bed. Like the vegetative deities, we arise to a new life. When spring comes, the year also gets up again.

Maybe it's coincidence or maybe it's the season, but I've had some rebirths in my life during this month. My stepmother phoned to say she's doing her spring cleaning and found a box of old family photos she wants to send me. I received an e-mail from my ex-husband's father's third wife's daughter (my ex-sister-in-law). We were friends before I moved to California but then lost touch. She and my ex-husband now talk via e-mail, and he told her he'd seen my Web site. (Now that's something to ponder.) She and I are catching up on twenty-five years of family gossip.

Reader, along with our closets, let's spring-clean our lives this year. My stepmother did some things I didn't like, and I've been angry for many years. It's time for me to let that anger go. What outworn angers or hurt feelings can you let go of? What old friends or family members can you reconnect with? Don't just name them. Take action. Get in touch.

Attis and Cybele

♀

When Attis decided to marry an Anatolian princess, it is said, Cybele drove him mad. He castrated himself, handed his genitals to her, and hanged himself from a pine tree. It was these actions that inspired Cybele's priests, called *galli* or *corybantes*, to sacrifice significant parts of themselves. When Cybele and her *galli* moved to Rome, their spring rites, which included ecstatic self-mutilation, scandalized the staid Roman Republicans. Some *galli* were punished by being put to death, which may have been what they wanted, anyway.

Attis is perpetually reborn. Other gods who die and are reborn around the spring equinox are Adonis, Baal, Dumuzi, Jesus, and Tammuz. All but one of these are known to be vegetation gods.

As part of the six-day rites of Cybele, women planted little Attis gardens of lettuce. They weren't making salads; like the tender young god, lettuce grows fast and wilts easily. Weeping and wailing, celebrants threw the wilted lettuce into the Tiber. Then they proclaimed the god's rebirth with a wild celebration that included dancing, singing, parading through the streets, and telling bawdy jokes. The day of jokes had its own name, the Hilaria.

Reader, let's use a nondestructive mode to commemorate Attis. Check on the seeds you planted on March 11 to honor Johnny Appleseed. Plant more seeds. If you're like I am with seeds, try nasturtiums. The seeds are big and grow fast. Or try sprouts. If you've got a really brown thumb, buy the Chia-pet that looks like somebody's head and name it Attis. Attis is also associated with ivy, violets, and pine trees. Plant ivy and whisper to it to grow as tall and wild as it wants to. Buy a bunch of violets and present them to someone you love. Meditate under a pine tree.

Concordia, Janus, Pax, Salus

♀

Concordia is the Roman goddess of civic harmony. Janus is the god of thresholds who carries the key to the door and a stick to hit intruders with. Pax is peace personified; her name was used to characterize a time that wasn't peaceful at all, the Pax Romana. Salus, like the Greek Hygeia, is a goddess of safety, health, and well-being. Originally an agricultural deity, she was shown on coins feeding a sacred snake.

When we honor these four deities, we are recognizing some basic elements of a happy home—harmony, security, peace, wellness. Neither the Roman Republic nor the empire provided much harmony, security, peace, or wellness except to its richest citizens (have things changed today?), but even the poorest plebian and lowliest slave could burn incense on an altar and make a small, hopeful sacrifice.

Reader, let's bring these deities into our lives. Let's acknowledge our partners—a life partner, business partners, partners on a board or in a civic or artistic project. Except for hermits, people are social creatures. People really do need other people. (Remember the Bob Merrill song Barbra Streisand sang in *Funny Girl*? It's trite, but there's truth in its sentimentality.)

Who are the people in your life? What values do they bring? What ideas do you share? How do their personalities complement yours? Think about the man you live, work, or play with and appreciate his strength and courtesy. Think about the woman you live, work, or play with and appreciate her strength and courtesy. Set up an altar to Concordia, Janus, Pax, and Salus and give thanks to them for your partner and the harmony of your household and your work. Give thanks for the door you can open and close. Give thanks for your health or ask for healing that is needed.

Lunar Goddesses and Gods. And Lunatics

♀

My friend Kathleen Zundell is a professional storyteller who leads women's full moon walks at a local nature preserve. We meet an hour before sunset, and Kathleen, who wears a T-shirt with a glow-in-the-dark full moon on it, talks about astronomy. She has cards showing the moon on all twenty-nine days of the lunar month. Once she handed out the cards and stood us in a circle so we could see how the moon moves through its phases.

As the moon begins to rise, Kathleen talks about lunar gods and goddesses and myths from around the world. Carrying our supper in a sack, we then set off down the path through the preserve.

You know that hush that comes upon the earth just at sunset? That's where we are, in that hush. We start out talking and giggling, and then we feel it. Everything gets quiet. We hear the little chirpy birds settling into their nests and the bullfrogs in the pond announcing their presence. We see herons standing tall, ducks and fish having a look at the sky. Once, from a distance, we saw a skunk. Orb spiders are spinning at this time of night; we're always careful to walk around their webs.

Reader, gather some friends and take your own moon walk tonight, full moon or not. You can start by singing moon songs. The old ones are best (you can Google the lyrics)—"Moonglow," "By the Light of the Silvery Moon," "Shine On, Harvest Moon," "Moon Over Miami." Sing loud. Make up silly moon-fairy names for each other—Moonbeam, Lucy Lunacee, Selena-deena. Look for the man in the moon and name as many moon gods and goddesses as you can. If there's enough moonlight, do a moon-shadow dance (just make it up) and watch your shadow dancing with you.

Aphrodite's Doves

April is Aphrodite's month. Originally a great, fecund, eastern Mediterranean mother goddess, she became the Greek goddess of every dish, spicy or mild, in the great banquet of sexuality. In Rome, April 1 was the Veneralia, when women stripped statues of Venus (a tamed Aphrodite) of their robes and bathed them in rosewater. The women bathed themselves in rosewater, too, then burned incense to Fortuna Virilis, goddess of "seeking good relations with men." Let's remember, however, that when Aphrodite mated with Dionysus, their offspring was Priapus.

Aphrodite's bird is the dove. In the *Aeneid*, where Aphrodite and Anchises are the parents of Aeneas, legendary founder of Rome, two doves lead Aeneas to the grove of the Golden Bough. Statues of Aphrodite at Paphos often show her holding a dove, coins from her birthplace on the island of Cyprus are stamped with a dove, and a flock of doves was released in her honor at the festival of Amagogia in Phoenicia.

In the Bible, the dove is associated not with Aphroditean lust but with purity and gentleness. When Noah released a dove from the ark, he learned the flood had ended when it flew back carrying an olive branch. That "voice of the turtle" in the Song of Solomon is a cooing dove. In the synoptic gospels, a dove appears above Jesus' head at his baptism, and he tells his disciples to be as wise as serpents and as harmless as doves. Later, the dove came to symbolize the third—masculine—member of the Holy Trinity. Old grave markers were often decorated with doves. But how many Christians know that the doves on their cars honor Aphrodite?

We know today as April Fools' Day. To the Romans, it was All Fools Day. They spent the day doing foolish things and playing pranks.

Veriditas

When you do a Google search for *veriditas*, you get several hundred hits on *Veriditas.net*, the voice of the labyrinth movement (more about that another day). Another hit proclaims "Ancient Satanism/Paganism Is Being Mainstreamed in Today's Churches" by the labyrinth movement, because the labyrinth is a "coiled serpent," against which we are warned to protect our loved ones.

Veriditas is a Latin word that means "greening." It's the greening power of nature, the divine force of life. As I understand it, *veriditas* seems to be much like *prana* and the *anima mundi*, or "soul of the world." Which reminds me of the sublime documentary film directed by Godfrey Reggio with music by Phillip Glass. *Anima Mundi* (1992) is only twenty-eight minutes long, but music and the images of animals and the land will break your heart and inspire you to contribute to the World Wildlife Fund, for whom Reggio and Glass made the movie.

It was the great medieval abbess and scholar Hildegard of Bingen (1098–1179) who gave us the word *veriditas*. Hildegard was her family's tenth child, so they gave her as a tithe to the church. In 1141, she had a vision that changed her life: "The heavens were opened and a blinding light of exceptional brilliance flowed through my entire brain . . . and it kindled my whole heart and breast like a flame. . . ."

At a time when nearly everyone on the European continent was illiterate, Hildegard wrote mystical books about her visions and practical books on health and healing. She wrote letters of advice to the pope and to kings and noblemen throughout Europe. She wrote hymns and sequences in honor of saints for her nuns to sing. Hildegard has a place setting at Judy Chicago's *The Dinner Party*.

This month we'll be exploring variations on *veriditas*.

Jane Goodall

※

Many years ago, I saw a TV documentary on the brain. Some animals may be as smart as human animals, the experts said, but they don't have language. We can't *understand* their languages, I thought, so we don't know the extent of their intelligence.

At one point in the program, a researcher at The Famous Primate Laboratory picked up a little rhesus monkey hardly bigger than the man's hand and talked about simian intelligence. Then, to show us its brain, he snipped its head off. Just like that! I can still see that little monkey's eyes. I was only marginally aware of People for the Ethical Treatment of Animals (PETA), so I sent out a prayer to Jane Goodall.

As a child, Goodall was inspired by Tarzan and *The Jungle Book.* She later worked with Louis Leakey, the paleontologist who discovered some of the oldest human remains in Africa. She's best known for her work with the chimpanzees in Gombe.

We know that chimpanzees differ from us in the structure of their DNA by just over one percent and that their blood chemistry and immune systems are similar to ours. We know that animals, both domestic and wild, have intelligence. We know they have souls. We shouldn't cut their heads off.

In 1977, Goodall established the Jane Goodall Institute for Wildlife Research, Education and Conservation. "Young people around the world," she writes, "*can* break through . . . the brick walls of overpopulation, defor-estation, soil erosion, desertification, poverty, hunger, disease, pollution . . . and human greed."[8] When she travels, she carries a stuffed chimpanzee named Mr. H. When people come up to talk to her, they touch Mr. H. These people, she says, give her reason for hope.

Megalesia

The rites of Cybele were so bloody that Roman citizens weren't allowed to participate. "So great is the aversion of the Romans," writes Dionysus of Halicarnassus, "to all undue display . . . lacking in decorum" that a more sedate festival, the Megalesia, was instituted. But by 161 B.C.E. (only forty years after Cybele's black stone and her *galli* arrived in Rome), Megalesian banquets had become so extravagant that the senate decreed a limit to how much a host could spend. The serving of foreign wines was forbidden. Silver dishes could not weigh more than 120 pounds.

The Roman Megalesia opened with a ritual at the temple of the Magna Mater (Cybele), where the priests offered the goddess a dish of simple herbs. This was because, as Ovid wrote, ancient people drank only pure milk and ate only "the herbs that the earth bore of its free will."

Reader, are you a vegetarian? I once had a friend who refused to eat anything with eyes. She was not happy the day she encountered potato eyes. I had another friend who refused to eat anything with a central nervous system. When I brought this up at lunch with pagan friends one day, someone remarked that plants react to stimuli and trees perhaps "talk" to each other.

I'm an omnivore. I have been a vegetarian. For days at a time. But no matter what kind of "-vore" we are, let's be vegetarians today. Go to your garden or the nearest farmers' market and select every green herb that appeals to you. Get red and purple ones, too. Invite your friends and get out a really big salad bowl. Add other veggies, some nuts or seeds, some sprouts, maybe edible flowers. Toss your salad with the best balsamic vinegar and oil you can find. Enjoy your simple banquet.

Ching Ming

Ching Ming, which is held during the full moon, is Chinese Grave-Sweeping Day. *Ching* means "pure" or "clean" and *ming* means "brightness." Living members of a family clean the graves of their ancestors. Some families begin their ritual by setting off firecrackers to get the ancestors' attention and scare demons away. Next, they clean the headstone, weed the area, pick up trash, and replace wilted flowers with fresh ones. Finally, they light incense and burn symbols of good fortune. The rising smoke takes the good fortune to the ancestors in heaven. It is also customary to honor the ancestors with wine and to feed them. As at the Mexican Day of the Dead, the family brings real food and lays it out on the grave. They have a picnic there for good luck.

Several years ago, I spent a ceremonial Saturday with pagans from several traditions. In the afternoon we went to a local cemetery. We found the older graves, read the epitaphs, and did a bit of tidying up. Then we went to the catacombs, where dead people were tucked into their niches in the walls. After asking for the blessings of the dead, we got quiet and simply listened. At first, all we could hear was the traffic nearby. But soon we could hear our own breathing, and then we began to hear rustlings and whisperings. Reader, do you remember the third act of *Our Town*, when the dead people in the cemetery above Grover's Corners are talking to each other? How the dead become detached from the living? On that day, we heard the dead talking to each other. They ignored us, but we knew they knew we were there.

Visit a graveyard today. Be still. See if you can overhear what the dead are saying.

The Green Man

Although his foliate head, or leaf mask, is a popular icon in our gardens, I suspect that the Green Man isn't quite as tame as we think he is. William Anderson writes that he "signifies irrepressible life" and is "an image from the depths of prehistory." He's the spirit of growth, the wilderness lover, the consort or son of the Great Creatrix. If we could understand the leafy words flowing out of his mouth, we'd learn the secrets of nature. Like the Lorax, he's saying, "Pay attention!"

As we learn from Anderson's book and its splendid photographs, the face of the Green Man appears on cathedrals all over Europe. We don't see him at first, but suddenly, among the saints or on top of a leafy column—there he is. He's looking down at us from spires, chancels, arches, tympanums, bosses, corbels, crypts, and tombs. He appears to be expressing emotions from serenity to rage; sometimes he looks like he's in a trance.

The Green Man may be related to the Paleolithic ithyphallic shamans painted on cave walls. Perhaps he's the unfathered brother of our familiar vegetation gods, Dionysus, Adonis, Osiris, and the rest. Foliate heads are found on early temples, but what on earth is this pagan fellow doing in Christian cathedrals? It's likely that the masons and stone carvers were recording a message about birth, death, and rebirth.

That message about rebirth is why, Anderson says, the Green Man is so popular today. He's come to symbolize the green movement. He's a friend of the earth who is whispering to us to wake up and grow up, to march and dance with him in celebration of our relationship with nature. Reader, what green thing can you do today? Donate money or your time to your city's tree-planting program.

Daylight Saving Time

Daylight Saving Time (DST), first conceived by Benjamin Franklin in 1784, was invented so we could make better use of daylight. It saves electricity (we turn the lights on later) and gives us more time after work.

From time out of mind, people told time by the sun. Whenever the sun seemed highest, that was noon, and there was no consistency in time from town to town. Consistent time wasn't needed. Before the Industrial Age, nobody cared what time it was. Mechanical clocks began to appear in the Middle Ages, but every shire and village still ran on its own idiosyncratic schedule. Standard time, time zones, and Greenwich Mean Time (GMT) were first proposed in Victorian England by men who wanted the trains to run on time. Most of England's clocks were set to GMT in 1855, though some public clocks in large cities still had two sets of hands, one for GMT, one for local time. Standard time and time zones came to the United States in 1883 to standardize train schedules.

DST was officially adopted in many European countries during World War I. During World War II, President Franklin D. Roosevelt instituted year-round "war time" so people could come home from the factories and cultivate the vegetables in their "victory gardens." Our current version of DST was signed into law by President Richard Nixon in 1973.

I have long wondered how the old solar deities feel about Daylight Saving Time. "Amaterasu, your wake-up call was an hour ago. Come out of that cave!" "Yo, Apollo! You're an hour late. Get the chariot fired up and get going." "Saule and Rosemerta, the crops have been growing for a full hour. Why aren't you out in the fields already?" "Hello, Ra! Get out of bed, you lazy old man."

Hana Matsuri

Hana Matsuri is a Japanese flower festival celebrating the birth of the Buddha. People gather at temples with offerings of hydrangea tea and flowers, then wind through the neighborhoods in flowery processions. Celebrants build ancestral shrines and decorate them with the most beautiful flowers they can find. In some places, people take wildflowers to their family shrines, which they clean, leaving beautiful flower arrangements as decorations.

This festival reminds me of our Western custom of floral tributes at funerals and public monuments. People build impromptu shrines with bouquets and candles where someone has died. Do you remember the floral tributes for Princess Diana?

Flower festivals are important in cultures all around the world. Many festivals occur when trees start flowering. Hindu and Buddhist feast days have flowers on altars and shrines, and participants scatter flower petals before statues of deities and heroes being carried in processions. In many European countries, from ancient times until the present, people wear garlands or wreaths or carry flowering green branches in the spring festival processions.

Let's honor this day with our own flower festival. Don't pick wildflowers that may be endangered, but find a florist or flower stall. Buy as big a bouquet as you can afford. If your garden is blooming, bring some of your own flowers indoors. Invent your own *ikebana* with interesting containers from your cabinets. Tidy up each altar and/or shrine in your home and decorate it with an appropriate floral offering. Put a bouquet in a pitcher on your kitchen counter. Put a bouquet in your biggest vase on your dining room table. Put a bouquet in your favorite vase in your bedroom. Improve the shining hours of your day by breathing in the scents and enjoying the colors.

Good Friday

The *Oxford English Dictionary* (OED) is my favorite resource in the whole world. It gives chronological examples of how a word has been used in English. The full definition of *god*, which prints out to eighteen pages, opens: "a superhuman person (regarded as masculine) who is worshipped as having power over nature and the fortunes of mankind. . . ." The first quotation given ("alle godes") is from an Old English psalter dated 825 C.E. The full definition of *goddess* is one page long (!) and begins: "a female deity in polytheistic systems of religion." Variant spellings from about 1340 to about 1600 are *goddesse, godesse, goddes, goddis,* and *goddace.*

"Good Friday" first appears in English in the thirteenth century. I've never understood what is "good," however, about a day when someone is tortured. But my intention here is not to debate theology; it's the words I'm interested in. So here's my theory about "Good" Friday. In Old English, spellings of *god* included *godu* and *got.* The word *good* has been spelled *gód, gode, godd,* and *goode.* I think people elided *god* and *good,* and it's really God's Friday. Even today, we often substitute *good* for *god,* as in "for goodness sake," and we know of minced forms of oaths and ejaculations that have been common since Shakespeare's day—"golly," "gosh," "gad," "gog," "ods" (as in "ods bodkins," which means "Gods body"), even "cocks."

I have a friend at the Oxford University Press. We have interesting e-mail conversations. When I made a wisecrack one day about the comparative lengths of definitions, she replied that the OED's creators (both men and women) gathered linguistic evidence. The disparity, she said, is not linguistic but social and historical.

Pax, OED. Let us make every day a *gode, godu, got, gód, gode, goode, godesse, goddis, goddace* day.

Harvey

The March Hare is the Easter Bunny before we tamed him. In Teutonic myth, he's the emblem of the goddess Eostre. The Chinese said the hare was an animal of augury who lived on the moon. There's also a famous statue of Ix Chel, the Mayan goddess of the moon, weaving, and childbirth, arm in arm with the sacred spring hare.

In the late 1940s, a play called *Harvey* by Mary Chase opened on Broadway and won the Pulitzer Prize. In 1950, it was made into a movie starring James Stewart as Elwood P. Dowd, who has wrestled with reality for thirty-five years and "won out over it." Harvey is a pooka—a tall, white, invisible rabbit—and Elwood's best friend. They hang out a lot in the local taverns talking to people. This relationship causes no end of embarrassment to Elwood's sister. Plot complications arise when she tries to have Elwood committed to the local sanitarium, Chumley's Rest. At one point in the movie, we see a portrait of Elwood and Harvey. Look at Ix Chel and the hare again. It's the same pose!

Rent this farcical, metaphysical movie tonight. One of my favorite moments is when the loutish sanitarium attendant, Wilson, looks *pooka* up in the dictionary—and Wilson's name suddenly shows up in the definition.

When Dr. Chumley learns that Harvey can stop watches, he asks Elwood if the pooka can spend some stopped time with him. Elwood asks where he'd go. Dr. Chumley says that he'd go to Akron with a pretty woman. He would send out for cold beer, and then he'd tell her things he's never told anyone else. And he'd want her to hold out her "soft, white hand" and say, "Poor thing, poor, poor thing." For two weeks.

Reader, if you met Harvey, where would you ask him to take you?

Moveable Feasts

Whenever someone talks about Jesus' having been buried for three days and three nights, I start counting on my fingers. It doesn't add up. "Three days and three nights" is actually an Aramaic idiom that means an indeterminate but fairly short time.

Easter is a moveable feast. It's left over from the lunar calendar and occurs on the first Sunday after the first full moon after the spring equinox. All three of the standard-brand religions have moveable feasts. Nearly every Jewish holy day, for example, is lunar, as are the Moslem holy days. The feast days of Hindu gods and goddesses are likewise moveable, and so are holidays celebrated according to the old Chinese calendar.

The United States has a number of secular moveable feasts, including President's Day, Memorial Day, and Labor Day. This happens because the U.S. government decided we're entitled to three-day weekends, so it moved national days, willy-nilly, to Fridays or Mondays. Some curmudgeonly people (like me) wonder if that's a good idea. While I am grateful for the three-day weekend (or would be if I worked in an office), I wonder if people know what they're commemorating on those artificial holidays. Does it matter that, say, Washington and Lincoln don't have their separate birthdays anymore? That our holidays seem to be arranged for the convenience of the corporate culture?

Here's an idea for a moveable feast: have a traveling dinner party. Start at one person's house with appetizers. Go to another person's house for the soup or salad course. Go to a third person's house for the entrée. Finally, go to someone else's house for dessert. This can be enormous fun, and the best part is that the host and hostess are not responsible for the entire (possibly expensive) meal. (It's also good to help clean up at every house.)

Cerealia

The eight-day Cerealia, which featured games and other plebian pleasures, began as the Megalesia ended (which makes me wonder when the Romans got any work done). Ceres, later identified with the Greek Demeter, was originally a southern Italian grain goddess.

About 10,000 B.C.E., hunter-gatherers in the Near East began using sickles with bone handles and flint blades to harvest grain. Marija Gimbutas tells us that a food-producing economy was established in the Aegean basin between 8000 and 7000. By 6500, Greece and other western Mediterranean lands supported a "full-fledged Neolithic economy" with domesticated sheep, goats, cattle, pigs, pigeons, and dogs. Neolithic peoples cultivated wheat, barley, vetch, lentils, peas, and flax. These were settled but not sedentary cultures. The Sesklo (northern Greece) and the Starcevo (the Balkans, Romania, Hungary) cultures had agriculture by 6500. By 5500, farmers in central Europe were growing wheat, barley, rye, mullet, oats, peas, lentils, opium poppies, and flax.

There were farming villages in Egypt by about 5000. A thousand years later, people in Turkestan had domesticated grapes, and the Chinese were cultivating rice. After 3000, olives were being raised in Crete, and maize was being cultivated in the Americas. The olive tree was taken to Italy by colonizing Greeks about 600 B.C.E. and 250 B.C.E., the Romans were introducing farming throughout their empire with ox-drawn plows, irrigation, crop rotation, and the selective breeding of plants.

Even with the growth of city-states in the European Renaissance, Western civilization was largely agricultural until the Industrial Age (late eighteenth century); a majority of soldiers drafted in World War II were farmboys. Today, it is only with the rise of agribusiness that twelve thousand years of agricultural history is being plowed under.

Vaisakhi

Today is the Sikh New Year's festival. Although they live in India (mainly in the Punjab state), the Sikhs are not Hindu. Their monotheistic religion, which was founded by Guru Nanak (1469–1539), rejects the caste system, asceticism, the priesthood, and bathing in sacred rivers. Women and men are said to be equal, and Sikh men are recognized by the five outward signs of their religion—uncut hair, steel comb, iron bracelet, short sword, and short trousers. The major temple of the Sikhs is the Golden Temple at Amritsar, which is surrounded by a sacred lake lined with marble steps. A white marble bridge leads to the temple, which is covered with golden sheets upon which are written words from their holy book; the original book is enshrined inside the temple and taken out on feast days. To celebrate Vaisakhi, people travel to Amritsar and listen to the teachings of the gurus.

It is useful to remember that Sikhs, Buddhists, Hindus, Africans, and Native Americans do not consider themselves to be pagans. Even though the original usage of the word *pagan* meant "uncivilized," today the word generally connotes people who are not Christians. To early Christians of the Roman Empire, any follower of a non-Jewish religion was a pagan, and Christian writers used *pagan* in their diatribes to disparage Greek and Roman philosophers like Plato and Plutarch. During the Renaissance, *pagan* was again used to describe Greco-Roman thought and culture, but it was now a term of high praise. In the ninteenth century, *pagan* was nearly synonymous with *classical*. It was only in the late twentieth century that *pagan* came to refer to our nature religion. Most modern pagans have European Christian or Jewish roots.

As pagans, we can be examples to others. We can respect religions that may not respect us.

The Green Language

Reader, have you heard of the green language? It's said to be a punning, multilingual, gothic, goetic, coded language. It's also said that Athena taught it to Tiresias, who apparently passed it along. If you can manage to learn it, it is further said that you'll learn the occult secrets of the ages.

I love books of weird history. You know the ones I mean—those scrumptious books about alchemy and bible codes, Mary Magdalen and the Holy Grail, Atlantis and Shambhala, Akhenaton and Fulcanelli, Rosicrucians and Freemasons, Gnosticism and lost gospels, dragons and ley lines, the pyramids and the sphinx, gods from outer space, crop circles and cathedrals. And—to tie everything together—the Templars. We *know* that the Templars are related to *everything that has ever happened.*

I have books that say the Pacific Ocean resulted from the moon being pulled out of the earth when Venus flew too close. That Leonardo da Vinci painted the Shroud of Turin. That the son of King Solomon and the Queen of Sheba took the Ark of the Covenant to Ethiopia, where it still resides. That Abraham learned monotheism from Akhenaton and that Moses was an Egyptian prince who purchased the Israelites to take along when he left home. That Atlantis, located near the Canary Islands, sank about the time of the Trojan War and the Exodus. If you've read *Holy Blood, Holy Grail*, then when you read *The Da Vinci Code* you knew within the first hundred pages that Sophie was the Lost Merovingian Princess. Huzzah!

Reader, we don't have to spend all our time reading highly serious stuff. Read some weird history. Maybe you'll catch a few hints of the green language. Even if you don't, just think of the fascinating things you'll be able to tell the guys at work tomorrow.

Tellus Mater

Let the district [*pagus*] have a feast: purify the district . . .
    And offer the year-cakes on the . . . hearths.
May the mothers of corn be pleased, both Tellus and Ceres,
    With [offerings of] spelt and the entrails of a pregnant victim.
Ceres and the Earth share a single function:
    The one gives the grain its origin, the other its location.
—Ovid, *Fasti*

Like most of the Roman gods and goddesses, Tellus Mater was originally Italian. "Earth Mother" is a literal translation of her name: *tellur* means
"earth." Early on, she had a consort named Telluno, but he was absorbed
by Jupiter.

As earth personified, she protected seeds from the time they developed in fruiting plants until they were gathered and sown back into the
soil. Although we may not like to hear about blood sacrifice, on April 15
pregnant cows were sacrificed and their unborn calves burned in Roman
temples as offerings to the earth.

In the *Fasti* Ovid writes about the Roman calendar and gives historical,
astrological, and religious information for each day of the year. Notice his
use of the word *pagus;* this is one origin of *pagan.* He says that Tellus and
Ceres were constant companions. I like to imagine them as two stereotypical,
old-fashioned Italian mothers. They're dark, plump women "of a certain
age" dressed in traditional black dresses, headscarves, and sensible shoes.
In the springtime, they walk arm in arm through the land gossiping about
their troublesome children, both human and divine. And as they walk and
gossip, Tellus and Ceres encourage the land, pregnant with springtime, to
give birth. They whisper their birthing secrets to the barnyard animals and
tickle the roots of the wheat and grapes.

Demeter and Persephone

After Kore was kidnapped by her uncle Hades and taken to his underground realm, she grew up and was somehow renamed Persephone. Demeter refused to let any green thing grow until she was reunited with her daughter. The life force of the earth died.

It seems to me that little girls today are suffering from a major lack of *veriditas*. The divine life force of girls is not being encouraged to grow and flower. What can we do for our daughters, granddaughters, and nieces?

Before anything else, we must cherish them. We must value each girl for her own self, not as our trophy child or projection holder. Let every girl be as smart as she can be. Don't let teachers ignore her raised hand, don't let peer pressure teach her that she has to play dumb.

We must keep our girls healthy. In a time when the artificial hormones in our food are inducing premature adolescence, we need to feed them healthier food. In a time when eight-year-old girls think they're too fat and start dieting, we need to teach these girls that real women don't look like supermodels. In a time when there are Amber Alerts every other day, we must teach self-defense to young girls.

Our little girls (and our little boys) are our hope for the future, the seeds planted by humankind's old trees before they fall down. We've had spectacular flowers in our generations on the earth, but they haven't been strong enough to stop the clear-cutting of our souls. Our girls will grow up to be mothers who teach their children to think and dream. Let us teach them to dream of a happier world and make it so. Maybe we can arrive at critical mass, and our little girls, grown up, will save the forests.

···APRIL 17···

Armageddon

According to AEGSA Web site, April 17 is said to be the day in 1468 B.C.E. when Pharaoh Tuthmoses III of the Eighteenth Dynasty won the battle of Armageddon. The battle, which involved more than 30,000 men, took place at the fortress of Megiddo (near Haifa in modern Israel). The Egyptian force defeated assembled armies that no doubt included Hebrew warriors. The writers of the Old Testament somehow neglected to mention this battle, but John, author of the Book of Revelation, picked it up to be his metaphor for the Apocalypse, or final battle of the world. Tuthmoses III is said to be Egypt's greatest warrior-pharaoh, and his victory at Megiddo was the beginning of Egypt's rise to imperial power.

Maybe it's just me, but I don't understand why we've always idolized warriors. From Joshua and Achilles, to King Arthur and El Cid, to Dwight D. Eisenhower and Colin Powell, we've celebrated men who lead armies that kill each other, conquer the land, and subjugate the women and children. I see bumperstickers that say "support our troops," and I wonder how to support people whose job is to kill. Some warriors, of course, became peacemakers. Peacemaking, it seems to me, should be the proper work of a general. Reader, what do you think?

On a beautiful green April day, I like to listen to the chants of Hildegard of Bingen and contemplate the greening power of peaceful gods and goddesses. Here's a translation by Norma Gentile:

> O Life-green finger of God,
> in you God has placed a garden.
> You reflect heaven's eminent radiance
> like a raised pillar.
> You are glorious.

Demeter

Demeter, one of the most archaic goddesses, started out in livestock. As a horse-headed goddess, she was raped by Poseidon and bore him a daughter who became a Fury. After Zeus, in disguise as a bull, raped her, she bore Kore. In wild Arcadia, she was represented with a horse's head and surrounded by snakes and beasts; she a dolphin held in one hand and a dove in the other. When she moved to Attica, she lost the wildness.

Her name can mean either "earth mother" or "grain mother." Like Ceres—the two are inextricably conflated—she is goddess of the surface of the earth and the cultivated plants and grains that feed us. Whereas offerings to Tellus Mater were slaughtered and frequently cooked (which made the sacrifices nice communal dinners), offerings to Demeter were given on a fireless, bloodless altar. Honeycombs, unspun wool, unpressed grapes, and uncooked grain were returned to the grain mother.

Demeter is the granddaughter of Gaia, the planet itself, and daughter of Rhea and Cronus. Rhea, whose name is Cretan, probably originated as a mountain goddess on that island. When the Achaeans (the tribe that won the Trojan War) came down from the north and conquered Greece and the Mediterranean islands, the various god systems were mixed and matched, turning Rhea and Cronus into Titans and creating the cosmopolitan Olympians.

Some Wiccan traditions include "cakes and ale" as part of their rituals. Everyone reserves a sip of their wine or juice and a bite of their cornbread or muffin. These are collected by the priestess. After the circle is opened, the wine is poured on the earth and the bits of bread are left in the garden for the fairies or any hungry critter. We're still making offerings to our grain mothers.

Under the Rainbow

Just because their kings converted (usually for political reasons), this didn't mean the common people became Christians overnight. We did not abandon our grain mothers. In *The Goddess Obscured*, by Pamela Berger, we learn of the metamorphosis of Tellus, Demeter, and Ceres into saints.

One popular medieval story, which became attached to St. Radegund, tells how Mary, Jesus, and Joseph, fleeing from Herod's soldiers, come to a field of grain. Mary (or the saint) begs the grain for protection. The young grain seems to nod. As the Holy Family steps into the field, the grain immediately grows so high that when the soldiers arrive they are completely hidden. When the soldiers ask the farmer if he has seen anyone pass by, he replies, "No, not since I sowed this very grain." Seeing the mature wheat and knowing it takes months for grain to grow, the soldiers go on their way.

On the very day I bought *The Goddess Obscured*, I saw the end of the rainbow. It was an *El Niño* season, and I was visiting a friend in Santa Barbara. One afternoon we drove to Montecito to visit the Sarada Convent. I headed right for the bookstore. When I happened to look out the front window, I saw a rainbow arching over the convent and touching the Pacific Ocean at the foot of the hill. I called my friend's attention to the beautiful sight. We oohed and aahed, then turned back to the bookshelves. As I was looking at the illustrations in *The Goddess Obscured*, I walked to the back window for better light. I looked out. And there, rising from the green, wooded hill behind the convent, was the other end of the rainbow.

Reader, what wondrous sign have you received that the Goddess is alive and paying attention to you?

Sun Enters Taurus

Taurus, my friend Lilith says, is very straightforward about his or her feelings, very matter of fact. With a Taurus, you know where you stand. I've had a lot of Taurus friends. One was a technical writer who was built like a bull, not tall but barrel-chested, with a voice that could be heard clear across the "bullpen" where a whole team of tech writers labored over aerospace proposals.

Veriditas "awakens everything to life," Hildegard says. "The air lives by turning green and being in bloom. The waters flow as if they were alive." *Veriditas* flows through the earth as vibrant energy in all realms, spiritual or physical. "The soul," she writes, "is the green life-force of the flesh." In the book of her visions, *Scivias*, Hildegard also writes that the soul gives "vitality to the marrow and veins and members of the whole body."

Pagans sometimes object to the word *soul*, thinking it's a Christian concept. That's not true. It's from a Teutonic or Gothic word, *sáwol*, meaning the vital, sensitive, intellectual, spiritual, rational principle in plants, animals, and human beings. That's also *veriditas*.

On the human level, what is *veriditas* if not our feelings? Like water, our feelings flow through us, sometimes underground but powerful, sometimes in gentle streams or rapids on the surface. Even people like my friend the taurine tech writer, who said his skin was as thick as the hide of a rhinoceros, have strong feelings.

I think using *feelings* works in this context without doing too much damage to Hildegard's thought. Perhaps if she lived in today's secular world and observed how modern pagans think (and feel), she might say that our greening feelings give us our vitality. No matter what we call it, *veriditas* flows through us, physically, emotionally, mentally, and spiritually.

Parilia

The Parilia was celebrated to honor Pales, a Roman pastoral god or goddess. Sheepfolds were decorated with green branches, animals were driven between purifying fires, and milk and cakes were offered to the deity. This celebration is the origin of the Catholic Blessing of the Animals.

April 21 is the day tradition says Rome was founded. In one story, Romulus founded the city. Another version is told by Rome's chief poet, Publius Vergilius Maro, or Virgil, in his epic poem, the *Aeneid*. Aeneas, the hero, is the son of Venus and Anchises, a Trojan. At the end of the Trojan War, as Aeneas is leading a band of survivors out of the ruined city, Poseidon tells the other gods to protect him because he will become king of a great people. Aeneas and his companions wander for seven years in search of their destined home, stopping in numerous famous locations, including Carthage (modern Tunisia). Dido, queen of Carthage, falls in love with Aeneas. When he abandons her, like Aida and Madame Butterfly, Dido commits suicide.

Finally, Aeneas and his brave (but no doubt weary) band of Trojans land at Cumae in Italy. Aeneas meets the Sybil, who tells him to pluck the golden bough and takes him to the underworld, where his dead father tells him to sail north to the Tiber River to a place where there are seven hills. Here Aeneas founds the city.

The story goes on and on. Virgil uses history and myth to put "predictions" of glorious Roman history into his characters' mouths. Aeneas will get the help of the Etruscans in the Italian wars. He and his descendants will rule for three hundred years. The Romans ("people of the toga") will conquer Greece and most of the rest of the classical world.

The Beltane Papers

Back in the 1980s, when the current wave of feminist scholarship was in its infancy, Helen Farias dreamed of publishing a magazine. Her first newsletter went out in April, 1984. Although Helen died in 1994, *The Beltane Papers: A Journal of Women's Mysteries* still exists, the masthead says, "to provide women with a safe place within which to explore and express the sacred in their lives, to educate, empower, encourage and entertain, to inspire, support and reinforce their perception of reality."

With a distinguished advisory council of thirteen of our leading writers and feminist theologians, thoughtful articles and columns, poetry, book reviews, and occasional fiction, *The Beltane Papers* has grown from a modest newsletter to a beautiful magazine. The magazine within the magazine, *Octava*, celebrates the eight sabbats with history, traditions, and rituals.

We pagans like to say we work by consensus, that we're abolishing the hierarchy and the corporate organization chart. About the only thing we agree on, however, is that that's easier said than done. We can point to pagan groups that have never gotten anything actually done and other groups that have imploded from the weight of egos parading as consensus builders. But *The Beltane Papers* has successfully walked the talk for twenty years. It is published by the Brideswell Collective, which was formed on Candlemas, 1992, as "a conscious experiment in women working together for a common goal." The collective is an all-volunteer, feminist, egalitarian group of extremely busy women, who work not in a central office but in their homes throughout the United States. The magazine is a tribute not only to the power of the Goddess and women working together, but also to the power of e-mail and good software. A magazine that uses a system of time based on the discovery of agriculture functions smoothly in the twenty-first century.

Venus, St. George, and William Shakespeare

Gardens are sacred to Venus. Today is one of the two annual Vinalias, when wine was poured on the soil.

From the Middle Ages until recently, St. George's day was an English fertility festival, with parades of dragons and hobbyhorses, morris dancing, and general merriment. England's patron saint since his adoption by Edward III, the "historical" St. George was either an Arian bishop of Alexandria or a martyred Roman warrior. The mythical St. George reminds us of Bellerophon, the hero who slew the chimera, which to the Greeks was a fearsome monster with a lion's head, a goat's body, and a serpent's tail. To us, a chimera is only "an illusion or fabrication of the mind."

Today is Shakespeare's birthday. He's said to have been an ignorant country boy. Early in 2004, Michael Wood presented *In Search of Shakespeare* on PBS, in which he traces obscure records of Shakespeare's life and shows where and how Shakespeare received his education.

Scholars of the occult—most famously Manly P. Hall—insist that the mysteries of Rosicrucianism and Freemasonry can be dredged out of Shakespeare's plays, which makes Sir Francis Bacon their true author. My favorite alternative theory comes from a PBS *Frontline* program, *Much Ado About Something*, which proposed Christopher Marlowe as the real Shakespeare. Marlowe, also born in 1564 and an equally great dramatist, had a university education. A notorious hell-raiser and spy in the police state that was Elizabethan England, he was stabbed in a bar fight and died in 1593. But what if that was a cover story? What if he escaped? Several critics speculate that Marlowe went into exile in Italy, where many of Shakespeare's plays are set. Perhaps he wrote the iambic pentameter and sent the plays to London, where Shakespeare wrote the prose parts.

Trees

When I was a kid, our neighbor had a huge, giant, enormous weeping willow tree. It was taller than their two-story house, and the canopy its foliage made as it dipped to the ground was twenty feet in diameter. Spring, summer, and fall, we made that tree our private universe. We acted out epic (comic book) dramas there. One of our fathers built a platform up where the strongest branches made a V, and that became our treehouse. I remember climbing so high the branches could hardly bear my weight. I learned to leap, like Tarzan, from swaying branch to swaying branch. My brother fell out of the tree a couple of times, but I never did. I was queen of that arboreal universe!

We kids thought we'd invented that universe. Then I grew up and learned that trees have been honored as long as people have been able to take shelter under them, use them as landmarks, burn them as fuel, turn their trunks into lumber, or eat their fruit.

We know the Celtic tree alphabet and its tree months. We're familiar with the shamanic *axis mundi*, with Ygdrassil and the nine worlds of Norse mythology, with the Sephirotic Tree of Life and its four worlds, with the Tree of Knowledge in the Garden of Eden. We've heard the tales of the Royal Oak that sheltered Charles II from Cromwell's army and the Bodhi Tree under which the Buddha found enlightenment. We've heard of the Irmimsûl, the great Saxon Pillar of Heaven that Charlemagne chopped down. We've heard of Liberty Trees, hung with flags and caps during the American and French Revolutions.

Culture, kings, and kids—everyone has a tree story. Reader, did you climb trees when you were young? Did you have a treehouse? Do you still?

Re-Formed Congregation of the Goddess, International (RCG-I)

Founded by Jade River and Lynn Levy and incorporated in 1984, RCG-I is the oldest and largest officially recognized women's religious organization in the United States. RCG-I's Web site states that members "embrace a variety of spiritual paths, the common element among them being a belief in female divinity and a commitment to positive spiritual practice." The Women's Theological Institute offers three programs of self-directed spiritual development. The Cella Program is like an independent university where women create their own courses of study and complete projects in areas like ritualism, healing, and administration. The Crone Program, for women over fifty-three, "builds on a woman's past, but focuses on creating a future." The Guardian Program is for women "who identify with the amazon archetype." At rituals, guardians hold the energy of the circle by standing or walking outside it. They have also been known to chase intruders away.

In her book, *To Know*, Jade traces the history and theology of Dianic Wicca. "It is difficult," she writes, "to describe the relationship between women's spirituality and neo-Paganism. Perhaps the best analogy is that they are two streams flowing into the same river." I especially like the RCG-I Affirmation of Women's Spirituality:

- *To Know* . . . that I can create my own reality and that sending out a positive expectation will bring a positive result. . . .

- *To Will* . . . that I shall try never to use my energy unwisely or to limit the free will of another. . . .

- *To Dare* . . . to be myself [and] to take responsibility for myself [and] to be strong and independent. . . .

- And *To Understand* when to speak and when to keep silence.[9]

Marcus Aurelius

Marcus Aurelius Antoninus, Roman emperor from 161 to 180, was one of the "good" emperors, a philosophical monarch who was considerably less dramatic than the likes of Caligula and Nero. He founded a Mithraic temple on the Vatican Hill that was desecrated by the Christian Prefect of Rome in 376.

His *Meditations*, which he wrote in Greek, expound the principles of Stoicism, a school of philosophy established in Athens by Zeno of Citium in the fourth century B.C.E. The basic principle of Stoicism is that man must live in accordance with nature and his chief aim must be the attainment of perfect reason. Wisdom and virtue are the only true values. The original "stoic attitude" accepts the limitations of life and the inevitability of death. Today, Marcus is considered to be one of the great pagan thinkers. "All that is harmony for you, my Universe," he wrote, "is in harmony with me as well. Nothing that comes at the right time for you is too early or too late for me. . . . All things come of you, have their being in you, and return to you."

There's a dichotomy of religious expression that goes all the way back to the Greeks. Followers of the mystery "cults," like those of Cybele and Serapis, sought ecstasy and emotionality in worship, whereas the Stoics cultivated reason. Today we see this as a difference between evangelical Christianity and mainstream Protestantism. We also see it among pagans. Some people love to drum and dance and strip off their clothes and fall into a trance. Others want a more intellectual ritual with drumming, for sure, but also teaching we can get our mental teeth into.

Reader, when you design a ritual, what is your focus? Do you prefer ecstasy or intellectual rigor in your practice of your paganism?

Farewell, Promised Land

Sometimes the *veriditas* gets leached out. I was searching my book-shelves for books about trees when I came upon *Farewell, Promised Land*. The photograph on the cover shows a pier extending into a lake. There's a locked gate halfway down the pier. The "promised land," the authors write, "has been filled in, paved over, drained, torn down, burned out—inevitably crowded out. Too much has been removed from the wild—made tame or destroyed."[10]

I remember a news story about a major developer who was building a gated community in northern Los Angeles County. There was one major road into the "exclusive enclave." Practically in the middle of the road stood a five-hundred-year-old oak tree. When the developer said he would have to chop the oak down so he could widen his road, people gathered to save the tree, and a man took up residence in its branches. The reporters didn't mention that any protestors were pagan, but I'll lay money that some were. What finally happened? The developer fenced the tree and arrested the tree-sitter for trespassing. A company was hired to move the oak. According to later reports, it had been replanted down the road. Last I heard, it was still alive, though weak.

If I went into a wilderness I'd probably never find my way out. Nevertheless, I think of forests and I sigh. There is enormous natural beauty in every one of our fifty states, wild and precious green land everywhere on the planet. But there are also the realistic demands of human society. We cannot live on the planet without changing it. Building a log cabin means destroying a small part of some wild place. Reader, what can we do to plant some *veriditas* in the hearts and minds of people who need a place to live?

Floralia

> Come live with me, and be my love,
> And we will some new pleasures prove
> Of golden sands, and crystal brooks,
> With silken lines and silver hooks.
> —John Donne, *The Bait*

Today is the first day of the Floralia, a three-day love festival. Flora was a Sabine goddess of youthful pleasures, whose worship is said to have been introduced into Rome by King Titus Tatius. For the Floralia, inaugurated in 238 B.C.E. as a dictate of the Sibylline books, people decorated themselves with flowers and engaged in a feast of unrestrained love and merriment. There were also games and lewd theatrical performances. (And we think Mardi Gras invented bawdiness.)

If I went to a Floralia, I'd hijack a time machine and kidnap the poets below and take them with me. Here are my favorite lines from Donne's *Elegy 19, To His Mistress Going to Bed*:

> License my roving hands, and let them go
> Before, behind, between, above, below.
> O my America, my new found land,
> My kingdom safeliest when with one man manned,
> My mine of precious stones, my empery,
> How blessed am I in this discovering thee!

And these lines are from Marvel's *To His Coy Mistress*:

> Had we but world enough, and time,
> This coyness, Lady, were no crime . . . .
> But at my back I always hear
> Time's winged chariot hurrying near;
> And yonder all before us lie
> Deserts of vast eternity.

Labyrinths

The labyrinth is a spiral pattern that dates back at least four thousand years and is found on pottery, tablets, and tiles. Unlike a maze, a labyrinth has one path that leads to the center and back out again. You can't get lost in a labyrinth. It's not a rat race, there are no dead ends or false turnings. The Web site *Veriditas.net* says it is "a path of prayer, a walking meditation, a crucible of change, a watering hole for the spirit and a mirror of the soul."

The labyrinth at Chartres Cathedral, inlaid in the stone floor when the cathedral was built in the early thirteenth century, had been ignored for centuries and covered by chairs. In 1996, Dr. Lauren Artress duplicated the Chartres labyrinth at Grace Cathedral in San Francisco and began using it as a meditation and healing tool. Today, using the *Veriditas.net* "labyrinth locator," we can find labyrinths all over the United States. There are also books that teach you not only how to properly walk the labyrinth, but also how to draw one and how to make a "finger labyrinth."

I once belonged to a Goddess circle that constructed a labyrinth on the beach at dawn on the summer solstice. We drew the path with kelp, put fruit and flowers in the center, and invited everyone we knew to walk with us. Now I go to the labyrinth at a local Unity Church.

As you stand at the opening, you can see the entire path, which is marked with river pebbles. You begin walking, back and forth, making sharp turns, and you're traveling through the whole wide world. Even as you focus so you won't trip, your mind goes somewhere else. Just when you think you'll never come to the center, you make a final turn and there you are.

Walpurgis Night

Although May Day—Beltane—means fertility rites in the fields, May Eve, or *Walpurgisnacht*, has a sinister reputation. It's the night German witches ride on broomsticks and he-goats to the top of the Brocken for revelry on the highest point of the Harz Mountains. In the Walpurgis Night scene in Goethe's *Faust*, written in 1808, Dr. Faustus meets Mephistopheles. This devilish personage introduces him to Lilith, a "pretty witch," who coyly says, "Ever since the days of Eden/Apples have been man's desire./How overjoyed I am to think, sir,/Apples grow, too, in my garden" (Greenberg translation).

We're probably most familiar with Walpurgis Night from the segment in Disney's *Fantasia* (1940) set to Mussorgsky's *Night on Bald Mountain*. I've just found another Walpurgis Night movie: *Valborgsmässoafton* (1935), starring Ingrid Bergman, is a Swedish melodrama about office love and an abortion.

Walpurgis Night also reminds us of the Wild Hunt. There are two versions of this medieval legend. In one, Diana leads a coven of wild women across the skies. In the other, the Huntsman, whose name may be Herne, leads his dogs and hunts the unwary.

St. Walburga was an eighth-century nun. Born in Sussex, England, she was called to missionary work in Germany. When the ship taking her across the North Sea was assaulted by a terrible storm, Walburga knelt on the deck and prayed. The sea became calm. She was later appointed abbess of a double community at Heidenheim. She is sometimes shown holding three ears of corn, which may have connected her in the peasants' minds with their old grain mothers. Her connection with May Eve came about because her relics were carried to Eichstatt on May 1, 870. The saint, the *Catholic Encyclopedia* assures us, has nothing to do with the pagan festival.

Isis Oasis Sanctuary

On May 1, 1978, Loreon Vigne, artist and priestess of Isis, purchased ten acres of land near Geyserville, California, seventy-five miles north of the Golden Gate Bridge. The land was already sacred. It had once been a Pomo tribal ceremonial ground and, later, the setting for a Baha'i school. It is now the Isis Oasis Sanctuary, whose centerpiece is a five-hundred-year-old fir tree. Seeing this sanctuary, we can easily imagine that a goddess from the black land beside the Nile can find honor and happiness here at the Russian River. In addition to the fir, there are a swan pond, waterfalls, and an aviary, as well as a temple and meditation space.

Loreon's intent is to keep the wisdom of the ancient Egyptian tradition alive with "magical rites, scroll teachings, and studies of the forty-two laws of Ma'at at our Grand Temple before an altar to the Goddess Isis." The Temple of Isis, which is a lyceum of the Fellowship of Isis, is open for spiritual events, including regular Sunday-afternoon services, healing retreats for women and men, goddess festivals and workshops, craft weekends, and guest speakers. The redwood theater is open for cultural events like concerts, films, plays, and dance performances.

We've read about temples and sanctuaries from Lindisfarne to Malta. Novels and nonfiction books tell us how people were healed in mind and body. They could take the waters, receive massage, ask an oracle for advice, sleep and incubate beneficial dreams, and experience true mystery. People like Loreon are establishing sanctuaries where we can revive the old wisdom and use New Age healing modalities, too.

We like to dream about reviving the ancient pagan world. That's not possible, but buying and healing parcels of land and building temples is perhaps a viable way to build a pagan future in the world.

Guinevere

In Alfred, Lord Tennyson's *Idylls of the King*, King Arthur's court is faux-medieval and high Victorian at the same time. Any work of Victoria's poet laureate couldn't be anything else. But what do we know about a historical King Arthur? There are dozens of books about Arthur and his court. Was Arthur a sixth-century Romano-Celtic chieftain? In 1191, monks discovered the bones of Arthur and Guinevere in a ruined abbey on Glastonbury Tor. They took them to King Henry II, but the bones have long since disappeared. Were they genuine? Was the Arthurian court pagan, Christian, or both? Does it matter?

Was there a real Guinevere? It is possible that she is a Welsh triple goddess, for variants on the Arthurian legend say he married three women, all named Guinevere. The ancient tradition says that the king must "marry" the land. If he is happy and well, so are the land and the people; if he is wounded, so are they. This is vividly shown in John Boorman's cheesy but fascinating film, *Excalibur*.

Early in Lerner and Lowe's musical *Camelot*, Guinevere sings "The Merry Month of May" and invites several knights to ride with her. Then she meets Lancelot. What do people always remember about Guinevere? She betrays Arthur, whom she loves, by sleeping with Lancelot. Like other Celtic goddesses (Maeve and Blodewedd), Guinevere can make a king through sacred marriage and unmake him by choosing a new hero.

In May, betrayal lies in the future. Guinevere is the May Queen. We can't help but fall in love with her. We witness her life and all of her moods—occasionally divine, altogether human, sometimes regal, sometimes prissily religious—when we read the Arthurian novels of Marion Zimmer Bradley, Mary Stewart, T. H. White, and others.

Tending Our Gardens

❧

Is there a pagan among us who does not have a garden? My garden consists of plants in pots, some lined up on crates and tables outside my windows along the building's common patio, some hanging in wrought-iron holders up the stairs to the second story. It gets chilly enough in Southern California that some of my plants die back in the winter, but most survive all year. Because the front of the building faces west, in the summer I have to move plants into shade and water them frequently. Because it's a potted garden, I need to be tending it every day so the plants don't die.

Reader, how do you tend your garden? If you live where it gets cold, what kind of gardening do you do in the winter? Do you study seed catalogs and plant books and make lists? When do you begin your spring dreaming and planting? Are you fortunate enough to have a yard and a real garden? I've heard that women prefer flowers, whereas men generally grow edibles.

We also plant metaphorical gardens. Maybe they should be called karmic gardens. The word *broadcast* comes from the way farmers once sowed seed. They'd take a handful out of the bag over their shoulder and fling it out across the ground to fall where it might or be carried away by the wind. Let's think about the seeds we're broadcasting. Some of our seeds fall close to home, but many fly across the Net and the Web and end up who knows where. That makes for very big gardens. And some unexpected blooms. You know what they say—what goes around comes back around. As you sow, so shall you reap.

May is the month of flowers. Let's talk about gardens and flowers.

···MAY 4···
Bona Dea, Sacred Hawthorne, Dressing the Well

❤

In the Roman Republic, Bona Dea ("good goddess") was a mysterious women's goddess. She may have been an earth goddess, but we can only speculate about her identity and rites. Because several poets mention over-hearing the sounds of hilarity, it's possible that Bona Dea's rites were something like a Roman girls' night out. In 62 B.C.E., they were held in the house of Julius Caesar, although Julius was *not* there that night because men were not allowed to participate. One night, Publius Claudius disguised himself as a woman, snuck into the rites, and was found out. There was a major scandal, but even he did not reveal the mystery.

Hawthorn is also called white thorn, May tree, haw-tree, and thorn apple. It's a member of the rose family that produces white flowers early in May and little red fruits afterward. In Ireland, it's a holy tree, the destruction of which is said to be followed by the destruction of one's wealth, cattle, and children.

In Britain, Ireland, Greece, and Rome alike, people performed purification ceremonies in early May, one of which centered on the local sacred well. Nearly any well is sacred, and wells throughout Europe were marked by hawthorns. During the first week of the month, the young women "brought in the May" by gathering flowering branches to be used for decoration, divination, and healing. The women also "dressed the well," by hanging new scraps of white cloth (often torn from their clothing) on the hawthorn to request healing or purification.

If you live near or can find a sacred well, dress it today. If there's no well nearby, dress a tree and make a wish for healing with each scrap of white cloth you tie to a branch. While you're there, pick up the trash around the well or the tree.

Wesak

When the moon is full in Taurus, a worldwide festival celebrates Prince Gautama's attainment of Buddhahood. It is said that during this moon cycle the Buddha himself returns to earth to bless the planet and all its peoples, and that increased communication between the visible and invisible planes is possible. Those who are sensitive to this Buddhistic energy can feel it. Mainstream metaphysics tells us that the Wesak energy is the result of the Buddha and the Christ working together to bless all humanity.

Some years ago, I attended regular full-moon meditations at the house of a Scottish lawyer and his Latina wife. They were devotees to Satya Sai Baba and kept a special chair for him. Other people who meditated with us were Buddhists, Jews, agnostics, and several varieties of Christians. We would gather with the intention to bring harmony among religions.

One Wesak, Sai Baba came via an inner plane. I admit I didn't see him myself, but I felt a strong energy and I did see the *vibhuti*, his sacred ash. Other people did see him. More recently, I have attended pipe ceremonies led by a medicine woman and pipe carrier who is a friend of mine. When I received my Green Tara refuge and initiations, I was the only witch and non-Buddhist in the room, and nobody had a problem with it.

Reader, my point is that it's good to get out and see what other people are doing. You probably attend sabbats regularly, but do you engage in more ecumenical spiritual practices? Just as there are fundamentalists in all religions (including ours), so are there people of goodwill in all religions. When was the last time you had a meaningful conversation with a Buddhist monk, a rabbi, an imam, or a Christian clergyperson?

Inghean Bhuidhe

❦

Inghean Bhuidhe (pronounced een-AWN boo-EE) is the "yellow haired girl" associated in pagan Ireland with sacred wells. She is the middle sister of a triad of goddesses responsible for the growing cycle of crops, a mother goddess who represents the coming of summer and ripening of the crops. Even though she became a Christian saint, her wells were still sacred, and her day is the first day of summer.

The youngest sister of the triad, Latiaran ("breast of light"), is the crone goddess who recycles the harvest season into the planting season. Latiaran went to the smithy every morning to fetch a "seed of fire." One morning, the smith told her she had pretty feet; when she looked down, her apron caught fire, but she was not burnt. The eldest sister, Lasair ("flame"), is the maiden goddess of budding flowers in the spring. Before she became a Christian saint, she lived in a fiery red castle.

It's interesting that in this triad of goddesses the first is the harvest crone and the last is the one who buds. We're accustomed to thinking of the cycle as moving from maiden (budding) to mother (ripening) to crone (harvesting), but here we begin with the recycling of the harvest. In Greece, when Hera was bathed in the sacred rivers in the springtime, her crone aspect was washed away and her virginity restored.

Thus are we told that when we plant we need to consider what we will harvest, and when we harvest we must consider what will next be planted. This wisdom is useful not only for farmers, but also for anyone who does magic. Reader, when we do a spell, do we have our outcome clearly in mind? Have we given any thought to what will be planted next in that same field?

The Language of Flowers

Here's flowers for you:
Hot lavender, mints, savory, marjoram,
The marigold, that goes to bed wi' the sun,
And with him rises weeping: these are flowers
Of middle summer. . . .
—William Shakespeare, *The Winter's Tale*

Shakespeare's plays are full of flowers, not only as props but also as metaphors. Perdita, the king's lost daughter, speaks the sad words given above. Another flowery Shakespearean girl is Ophelia. When Hamlet's feigned insanity drives her mad, she famously wanders across the stage muttering, "There's rosemary, that's for remembrance. . . . "

The language of flowers reached its greatest popularity during the Victorian era (1837–1901), when social conventions prevented people from saying aloud what they were thinking or feeling. While Victoria was on the English throne, people had "limbs," poultry leg and breast meat came to be called "dark" and "white," and piano legs were modestly covered.

Lovers had to find subtler ways to speak. If a suitor handed a girl a bouquet right side up, that meant he had positive thoughts about her; upside down, he had negative thoughts. Every variety of rose or lily had its own meaning, and so did potted plants (the begonia signifies "a fanciful nature"), herbs (parsley is "useful knowledge"), and spices (cinnamon means "my fortune is yours").

Reader, learn the language of flowers. Instead of sending a *billet-doux* to your honey, send a tussie-mussie, which is a small bouquet wrapped in a lace doily. Do you know a sage or a crone having a birthday? Does he already have too many neckties or she too many kitchen gadgets? Ivy means "fidelity and friendship." The cattleya orchid signifies "mature charm." Your friends will be delighted by the flowery language.

Dame Julian of Norwich

❦

We don't even know her real name. She lived through the Black
Plague twice before she was twenty, and when she was thirty, she became
so ill she received last rites. As she lay close to death, she received a series
of sixteen visions, or showings, of a loving god. Her joy was so enormous
she said she'd found all she ever wanted. She lived the last twenty years
of her life as an anchorite in a tiny room beside St. Julian's Church in
Norwich, England. Her cell had no door—only a single window to which
people came to ask her blessing. As was the custom, she took her name
from the name of the church, and so we know her only as Dame Julian
of Norwich.

Dame Julian (1342–ca.1417) was the first woman to write in English.
At a time when women could be punished for addressing theological topics, she wrote, "Because I am a woman, ought I therefore to believe that I
ought not to tell you about the goodness of God, when I saw . . . that it is
his will that it be known?" In a misogynistic society, she found loving
motherhood in the father god: "I am . . . the power and goodness of
fatherhood; I am . . . the wisdom and lovingness of motherhood . . . "
(translation by Colledge and Walsh).

When we read the words of medieval mystics like Hildegard and
Dame Julian, we're tempted to see them as proto-pagans. Please don't
make this mistake. These women were Christian mystics and would be
horrified to be reinterpreted. What we can bring away from their words
is the fact that a few women courageously spoke and wrote about an
inner mysticism that goes beyond the limits of a particular interpretation
of a particular god.

Lemuria

To the Romans, *lemurs* (also called *larvae*) were the disembodied, wandering spirits of dead ancestors. Because the dead came back in February and May, Romans performed rites of exorcism during these two months. Ovid tells us how the paterfamilias banished dead family members. The father would rise from his bed at midnight and, remaining silent, make certain (obscene) gestures to dismiss the *lemurs*. Then he would wash his hands three times. Next he would put black beans in his mouth and spit them out, saying (nineteen times), "Thee I send forth." The ghosts were supposed to pick up the beans and go away. If any remained, he would say, "Shadows of my fathers, depart!"

I'm not sure how the linguistic connection was made, but Lemuria is also the name of a drowned continent said to lie under the Pacific Ocean. In *Isis Unveiled* (1888), Madame Helena Petrovna Blavatsky wrote that the Lemurians were giants who flourished a million years ago, which made Lemuria older than Atlantis. In 1926, an ex-British army officer named James Churchward wrote about the destruction of Lemuria, or Mu, claiming the Lemurians had colonized Central and South America. H. P. Lovecraft also wrote about the Lemurians, and there's a group of people in Illinois who claim Lemurian descent.

Lemurs are arboreal primates to whom Carl Linnaeus gave the Latin name because they have ghostly eyes and nocturnal habits. The word *larva*, given to the wingless form of a newly hatched insect, comes from the alternate Latin name of the *lemur*. From a bean-spitting paterfamilias to a lost continent to primates and immature insects—Reader, how much more fun can we have on a page?

Look for your own ancestral ghosts at midnight. Unless you want to ask them family secrets, spit black beans at them and banish them to lost Lemuria.

Inner Gardening

I'm a majorly inner gardener. As I sit here at my computer next to the window, I look at my plants out on the patio and promise to water them . . . and then I get distracted trying to figure out how to properly prune a sentence. When I look again, I see wilted leaves. It's hot this week. One of my plants turns into a crispy critter every couple of days. I click on "save" and rush out the door with the watering can.

I love the outdoors—as long as it's out there and I'm in here and there's a nice window between us. I believe that every bit of land on the planet is holy land and that all wilderness is sacred. It doesn't need my footprints on it. I'm with Woody Allen: I don't like to get the outdoors on me. I don't even like to get climate on me.

I'm one of the few pagans I know who almost never goes to outdoor rituals. The night's too dark, and I trip over things I can't see, which is just about everything. The ocean's too big and the tide's coming in. The beach is too crowded and dirty and I don't like to get sand between my toes. The woods are too full of rocks and roots and bushes, to all of which I'm probably allergic. The lions and tigers and bears are unfriendly. The desert's too hot, and the smoke from the sacred campfire makes me cough.

Inner gardening is more than plants in pots. The phrase is a metaphor for the cultivation of our spirit. Our plants, no matter where they're growing, teach us how to stay green and bloom. We can learn that cultivating our plants reminds us to cultivate our relationships with our families and friends. (More about this later.)

Eisheilige

In southern Germany, the *eisheilige*— the "iceman days"—is the brief cooling trend in May. The "ice saints," Mamertius, Pancratius, and Servatus, were celebrated on May 11. Along with Cold Sophie, these "strong lords" are pagan figures who were turned into Christian saints were said to bring cold weather during planting season. They'd kill a budding tree or a field of sprouting wheat the minute they touched it with their frosty fingers or blew on it with their freezing breath. Farmers learned early on not to set plants out until after the ice saints had come and gone.

Sometimes we find ice saints in our lives, people whose presence chills our blood and infects our happiness with frostbite. They're self-righteous, hypocritical, and extremely annoying. They're bigger control freaks than we are and insist that a household chore or a ritual has to be performed "their way or the highway." Sometimes they threaten physical harm. Sometimes they're psychic vampires who steal our energy. Sometimes they're thieves who steal our stuff or our work.

They're all poisonous people. We need to get them out of our lives. One banishing technique I like—but which must be done with finely focused aim and a strong intention to harm none—is to put the ice saint right where he or she belongs: in the freezer. Write the person's name and behavior on a piece of paper and bind it with black thread and thirteen knots. Say out loud exactly what the ice saint does that is dangerous. Say out loud that you want to bind *the behavior*. You're not out to injure the person, just to protect yourself and get him or her out of your life. Put the piece of paper in a little jar, fill it with water, and put it in your freezer. Then take real-life action to get the ice saint out of your life.

Roses

Once upon a time, Chloris, a Greek flower goddess, asked the Three Graces to help her create a beautiful new flower. The Graces gave it joy, brightness, and charm. Soon Aphrodite gave the flower beauty, and Dionysus contributed a special nectar that turned into perfume. Finally, Zephyr, the god of the west wind, blew away the clouds so the flower could open her petals to the sun. Thus was born the rose.

The cultivation of roses probably began five thousand years ago in China and the Middle East. A Minoan fresco dating back to 1500 B.C.E. shows a *gallica*, or damask, rose. According to the Persians, a nightingale began to sing when the first rose bloomed. In the fifteenth century, the Rosicrucians selected the rose, which was emblematic of the heart, and mounted it on a cross to be their symbol.

The Roman philosopher Pliny lists thirty-two medicines made from roses. Rose oil has been used since the days of the Greeks for healing and meditation. Rose water is a skin tonic. Rose syrup calms the heart and cures an upset stomach. Rose sugar gives its flavor to pastries. Rose petals relieve uterine congestion and cure PMS. Rose hips provide vitamin C. Attar of roses has long been used in aromatherapy.

Because the Romans used rose petals and oil as aphrodisiacs, the early Christian church abhorred the flower. By about 400 C.E., however, the white rose had become the symbol of the Virgin Mary, and the red rose came to symbolize the blood of the martyrs. Roses were carried back to Europe and planted in nearly every country by knights returning from the Crusades. In the thirteenth century, the *rosarium*, a meditation garden filled with roses, gave its name to the rosary, a garland of roses dedicated to the Virgin Mary.

Our Lady of Fatima

❧

After the death of her son, Mary Theotokos (Mother of God) retired to Ephesus. If you go there, you can see the little house she is said to have lived and died in. In 1950, her bodily assumption into heaven was declared by Pope Pius XII. In 1997, Catholics around the world petitioned Pope John Paul II to proclaim her "Co-Redemptrix, Mediatrix of All Graces and Advocate for the People of God." By a vote of twenty-three to zero, a Vatican commission advised against the new doctrine. They no doubt thought it would bring her too near to godhood. Excuse me—*goddesshood.*

Mary seems to enjoy visiting her children. She appeared six times in 1917 at Fatima, Portugal. These apparitions have been recognized by the Church, as have her earlier apparitions in Guadalupe, Mexico (1531), and at Lourdes, where she appeared eighteen times in 1858. In the twentieth century, she appeared at least 392 times. Sites of her apparitions include Amsterdam; Medjugorje, Bosnia-Herzegovina; Rwanda (before the 1994 genocide); Queens, New York; and Santa Ana, California. (Every time I thought I'd come to the end of this list, I found another apparition.) In addition, millions of people visit her shrines, both the famous ones (Lourdes and Czestochowa) and the less famous ones. People have seen her likeness on office buildings and on a wall in the subway in Mexico City. There is a circuit of Marian sites to which people travel from all over the world.

Even though Pope John Paul II publicly gave Mary credit for saving him from the assassin's bullet in 1981 and for the fall of communism in Europe, the Catholic Church has consistently discouraged the popular elevation of Mary to goddess status. Is it time for the handmaiden of the Lord to be recognized as more than a maid?

What's Your Garden I.Q.?

1. A ladybug is:
   a. A female insect
   b. An insect named for the Virgin Mary
   c. An insect that infests sunflowers
   d. A variety of large aphid

2. Which is the real flower?
   a. Foxglove
   b. Vegetable lamb
   c. Chickpea
   d. Skunk cabbage

3. Which is not a real plant?
   a. St. John's wort
   b. St. Patrick's cabbage
   c. St. Ignatius's bean
   d. St. Paul's rose

4. Which grew in the Garden of Eden?
   a. Arborvitae
   b. Judas tree
   c. Tree of heaven
   d. Tree of knowledge of good & evil

5. Which flower inspired an investment scheme that boomed and went bust?
   a. Tulip
   b. Rose of Jericho
   c. Orchid
   d. Jasmine

6. Who was never a garden god?
   a. Xipe
   b. Priapus
   c. Pomona
   d. Vertumnus

7. Who is a garden saint?
   a. Saint Fiacre
   b. Saint Gazebo
   c. Saint Ullulla
   d. Santa Gertrudis

8. If you find a Chicago fire in your garden, you should:
   a. Put it out
   b. Move away from Illinois
   c. Eat its red fruit
   d. Admire its red foliage

9. Which of the following gave his name to a beautiful plant?
   a. Erwin Schroedinger
   b. Michel Bégon
   c. Richard Feynman
   d. Werner Heisenberg

10. What is kudzu?
    a. Rude gesticulation and mouth noises
    b. *Passiflora edulis incarnata*
    c. A beautiful nuisance
    d. The magical plant Jupiter gave to Juno to make her pregnant.

Answers: 1-b, 2-a, 3-d, 4-d, 5-a, 6-c, 7-a, 8-d, 9-b, 10-c

Mercurialis

Mercury, who was identified with the Greek Hermes, is the Roman god of intellect, communication, and travel. He is the messenger of the gods and the patron of merchants and thieves. The *Mercuriales*, "Men of Mercury," was probably the largest Roman corporation. May 15 was their corporate holiday when they paid homage to Mercury to assure their continued success.

As the planets journey around the sun, occasionally they seem to be moving backwards. Astrologers call this apparent reversal "retrograde motion." When a planet is retrograde, things generally go wrong with whatever is ruled by the god the planet represents. When Venus is retrograde, for example, affairs of the heart can break apart.

Because Mercury is the innermost planet and moves fastest, it goes retrograde most often, though its retrograde periods seldom last longer than a month. This is fortunate because when Mercury goes retrograde, his name seems to change to Murphy and his Law takes over our lives. Our cars break down. Our computers do stranger things than usual. Contracts and agreements get lost in translation. People miss telephone calls, faxes, e-mails, and meetings. I used to know a printer whose presses broke down during Mercury retrogrades. A friend who was watching a video of a Fleetwood Mac concert told me *The Andy Griffith Show* suddenly appeared in the middle of it. During a recent Mercury retrograde, my car key broke off in the ignition, the temporary mail carrier busted my mailbox, and I got a hospital bill for $5,860 for a procedure I didn't have.

Reader, perhaps Mercury retrograde is our opportunity to practice nonresistance. What we fight hardest is what usually comes to us. Maybe we should just go with Mercury's flow, do no serious work, and try to relax. When Mercury goes direct again, we can fix what broke.

Our Community Garden

Soil, fertilizer, water, and light nourish our plants and make them grow. If we visualize our pagan community as a garden, we find flowers, trees, herbs, and, yes, a few weeds. Let's call upon the four elements to help us nourish our community garden.

Where are we grounded? In the earth. We wear T-shirts that proclaim, "I worship the ground I walk on." At the end of our rituals, we touch the earth, if only symbolically, and let her absorb and recycle our excess energy. Where are we planted? Where we'll bloom. We don't live in a pagan paradise, so it's our job to send down roots. Eventually our roots and branches form a sphere. As above, so below. When we bloom, hopefully we're sending out a precious scent that attracts our neighbors and brings them into our circle.

We often need to add fertilizer. Do I need to mention how much pagan . . . er . . . manure we can dig up? High priestesses so high they're interstellar? High priests whose highness is suspect? Ignorant and exclusivistic Web sites? Not everything stinks, however. The manure helps us define and refine our beliefs. We learn, for example, to distinguish tired old myths (like those apocryphal nine million burned witches) from authentic history. Just as compost—organic fertilizer—can become very hot when we put it to work, so can our "heated discussions" help us grow in toleration. Sometimes our brains get fertilized and we learn something.

As we cultivate our garden, we water it. Let's water our community with clear emotions. Even if we don't always like each other, we can express love and accept different opinions.

Finally, plants grow toward the sun. Let's let the sun represent both intellectual clarity and the warmth of friendship.

A Language of Flowers Ritual

❦

Earlier this month we learned about the language of flowers. We already know that flowers and herbs have magical powers, so let's design a ritual that uses the power and the language of flowers and herbs. Let's use this nonverbal language to tell our circle or coven mates of our feelings for them.

Without even getting into whether or not we want to invoke Findhornian devas or cute little flower fairies, begin by casting the circle. Instead of invoking the usual elemental powers, select an herb to stand in each direction. Start with a book of herbal magic and a dependable list of correspondences. Identify an herb or a flower for each elemental power. Turn to the language of flowers and decide what messages these herbs and flowers project into our circle. If we select sage for air, for example, its message is "wisdom." If we select an olive branch for fire, its message is "peace." If we select the lotus for water, its message is "eloquence, mystery, truth." If we select a fern for earth, its message is "fascination, magic, sincerity." These are qualities we surely want to manifest in our circles. You can also cast the circle by sending an herb or flower around with a kiss. We might use an African violet ("such worth is rare") to cast the circle this way.

Everyone should bring a small growing plant. The working of this ritual occurs as each person presents a plant to someone else in the circle. We can, for example, give someone a potted ivy—"friendship." After the ritual, the receiver takes the plant home and tends it, and the friendship grows. Look up the language of flowers and see what kind of conversation you can plant in your circle, coven, or community. Let it bloom.

Apollo

Apollo (he had the same name in Greece and Rome) was a god of healing (he was the father of Asclepius, god of medicine), prophecy (he owned the oracle at Delphi), the arts (ditto the nine Muses), music (he invented the lyre), and archery. After he shot his entire quiver into the Python at Delphi, he decided he should be honored for this "service to mankind" and inaugurated the Pythian Games, which began as a music competition. Athletic and equestrian events were added over time.

Apollo is *machismo* personified. Though he is always depicted as a beardless young man (an *ephebe*; compare Michelangelo's *David*), he is famous for his lusty pursuit of young women and men. He also liked to challenge other gods to contests he was sure he could win. When he challenged Pan to a music contest, Pan played his syrinx more beautifully than Apollo played his lyre. King Midas was the judge of this contest; when he gave the prize to Pan, Apollo gave him a pair of ass's ears. When Apollo noticed that Eros had an itty-bitty bow and golden arrows, he challenged him to an archery competition. Eros shot Apollo with one of his golden arrows, causing him to fall in love with the first woman he saw. This was the nymph, Daphne. Eros then shot an iron arrow into Daphne's heart, turning her against love. Apollo chased Daphne until she prayed to Gaia for succor and was turned into a laurel tree. Chastened at last, Apollo wore a wreath of laurel leaves thereafter. Laurel wreaths were also awarded to winners at the Pythian Games.

Reader, why not hold your own Pythian Games today? Write a poem. Play some music. Chase your boyfriend or girlfriend around the yard. Engage in some lusty personal healing.

In the Nursery

❦

As I look out the window, I can see that some of my plants are wilting. I may be visiting the garden store pretty soon for new plants.

Garden stores used to be called nurseries. According to the *Oxford English Dictionary*, a nursery is a room or area in a house set aside for the care of children, a preschool class ("nursery school"), a place where people are trained in job skills, a natural habitat in which animals breed and raise their young, and a place where young plants and trees are grown until they're large enough to be moved.

What do these definitions have in common? The care of the young and tender. It's inner gardening again. Just as we set aside a room for our babies and perhaps hire someone who used to be called a nursemaid to watch over them, so do we also set aside metaphorical space for our friends and family. Just as a gardener (the nurseryman) prepares potting beds and tables and cares for the growing plants, so do we nurse and nourish our relationships.

If we don't, we should. If you have a garden, you check the soil and water it when it's dry. You check for mealy bugs and other pests. When you see leaves turning yellow, you try to find out what's wrong. You rotate your plants so they face the light.

Reader, we need to take the same care with our relationships. Keep up with what's going on in your friends' lives. Add fertilizer and water, so to speak, by making phone calls and having genuine conversations. Be alert for the little buggy things (a misspoken word, a forgotten event) that can wilt or kill a friendship. Let's create a nursery in which we "plant" our family and friends and care for them.

Mjollnir

The Germani, who lived between the Rhine and Lithuania, shared much of their culture with the Celts and the Norse, to whom the Romans thought they were related (*germani* means "related"). Thor, the Germanic thunder-god, was thus likened to the Celtic Taranis and the Roman Jupiter. These are the guardians of oaths and carriers of weapons that cause thunder and lightning. Thor's weapon is Mjollnir, the hammer he uses in the spring to break up the winter ice. Mjollnir, which like Freya's necklace was constructed by the dwarves, is sometimes a battle-axe and sometimes the symbol of the lightning that strikes the earth to fertilize it. Heathens wear Mjollnir amulets, just as Christians wear crosses, to symbolize their faith.

What we know about the Germanic tribes comes largely from the *Germania*, written by Roman historian Tacitus, and the Viking sagas of Snorri Sturleson. The primary Germanic trinity is Odin, Frigg, and Thor, the latter being either the son or the ancestor of Odin. (One theory is that Thor was originally a local farming god who had to be worked into the new pantheon.) Robust and bombastic but honorable, Thor is friendly to human beings and neither mysterious nor philosophical. When the German tribes were Christianized, he was called St. Thor or renamed St. Olaf.

Thor gave his name to Thursday, which was the first day of the Germanic week. Thor's Day was a holy day when oaths were taken and civil contracts were made on Thor's hammer, or on the local blacksmith's hammer, which was said to be the same thing. Winter's Day and Summer's Day occurred on Thursdays.

Reader, Thor can be construed to be a god of the working classes. Wherever you work and whatever your work is, honor him in the work you do on Thursday.

The Four Children of Leda

Greek mythology is nothing if not complex. Once there was a nymph named Nemesis, also called Leda, with whom Zeus became infatuated. He chased her through a number of animal forms. At last, exhausted and desperate, Leda changes herself into a wild goose. Zeus becomes a swan and drives her to Sparta. There she lays a hyacinth-colored egg. A mortal woman named Leda, wife of King Tyndareus of Sparta, finds and cares for the egg, from which Helen (later of Troy) hatches.

In another story, Leda, queen of Sparta, somehow attracts the attention of the king of the gods, who takes on a swan form and rapes her. Now we come to Leda's children: Helen, Clytemnestra, Castor, and Polydeuces (known to the Romans as Pollux). Helen married the Spartan king, Menelaus, and was kidnapped by the Trojan prince, Paris, which started the Trojan War. Clytemnestra married the Mycenean king, Agamemnon, who assembled the mighty army that sailed to Troy. She was later killed by her son, Orestes. Castor and Polydeuces were Spartan heroes who sailed on the Argonaut with Jason to fetch the Golden Fleece, fought in the Trojan War, and battled their way through a bloody family plot of betrayal and revenge.

One account has it that Helen, Castor, and Polydeuces hatched from the egg that Leda laid after her encounter with the swan. Tyndareus (remember him?) lay with her the same night and sired Clytemnestra. Alternatively, twins Helen and Polydeuces were born from the egg, and twins Clytemnestra and Castor were the children of Tyndareus.

When Polydeuces was killed in battle and hauled up to heaven, he refused to stay there. Meanwhile, Castor was yelling, "Let me not live longer than my brother." So Zeus set them together in the sky, where they became the constellation Gemini.

Sun in Gemini

❦

Gemini, my friend Lilith the astrologer says, will talk about anything under the sun. I have a friend with a late May birthday who calls himself an airhead. He's not, but we sure have interesting conversations. Gemini, ruled by Mercury, is a mutable (fluid and changeable) sign. That means Gemini people are intellectual and quick-witted. They become bored if the conversation isn't interesting enough.

I don't think I've ever met a pagan who wasn't an honorary Gemini. We come together in covens and circles, in public rituals, in gatherings. And we talk. We talk about gods and goddesses and what kinds of rituals we prefer. We gossip about famous pagans. We'll talk about anything under the sun or the moon, and when we're not face to face, we continue our conversations via e-mail, lists, and chat rooms. We are *forever* communicating.

Reader, you talk to your coven or circle mates at least once a month, but how well do you really know each other? We don't always know each other's personal stories. Some people think we can do effective magical work without knowing each other on a personal level, whereas others believe the personal connection is vital to a successful working.

Gemini is a good month for storytelling. Depending on the size of your group and how long you want to spend together, tell stories about yourself. Tell a story of your childhood. Maybe, like me, you had an invisible twin when you were two years old. Tell the story of how you came to paganism. Tell the story of how you found your first teacher or first coven and what wise and foolish things you learned. Finally, tell a fantasy story of how your life would be if the standard-brand religions did not rule the world.

··· M A Y 2 3 ···

The Trail of Tears

❦

The removal of the Cherokee is one of the most shameful episodes of American history. It's the product of our hubristic nineteenth-century belief in "manifest destiny."

The Cherokee nation had long lived in north Georgia, but by 1830 the white American population had increased sixfold. Gold was discovered on Cherokee lands while Andrew Jackson, a general turned populist president, was in the White House, and Congress passed the Indian Removal Act of 1830. The Cherokee took their case to the U.S. Supreme Court, where Chief Justice John Marshall ruled that the Cherokee nation was sovereign and the removal laws were invalid. But tribal politics destroyed this victory when a minority sided with John Ridge, a Cherokee who advocated removal. Ridge signed the Treaty of Echota in 1835. That gave Jackson the legal document he needed. The removal began.

The U.S. army herded men, women, and children along a thousand-mile trail out of north Georgia and through Tennessee, Kentucky, Illinois, Missouri, and Arkansas. They arrived in Oklahoma in the middle of the freezing winter of 1838–39. Ill led and ill fed, four thousand people died. Their sad journey came to be called *Nunna daul Tsuny*, or "trail where they cried."

It is said that the mothers grieved so much that their chiefs prayed for a sign to lift their spirits and give them the strength to care for their children as they walked through wilderness and across major rivers. Wherever a mother's tears fell to the ground, we are told, a new flower grew—the Cherokee rose. It is white for the mothers' tears. Its gold center symbolizes the gold taken from the Cherokee lands, and it has seven leaves on each stem to represent the seven Cherokee clans. You can read more in *Selu: Seeking the Corn Mother's Wisdom* by Marilou Awiakta.

Mother's Day, Queen Victoria, the Three Maries

May's a maternal month. Some cultural historians say the idea for Mother's Day arose from the Matronalia. The U.S. Congress passed a joint resolution in 1914 designating the second Sunday in May as the official Mother's Day.

Queen Victoria of England (1819–1901) was the great mother figure to the subjects of the British Empire, upon which it was said that the sun never set. In her own lifetime, she was worshipped as a goddess by a sect in Orissa, India, and she became the flesh and blood mother of generations of European royals. She had nine children, forty-two grandchildren, and eighty-seven great-grandchildren, to a current total of 953 descendants. These Victorians married into thirty-three royal families and ruled in most of Europe. We're most familiar with the present-day dynasty of English royals, starting with Victoria's son, Edward VII (the playboy who gave his name to a cynical and debauched *fin de siècle* era), and continuing with George V, Edward VIII (who abdicated and became the Duke of Windsor), George VI, and Elizabeth II. Few of Queen Victoria's descendants occupy thrones today, but that's not for want of trying.

Shortly after the Crucifixion, it is said, a boat left Jerusalem without sails, oars, or supplies. It drifted across the Mediterranean and miraculously came to shore near Marseilles, France. Among the refugees in the boat were the Three Maries—Mary Jacobe, the mother of James and sister of the Blessed Virgin Mary; Mary Salome, mother of two apostles; and Mary Magdalen, said to be the wife of Jesus and mother of his daughter. Also on the ship was their servant, Sarah the Egyptian, who became a goddess to the local gypsies. People from around the world gather in Sainte-Maries-de-la-Mer, Provence, today to celebrate Sarah and the Maries.

Star Wars

❦

When the first *Star Wars* movie opened on this day in 1977, from it flowed a major industry that today includes a huge official Web site and enough products to populate any galaxy.

Joseph Campbell wrote that myth is "the secret opening through which the inexhaustible energies of the cosmos pour into . . . manifestation. Religions, philosophies, art . . . the very dreams that blister sleep, boil up" from it.[11] As nearly everyone knows, George Lucas studied Campbell's works, along with mythology in general, to create his archetypal story of a Manichaean battle between good (Luke Skywalker, as instructed by Obi-Wan Kenobi and the Jedi Knights) and evil (Darth Vader). One Web site I looked at lists other sources for the story, including earlier science-fiction films, Buck Rogers, the tales of King Arthur's court, stories of magic and sorcery (like those by Tolkein and Castaneda), fairy tales, and war movies.

I was fortunate to be present at a lecture given by Ray Bradbury shortly before the second *Star Wars* movie opened. Bradbury compared Obi-Wan Kenobi and Yoda to Merlin and other magical mentors. I don't remember if Bradbury mentioned Gandalf or Dorothy's three teachers in Oz (think about it), but I'm sure we could name a dozen more mentors in myth, literature, and movies. (We get the word *mentor* from the *Odyssey*. Mentor, Athena in disguise, aids Telemachus, son of Odysseus.)

Reader, have you ever had a mentor? If you did, what did you learn in addition to "book learning"? What qualities of humanity did you learn? If you haven't had a mentor, are you willing to seek one out? How would you recognize this person? Are you willing to serve as a mentor to a pagan boy or girl who needs to learn more than how to cast a spell to become popular?

Pagan E-zines

❧

Periodicals were invented in eighteenth-century London. The first and most famous magazine was the *Spectator*, produced by Joseph Addison and Richard Steele from March, 1711, to December, 1712. The setting was the reign of Queen Anne, last monarch of the Tudor-Stuart dynasty before the Hanoverians (who changed their name to Windsor during World War I) were brought in to be properly Protestant. Literary men gathered at coffee-houses for high-flown discussion, which Addison and Steele would report, which the men would then read and discuss, creating an elite and learned literary cycle. Today's print magazines are still gossipy. Now we also have electronic magazines (e-zines) that cater to every sliver of interest.

Pagan Muse was launched as a quarterly print newsletter in 2000. Edited by Jodi Ierne, it includes "everything from rants to kitchen tips to fiction to public service announcements." One feature is the short-fiction contest, which has become increasingly popular as more pagans think of themselves as writers. *Pagan Muse*'s sister (or daughter) is the *Teen Witch Newsletter*, a Web site, forum, and "a safe haven for kids to turn to and learn from."

Matrifocus, whose first issue appeared at Samhain, 2001, is a seasonal e-zine for Goddess women and anyone interested in the Goddess religion. "On the pagan cross-quarters," editor Sage Starwalker says, "we publish articles and art by women that are woman-, Goddess-, life-, and earth-positive." Visit *Matrifocus* and you'll find works by regular columnists, articles by our top pagan authors, reader contributions, and stunning graphic design and art.

Reader, do you want to be a writer? Go to *Pagan Muse* or *Matrifocus* and read carefully. Find out what kinds of articles and poetry they publish. Get the writer's guidelines. Then do the hard part. Start writing.

Walking in the Light

Whether the sun is shining or it's raining, we're well into the season where everything is growing lustily and waving its little green arms to get the bees' attention. When I took my walk this morning, I walked under jacaranda trees whose clouds of violet flowers make whole city blocks look like paradise. I saw blooming roses and bougainvillea climbing walls and tiny yellow flowers pushing up through the cracks in the sidewalk. When I passed the local McDonalds, I had to stop. There I saw a small fig tree and a weeping willow hovering over a bed of statice, star jasmine, and alyssum, all of it surrounded by grass so green I wondered if I'd been transported to Oz.

It's the light of late spring and early summer that makes those colors. What is the quality of the light where you live—warm, glittery, glaring, dazzling, brilliant? How is today's light different from, say, February light or August light or November light?

How does light affect you emotionally? Do you feel different on a sunny day than when it's overcast? Did the lengthening days of spring make you joyous? Do the bright days of the beginning of summer fill you with confidence? Will the shortening days of fall make you melancholy? Will the short winter days make you irritable?

Walking in the light has a literal meaning—walking during the day, in the dark with streetlights, or maybe under a full moon. How does it feel to walk in the dark? Do you feel safe? Some people say we should shine our light into the darkness.

All of the above has a metaphorical meaning. We're walking in light that signifies spiritual awareness or divine protection. Are we lighting the path for people who come behind us?

The Sierra Club

The Sierra Club was founded on May 28, 1892, with 182 charter members and John Muir as its first president. These naturalists and conservationists didn't waste any time putting activism into action. In their first organized campaign, they led an effort to defeat a proposed reduction of the boundaries of Yosemite National Park. By 1900, the club had already worked to set the Grand Canyon and Mt. Rainier aside as national parks. In 1916, the club supported a bill to establish the National Park Service and supported the formation of the Save-the-Redwoods League. The club continued with its conservation work through the Great Depression, when few people cared about anything except their next meal. During World War II, the club opposed the repeal of the Antiquities Act, which allows the establishment of national monuments.

The Sierra Club has always been politically active. Issues listed on its Web site are issues pagans and other thinking people care about: clean water, global population, human rights, protecting national forests and wilderness, creating responsible trade, and stopping sprawl and global warming. Members are keeping a critical eye on these issues, on candidates in local and national elections, and on judicial nominations. The Sierra Club is the father of dozens of younger organizations, some of which engage in forest theater, others in e-mail campaigns to save our wild areas.

Reader, should we stay in our circles and temples and remain above messy political fights? Before you say we're above such mundane concerns, ask yourself: do other religions stay out of politics? Whether we are conservative or liberal, no matter what political party we belong to, what do we *as pagans* stand for? What do our ancient pantheons tell us about living in the modern world? What actions can pagans take to make changes in the world?

Flower Essences

We've been using roots, stems, leaves, buds, flowers, and fruits and shoots for physical and metaphysical healing for about as long as people have been susceptible to disease (and dis-ease). While a bouquet perks our spirits right up, the essences of the flowers also have healing properties. The flower essence—which is different from its essential oil—is derived from picking the bloom at dawn at the height of its vitality and soaking it in pure spring water and pure sunlight. The essence is gently cooked, filtered out of the water, preserved in brandy, and diluted to homeopathic doses.

Edward Bach, a British physician, discovered flower essences in the 1930s. There are thirty-eight Bach Flower Remedies, which include the essences of trees and herbs that help to heal emotional imbalances of many kinds. My favorite is the Rescue Remedy, which calms the emotions during emergencies. Its ingredients are impatiens (for those who want everything done *now*), clematis (for people who escape reality by withdrawing from it), rock rose (which heals fright, panic, terror, and hysteria), cherry plum (for those who fear losing control), and star of Bethlehem (for distress following shock or trauma).

Flower Essence Services' Quintessentials use one hundred North American herbs and flowers, from aloe vera to zinnia, not used by Dr. Bach. The Australian Bush Flower Essences uses another sixty plants, one of which, waratah, "enhances positive transformation for those going through the 'black night of the soul.'"[12]

Reader, this is *not* to say we should forswear treatment by the medical profession. Alternative modalities can strengthen our immune system or soothe our emotional bodies while allopathic medicine is healing our physical bodies.

Frigg

Frigg, whose name means "beloved" or "lady," is the wife of Odin.
Keys and the spindle are sacred to her, and the Norse knew the constellation Orion as Frigg's spinning wheel. Frigg is also a prophetess; Saga
("seeress") may be one of her names. She and Odin sit together in a magical chair, *Hlidskialf*, from which they can see all beings and activities
throughout the nine worlds of the Norse universe.

As I was doing research on Frigg, I came upon an interpretation of
Ragnarok that is new to me. Lynda C. Welch points out that only two
goddesses are mentioned in the accounts of Ragnarok. One is Sol, a sun
goddess who is killed by a wolf, but not before she gives birth to a daughter who is brighter than she is. The other is Hel, the goddess of death and
the underworld.

Because of their prophetic powers and their impressive battle skills,
Welch suggests we would expect Frigg, Freya, and the Valkyries to be
present at Ragnarok. But where are they? The great Norse goddesses are
conspicuous by their absence.

The skies "fall to utter darkness," Welch writes, "devoid of all signs of
life." Like Tiamat and the Chaos that give birth to Gaia, Nyx, and other
eldest goddesses, the dark Norse night is the womb waiting for the spark
of life. It is the void (*Ginnungagap*) that precedes creation. Cleansed with
fire and water, Midgard "remains not only intact, but refreshed and
renewed." The giantesses and earth goddesses are about to arrive. Finally,
near the end of the story, golden chess pieces appear lying in the grass.
Gold is always associated with Frigg and Freya. The goddesses, Welch
says, are "resting in the wings of this powerful myth."[13]

Saecular Games, Dis, and Proserpine

❦

The Saecular Games were instituted in 17 C.E. by Augustus, the first
Roman emperor, to mark the end of one *saeculum*, or longest span of a
human life—100 or 110 years—and the opening of a new one. During
the games, offerings were made to the chthonic deities, Dis and Proserpine
(better known as Pluto and Persephone). Dis is the Italian god who carries
souls to the underworld, where great treasure lies hidden, and Proserpine
nurses the tender first shoots of spring, which grow into the vast harvests
upon which Rome's fortunes depended. Five hundred years later, the historian Zosimus blamed the neglect of the Saecular offerings for the decline
and fall of the Roman Empire.

Knowledge of classical civilization and mythology disappeared with
the fall of Rome, for the early Fathers of the Church declared that no
learning but Christian learning was permitted. This led to the illiteracy
and ignorance of the Dark Ages, which lasted until the tenth or twelfth
century. It was the Arab and Byzantine civilizations that preserved pagan
literature. The classical gods and goddesses didn't return to the world until
after the fall of Constantinople in 1453, when pagan works were smuggled
into Renaissance Italy by agents of the Medicis.

With the rise of Italian Humanism, gods and goddesses began to reap-
pear in art and literature, but because Europe was still ferociously Christian,
they were demonized, as in Milton's *Paradise Lost*. They were also turned
into allegories and given new, moral meanings. Ceres looking for her
daughter was seen as the Church looking for the souls of the faithful
who had strayed from the fold. Her two torches were the Old and New
Testaments. Mars and Neptune represented earthly tyrants, Pluto symbolized evil prelates, and Saturn, Jupiter, and Apollo represented virtuous
ecclesiastics.

Marilyn Monroe, Anubis

Thanks in part to her death at age thirty-six, Marilyn Monroe is one of the deathless goddesses of the silver screen. Unlike the sublime Marlene Dietrich, she didn't live long enough to become a caricature of herself; unlike the equally sublime Katharine Hepburn, she didn't live long enough to outlast Hollywood's killer tentacles. No matter what happened to Marilyn in real life, she will be forever Sugar Kane and Lorelei Lee. Marilyn is Venus who entertains us. This goddess sings and dances and acts.

Reader, does it seem to you that Hollywood is like Cronus, the old Titan who eats his children? Goya's painting *Cronus Devouring His Children* is horrifying, and we seem to see it acted out nearly every day in tabloid stories about movie and sports stars and their follies and drug addictions. We seem to know every detail of Marilyn's awful childhood: her psychoanalysis, problems with alcohol and pills, miscarriages, troubled marriages. Did Hollywood eat her up?

Anubis is the Egyptian jackal-headed psychopomp. Like Hermes, he is a deceptively gentle fellow who guides human souls to the underworld, where he presides over embalming the dead and weighing their souls. Anubis may be the fourth son of Ra, or perhaps he's the son of Osiris or Set and Nepthys. He was adopted by Isis and helped her find the pieces of Osiris's dismembered body and restore them to life. I have a friend who is devoted to the Egyptian pantheon and says that Anubis often comes to visit her disguised as a large black dog. She and the god are on excellent terms.

Anubis and many of the other Egyptian gods and goddesses often take on animal forms. Many people have animal totems. We'll be talking about our cousins—four legged, many legged, feathered, and finned—often this month.

Juno

Just as each Roman man had his *genius*, or guardian spirit of masculinity, so did each woman have her *juno*, or guardian spirit of femininity. Juno ruled every woman's entire life and every feminine occasion. As Juno Pronuba, she arranged marriages; as Juno Cioxia, she ruled the first undressing of the bride by the bridegroom; and as Juno Lucina, she presided over childbirth and the opening of a newborn child's eyes to the light. It was the custom of pregnant women to unbind their hair and untie every knot in their clothing so that nothing should restrict the safe delivery of the child. (Juno also had an aspect called Viriplaca, she who settles arguments between spouses; this aspect seems not to have been on call during the married life of Juno and Jupiter.)

In Roman civic life, Juno stood with Jupiter and Minerva as the Capitoline triad that ruled the city. In one of her other aspects, Juno was *regina*, "queen." In another she was Juno Moneta, the "warner." The sacred geese of her temple once squawked so ferociously that the city was warned of a Gallic army outside the walls. Generals would thereafter come to Juno Moneta's temple for support, both popular and monetary, which is why we find an echo of this goddess's name in "money."

Thanks to Juno's power, June is the most popular month for marriage. Perhaps every June bride should set up a series of altars for the many aspects of this ancient Italian goddess of feminine power. I'm going to the wedding of a couple of young women I'm very fond of. It's going to be on their lawn and, like every other pagan wedding I've ever been to, there's sure to be drumming, people in spectacular dress, and tons of good food.

Cats

Today is the anniversary of the euthanasia of my first beautiful Maine Coon cat, Heisenberg, who was the friend of everyone—human, feline, canine—he ever met. He was sixteen years old and had an inoperable tumor. I have his ashes, which are golden, in a little box beside Bast on an altar, and I miss him every day. More recently, I also euthanized my other cat, Schroedinger. She was over twenty years old and had become exceedingly feeble. While she lived, she was queen of the house, and I was her chambermaid. I have recently adopted two new rescued Maine Coons, also named Schroedinger and Heisenberg.

Archaeo News featured an item on the oldest known evidence of people keeping cats. Archaeologists found a cat buried with a person in a Neolithic grave on Cyprus, which suggests that the domestication of cats began about 9,500 years ago. This is earlier than the earliest evidence of domestication of cats in Egypt (2000–1900 B.C.E.). The proximity of the feline and human remains in identical states of preservation suggests that a thirty-year-old person was buried with not only polished stone axes, flint tools, and ochre pigment, but also a feline companion. "Cats might have had religious as well as material significance to the stone age Cypriots," *Archaeo News* quotes the archaeologists as saying.

The headline said "pet cat," and the human is called the cat's "owner." We always say "owner" and "pet" in conversation. But I'm not sure we can own other beings—especially cats. Domestic cats live with us and depend on us for food, kitty litter, and petting. They may become our familiars (our family?), and they have historically kept down infestations of rodents. They've always earned their keep. But cats (and dogs and gerbils and parrots and snakes) are their own selves. How can we "own" an independent spirit?

Operation Migration

What is it about the sight and sound of migrating birds that makes us want to fly away? I once lived near Crab Orchard Lake in southern Illinois, which is a rest stop on a major migratory flyway. One morning I heard honking. I went outside and looked up to see Canada geese flying not ten feet above my roof. I thought of Daedalus and Icarus and their wax wings and promised every god I knew of that if they gave me wings I'd stay out of the sun. Watching that flying V of geese, I remembered that some of the most ancient goddesses of Old Europe are the bird goddesses.

A couple centuries ago, whooping cranes were numerous enough to fill the skies above North America, but thanks to hunting and land "development," the crane population dropped to fifteen birds. Now there are just over four hundred living cranes, about three hundred of them in the wild.

That's where Operation Migration comes in. This nonprofit organization, whose mission is to promote the conservation of migratory species, hatches whooping crane eggs at the Patuxent Wildlife Research Center in Maryland. To avoid imprinting (so the chicks don't think they're people), the human caretakers wear white suits and carry puppets that look like adult cranes. When the chicks are old enough, they are taught to migrate. In a PBS *Nature* program called "Flying School," we see how Operation Migration uses ultralight aircraft to lead the cranes from Wisconsin to their winter home in Florida. Watching half a dozen young cranes flying as Willie Nelson sang "On the Road Again" brought tears to my eyes.

Humankind brought whooping cranes—and how many other species?—to the brink of extinction. Now people are rescuing the birds and taking them back home to the wilderness.

Sheela na Gig

There's something about an older woman who shows an "unnatural interest" in sex that scares the bejeebers out of some men. A century ago, Sigmund Freud opined that the *vagina dentata*, or toothed vagina, would gobble a man right up. But the idea didn't originate with him. Early Jews spoke of the vagina as *beth shenayim*, a dangerous "toothed place," and the Greeks had a myth of the *laminae*, or lustful she-demons. In medieval drama, demons ran in and out of a Hell Gate that was dome-shaped like a vagina. This was, of course, a theological statement as well as a dramaturgical one. Like audiences at today's slasher movies, medieval audiences loved to be terrified.

How did the image of an ugly old woman holding her vagina wide open get carved into so many church facades? No one knows for sure. One scholar tells us that Sheela is a representation of St. Gobnatt, whose saint day is today, and that na-Gig comes from Gyg, a Norse giantess whose name means genitalia. This is not helpful information.

In the stories of Amaterasu, the Japanese solar goddess who is insulted and retreats into a cave, and Demeter, the Greek grain mother who sits down in despair by a well in Eleusis, it is an old woman doing a lewd dance that brings comfort to the goddess. In both stories, the hag raises her skirt, reveals her private parts, does wiggly dances, tells obscene jokes, and makes the goddess laugh. The hag brings the goddess back to her people.

Maybe the medieval dramatists had it partly right. Maybe the vaginal Hell Mouth is the gate to death *and rebirth*. Maybe we pagans understand the symbolism of old Sheela. Maybe she's showing us the path to transformation.

The Insect-Human Connection

Joanne Lauck talks to insects. They talk back to her. Her book, *The Voice of the Infinite in the Small*, tells how people and insects can get along together.

We know that there are more insects on earth than any other life form. Most insects are beneficial: they take pollen from plant to plant, they give us honey, they clean up our messes and recycle dead things for us. (The only insect I can think of that has no discernable worth is the flea.)

Our animosity toward insects, Joanne says, comes partly from a fear of being bitten. It's also fear of the unknown—"I didn't know what it was, so I killed it." These days, that fear is built up by the makers of insecticides and microbial handwashes, but all those products do is build stronger bugs with stronger immune systems.

Joanne tells us that cockroaches are a bit like cats. They're clean creatures whose waving antennae signal conversation and mutual grooming. I live in an old building, and the idea of a kitchen full of roach poison made me uneasy, so I decided to follow Joanne's example. When I spotted a roach one morning, I spoke to it. At the first word I said, the roach stopped, looked up at me, and wiggled its antennae. Joanne advises courtesy. "Gentle Sir Roach," I said, "you have as much right to live on the earth as I do. But I'm not sure I want to share my kitchen with you. Would you please go back to your tribe and ask them to live only in the spaces between the walls?" I'm sure my voice was as loud as thunder to the roach, and I felt really silly talking to a bug. But it worked. The apartments above and beside me are infested. Mine is not.

Athena

Gods and goddesses are major actors in the *Iliad* and the *Odyssey*, the epic poems sung by Homer circa 850 B.C.E. The *Iliad* tells the story of the wrath of Achilles during the last year of the Trojan War, which took place about 1250 B.C.E. (This was about the same time as the exodus of the Jews from Egypt.) Because Paris did not give the apple "to the Fairest" to Athena or Hera, these two goddesses became enemies of Troy. The *Odyssey* tells of the fantastical adventures of Odysseus, the king of Ithaca, during his perilous ten-year voyage home. In both books, Zeus tries to play on both sides at once, but he always inclines toward the Greeks. Much of what we know about Greek mythology comes from Homer's epics and the tragedies of the Athenian dramatists that derive from the same events.

The *Odyssey* is a collection of folktales, like the hero's journey through the underworld, put together around a larger-than-life central figure. Athena is initially angry at the Greeks because of the rape of Cassandra by Ajax, which Odysseus did nothing to stop. She relents, however, and makes Odysseus her favorite, though Poseidon and Helios continue to persecute him. Athena and Odysseus are a lot alike: crafty, cunning, resourceful, witty, self-important tellers of tall tales featuring their own exploits.

Gods and goddesses, often in human disguise, are in the action all the time, pushing the plot along. One of my teachers, a Tibetan Buddhist, says that gods and goddesses often manifest in our lives as people we know. Reader, has it happened to you that a god or goddess has become actively involved in your life? What was the situation? How were you feeling at the time? How do you know you were getting divine help?

First Viking Invasion of Lindisfarne

This day traditionally marks the sack of Lindisfarne in 793. Christian Britain had storehouses filled with treasure—gold and grain were equally valuable—that was attractive to the wilder northern tribes that still lived by subsistence farming. From this first raid, the Vikings went on to found Kiev and Dublin, sack Paris, explore the New World, and establish dynasties as far south as Sicily.

The Vikings were not the only barbarians. The word *barbarian*, comes from the Greek, whose speakers claimed that theirs was the only civilized language. Everyone else (with the possible exception of the Romans, but only after the Greeks had colonized Italy) barked like dogs. They went "bar-bar-bar." Those fur-wearing tribes who lived in the plains of Europe and around the Black Sea were "barbaric"—the Goths (the eastern Ostrogoths conquered Italy, and the western Visigoths founded Spain's medieval royal house), the Huns, the Vandals, the Slavs, the Turks, the Mongols, the Black Sea Scythians and Sarmatians, and the Germani and the Celts. They all resisted being conquered.

The Greeks and Romans were city folk, which is what *civilized* means. All those *civis* terms—*civic, civilian, civilized, civil law, civil rights, civil servant, civil defense, civil union, civil liberty*—differentiate between the insiders and the outsiders. History is written by the conquerors, and linguistics is probably written by those with the biggest mouths and liveliest pens. Like beauty, barbarism is pretty much in the eye of the beholder.

Reader, unless you can trace your ancestors to Greece or Rome from 600 to 100 B.C.E. and prove there was no intermarriage with other tribes, you are a barbarian. A lot of us live in cities nowadays; does that make us civilized barbarians? If society is dumbed down, will we go back to barbarism?

··· JUNE 9 ···

Vestalia Begins

The abbesses and their flocks are . . . Pallas, virgin Diana,
Juno, Venus, Vesta, Thetis; the reverence due to you is
expressed clearly enough by the cult of so great a deity.
—From a twelfth-century "moralized Ovid"
(quoted in Jones and Pennick)

Ovid and the other Roman poets were rediscovered during the late
Middle Ages and Renaissance, but as Christianity was Europe's only
true and official religion, the pagan gods and goddesses had to be reas-
signed proper Christian personae. Numerous editions of *Ovid moralisé*,
which transmigrated his bawdy fairy tales into religious allegories, were
published.

The Vestalia honors Vesta, the Roman goddess of hearth and home.
Her name comes from a Sanskrit root, *vas*, which means "shining." She
was originally associated with Janus Pater and Tellus Mater because fire
was required for both civic and domestic rituals. Ovid tells us that at the
Vestalia Roman matrons walked barefoot in procession to ask Vesta's blessings. They offered food to her in honor of the olden days when bread was
baked at every hearth, and millers and bakers also held this day sacred.
The food was taken on a clean plate to the Vestal Virgins, who tended the
city's sacred fire.

At noon today, stand before your home altar with a special candle and
light it, saying, "O Vesta, grant me your favor. Bless my home and hearth
and be present at my holy rites." Continue your Vestalia by cleaning
house. If you can, bake a loaf of bread; if you don't bake, visit your local
bakery and buy the finest loaf you can find. Invite friends for a potluck
and ask them to bring both food and candles for your sacred ritual fire.

The Muses

Be thou the tenth Muse, ten times more in worth
Than those old nine which rhymers invocate, . . .
If my slight Muse do please these curious days,
The pain be mine, but thine shall be the praise.
—William Shakespeare, *Sonnet* 38

Today is the natal day of the Muses, those energetic daughters of
Memory who were born near Mt. Olympus and transported into the sky
to become the constellation Sagittarius. Hesiod names three Muses:
Melete ("practicing"), Mneme ("remembering"), and Aoide ("singing"), but
we're more familiar with the Nine: Clio ("fame giver"), Euterpe ("joy
giver"), Thalia ("the festive"), Melpomene ("singing"), Terpsichore ("lover
of dancing"), Erato ("awakener of desire"), Polyhymnia ("many hymns"),
Urania ("heavenly"), and Calliope ("beautiful voiced"). We honor the
Muses whenever we visit their home, the museum. The first museum was
built in Alexandria about 300 B.C.E.

Poets have long invoked muses, usually generic and nameless, to
inspire them in their work. "Sing, goddess," Homer says, "of the wrath . . .
of Achilles." Dante's muse in *The Divine Comedy* is Beatrice, a girl he saw one
time at church. Shakespeare opens *Henry V* with this invocation: "O! for a
Muse of fire, that would ascend/ The brightest heaven of invention!" In
1928, Stephen Vincent Benét called for an American Muse "whose strong
and diverse heart/ So many men have tried to understand. . . ."

Reader, do you call on a goddess or god for inspiration? Before you
start your next project, find some symbol of it that you can hold in your
hands—your computer mouse, a craft or Craft item. Sit quietly, take several
deep, easy breaths, and invoke your muse.

Matralia

The Roman goddess of the dawn, Matuta, is identified with Aurora and Eos. The daughter of Hyperion and Thea, Eos drives a chariot across the sky, dragging the daylight behind her. At midday, her name changes to Hemera ("light of day") and in the evening she becomes the sunset goddess, Hesperide, whose gardens lie at the western edge of the world.

Matuta is also goddess of the sea and harbors, and as Mother Matuta she is the goddess of newborn babies. Her temple was situated in Rome's cattle market, where the Matralia was celebrated every June 11. One scholar tells us that this festival was open only to women "still in their first marriage," which reminds us that Roman women engaged in as much serial monogamy as Roman men did.

We also hear Matuta's name in Stella Matutina, an outer lodge of the Hermetic Order of the Golden Dawn. Stella Matutina is the morning star of the golden dawn. I found another Stella Matutina, a secular Franciscan movement founded in the late 1980s by a Roman Catholic married couple to whom "the Lord made his will known" that everyone in the world should live a "penitential lifestyle" as chaste brothers and sisters. This is interesting because the pagan dawn goddesses are as renowned for their enthusiastic sex lives as for their light work.

Reader, how do you celebrate the dawn? I have a friend who drinks a glass of water to honor the waters of the earth. Another friend lives in a hilly neighborhood of Los Angeles and climbs her hill to greet the rising sun. Someone else takes her daily walk at dawn and comes home invigorated by the new light. Another friend does her yoga asanas at dawn, and another writes in her journal by dawn's early light.

Little Chirpy Birds

As I wake up in the morning, I can hear the little chirpy birds in the neighborhood trees, and when I take my walk, I see them doing all the things a busy bird does. Here's a poem I wrote about them.

These little birds keep getting into my dreams.
You know the ones I mean—sparrows, wrens, chickadees,
the noisy little birds that swarm in the trees along the street
to sing the sun up every morning and down every night.
You can't see them for the leaves,
but you can hear them a block away,
these little chirpy birds singing fortissimo.

In my wakeup dream this morning
I am in the old place
(a friend once told me it was another planet, another time).
I am going along the covered road
toward the marketplace up on the cliff
or maybe
I'm going up the hill toward the great ambiguous university
where I never get to finish a class.
It's always silent when I'm there,
silent, forsaken, frightening,
I always seem to be alone,
silent, forsaken, frightened.

Today the little chirpy birds are there,
singing invisibly as big as the sun.
Their singing fills the dreamtime, the marketplace, the university,
until everything shines pure and crystal gold.
And then all these little chirpy birds, these invisible chirpy birds,
fill all the deserted classrooms
and sing until I have to sing with them.
I finish a class at last.

William Butler Yeats

We read W. B. Yeats's poetry and plays in our English lit classes. We do some research and learn that he was a leading Irish patriot of the early twentieth century who, in 1904, cofounded Dublin's Abbey Theatre. But we do not hear much in school about his magical activities. Yeats (1865–1939), who wrote about Ireland, about mythology, and about life, had a life-long interest in all things esoteric.

Although Yeats's grandfather and great-grandfather were clergymen in the Church of Ireland, his father was a freethinker who raised young Willie to scorn organized religion. After Willie heard Sir Walter Scott's romantic poem, "Lay of the Last Minstrel," he determined to become a magician-poet. When he failed the entrance exams for Trinity College, therefore, he went to art school, where he was drawn to the Pre-Raphaelites and theosophy. He met Madame Blavatsky in London and joined the Theosophical Society. He found the Theosophists too cerebral, however, and was initiated into the Golden Dawn in 1890, taking the magical name *Demon Est Deus Inversus* ("The Devil is the inverse side of God").

Reader, even this minuscule account of Yeats's early life gives us food for thought. Although he celebrates the *sidhe* and other elements of Celtic folklore, he was not, strictly speaking, a pagan or a Wiccan. There just weren't any Wiccans as we think of them during his lifetime. (Gerald Gardner didn't visit the New Forest until about the time Yeats died.) But it's interesting to consider Theosophy (which brought versions of Hindu and Buddhist wisdom to the West) and ceremonial magic (which is Judeo-Christian) and to see how these streams feed our pagan river. Do you know any ceremonial magicians? Have you attended a gnostic mass or other non-Wiccan high-magical ceremony?

Mary Cassatt

American Impressionist painter Mary Cassatt (1844–1926) started studying painting about the time the Civil War began. She soon wearied of being patronized by male instructors and male students, however, and decided to study the Old Masters in her own way. She moved to Paris, where she studied in the major European museums and became acquainted with the French Impressionists. Although the jury accepted one of her paintings for the Paris Salon of 1872, critics said her colors were too bright and her portraits were too accurate to be flattering. Rebelling against the orthodoxy of the Salon, she met Edgar Degas and Berthe Morisot, two more rebels, who encouraged her work. Ten years later, she had moved away from identification with any school and begun painting her famous realistic domestic scenes and mothers and children. By the 1890s, she had become a role model for younger American artists and advisor to art collectors. In 1904, France awarded her the Legion of Honor.

We have numerous pagan artists who may be as talented as any world-famous artist. Joanna Powell Colbert comes to mind. When I knew her several years ago, she was drawing her friends as goddesses; now we see her gorgeous work in our magazines. Other artists create illustrations, rubber stamps, greeting cards, and tarot decks.

Reader, our artists are trying to live as pagans and as artists, and they sell their work via the Internet and at pagan gatherings. It's important that we support them. Just like us, they have to pay the rent and buy cat food. Don't haggle over the price of a portrait of a goddess you love. Respect their images and don't glue them to jar candles (at least not without permission). Buy their greeting cards and send them to everyone you know.

Vesta's Temple Closed for Cleaning

On the day after the Vestalia, the temple of Vesta was closed for cleaning. The trash was swept out, hauled down an alley behind the Capitoline Hill, and thrown into the Tiber River. The temple and the public hearth were purified, and the blessings of the goddess restored to the city.

Cleaning our temple and getting rid of our trash is always a good idea, but can we continue to dump our trash into rivers and the ocean?

Back in the olden days, it was "out of sight, out of mind." I remember going fishing with my father and brother. I was drinking a Coke. Even though my father subscribed to several conservation magazines and never hunted, those were the days when people just threw stuff away. Recycling hadn't been invented yet. "What should I do with this empty Coke bottle?" I asked. "Throw it in the lake," my father said. And then he showed me how to hold it so it filled with water and sank to the bottom. It never occurred to us that I should take the empty Coke bottle home.

I shudder to remember that mindless act of pollution. Do I have any excuse? Well, I was only eleven years old. I was just doing what everyone did.

Reader, when we take out the trash, where do we take it? What are we teaching our children? Just a couple years ago, my daughter-in-law taught me a lesson when I plucked a flyer off the window of my car and dropped it for the street-sweeper to deal with. Without a word, she picked up that piece of paper and stuffed it into the trash bag in her car. We learn, we forget, we learn again, we keep on learning.

Whales

Say "whale," and people think of Herman Melville's great symbol of evil, Captain Ahab's obsession that kills nearly every man on the *Pequod*. Although *Moby-Dick* (1851) contains more information about cetaceans than any college student ever wants to know, it's a good book. Melville partly based it on a true event of the 1840s, when a sperm whale named Mocha Dick, which had nineteen harpoons in its hide, rammed a boat and caused the death of thirty men. The survivors resorted to cannibalism until they were rescued.

Say "whale," and people remember Monstro, the great whale inside whose stomach Pinocchio finds his father in the 1881 story by Carlo Collodi. Disney made them famous in the 1940 animated movie. Like *Moby-Dick*, *Pinocchio* is an allegory of good and evil. The puppet learns his lessons, and becomes a real boy.

At dinner the other night, I said "whale" to my friend, Teddy, who is a volunteer on whale-watch cruises. Each spring, she travels to Baja, Mexico, to visit the breeding grounds of the gray whales, which migrate to the lagoons there to give birth. The whales were threatened a couple years ago when industry wanted to turn the lagoons into salt reclaiming flats. Fortunately, the whales won that one.

In U.S. waters, whale-watch boats are permitted to come no closer to a whale than a hundred yards. The whales have no such restrictions. I remember a cruise when a curious whale swam right up to us. That whale and I looked at each other, eye to eye. In the Mexican lagoons, boats have no distance restrictions, and the whales swim under the boats and even nudge their babies up to greet the people. Considering the history of whaling, which these creatures must surely remember, that is mighty trusting. But the whales seem to like us.

Ludi Piscatari

The *ludi piscatari* ("fish games") was a festival for blessing fishing boats. Presumably, the fishermen were blessed, too, and I wonder if they also blessed the fish so they would be fruitful and multiply.

In 1850, Alfred, Lord Tennyson, the Victorian poet laureate, coined the phrase "Nature, red in tooth and claw." Wild animals were bloody. They hunted and ate each other. They might hunt and eat us—if we didn't hunt and eat them first.

My friend Teddy works in an aquarium. The petting pool is stocked with fish that normally don't bite. They are also well fed. One day, while she was introducing a class of third graders to the pool's inhabitants, the four-foot leopard shark, normally a gentle fellow that eats very small fish, attacked a foot-long sable fish. As the third graders watched, the shark shook the sable fish and bit it in half. Both halves dropped to the floor of the pool, and the shark swam in circles above it for a minute. It came back, picked up the front half of the sable fish, and swallowed it, head first. Then it picked up the other half and swam around, the tail dangling out of its mouth. Such a thing had never happened before in the aquarium.

The fish in the aquarium, Teddy reminded the children, are wild animals. They may live here, but they're not tame. Sometimes they display aggressive behavior. Sometimes nature really is red in tooth and claw.

Pagans like to adopt metaphysical "power animals." They're almost always wild animals, some of which can be ferocious—bear, cougar, scorpion, eagle. I like the *Medicine Cards* as much as anyone else, but I wonder . . . how wise is it to invoke and carry the power of a dangerous wild animal?

Glastonbury Goddess Temple

After humble beginnings, the Glastonbury Goddess Temple opened on Imbolc, 2002, and was officially recognized in the United Kingdom as a public place of worship on June 18, 2003. The temple is the first modern sacred space devoted to the Lady of Avalon who, we're told, "expresses Herself through the sacred landscape, mythology, and culture of the Isle of Avalon and in Glastonbury." The temple is open to the public for prayer, ceremony, meditation, and worship and is used by individuals for classes, healing, and rites of passage. During the annual Glastonbury Goddess Conference, it hosts large gatherings. The resident priestess, Kathy Jones, was kind enough to e-mail a statement of the community's beliefs to me:

- We believe in the Great Goddess, who is the One and the Many, who is immanent and transcendent, personal and impersonal, constant and changing, local and universal, within and without all of creation.

- We believe that the Goddess manifests and communicates Herself through the whole of Her Nature and the sacred land, through visions and dreams, senses and experiences, imagination, ceremony, and prayer.

Dion Fortune says two streams of myth meet at Glastonbury: the legend of the Cup (the Holy Grail) and the legend of the Sword (the Arthurian mythos). The Avalon of the Sword is the older and begins with the "tribes of primitive men." She also describes the Blood Spring, which rises from the oldest rocks, and says, "This was never a Christian well." She even connects Glastonbury/Avalon with Atlantis and says the Atlanteans visited the site long ago.[14]

Temples and sanctuaries like the Glastonbury Goddess Temple demonstrate that the Goddess is returning to her children. These places deserve our financial support.

James 1

Today is the birthday of James I (r. 1603–1625), England's first Stuart king. Like his Tudor predecessors, Henry VIII and Elizabeth I, James was a Protestant and head of a theological police state; unlike them, he believed in witchcraft and approved of persecutions. Shakespeare wrote *Macbeth* to commemorate James's ancestors. Remember the Wyrd Sisters? "When shall we three meet again? In thunder, lightning, or in rain?" They foretell Macbeth's rise and fall. In act III, Hecate appears and scolds them for dealing with Macbeth without her help.

Because seventeenth-century English Protestants wanted to read the words of their god for themselves, James authorized a new translation of the Bible. The Authorized Version is the one people still brandish at other people as the "unerring word," as if their god's eardrums resonate only to Jacobean English. Here is part of the translators' dedication to the king:

> But among all our joy, there was no one that more filled
> our hearts than the blessed continuance of the preaching
> of God's sacred Word among us, which is that ines-
> timable treasure which excelleth all the riches of the
> earth; because the fruit thereof extendeth itself, not only
> to the time spent in this transitory world, but directeth
> and disposeth men unto that eternal happiness which is
> above in heaven.

Reader, it's true that some people use this book of legendary history and sacred literature as a weapon and that there's a lot in it that reveals not a god of love but a jealous god. Nevertheless, that document is part of our cultural history. Western art and literature are filled with biblical subjects and allusions. Our nation was founded by people whose holy book this is. Find a good translation of the Bible and read it.

A Midsummer Night's Dream

It's midsummer. What better time to enjoy comedy, romance, and satire? What better time to meet famous mythological figures, lovers, working men, and fairies?

A Midsummer Night's Dream, first performed in 1595–1596, is my all-time favorite play. The fairies are as tall as regular people and just as foolish and quarrelsome. Puck is mischievous enough to twist the plot when he—like us—can't tell the two pairs of Athenian lovers apart. Bottom's translation into an ass echoes the translation of Lucius in *The Golden Ass*. And when the "mechanicals"—Elizabethan working guys—try to perform their tragedy, we groan and recall every earnest but painful high-school play we've seen.

Shakespeare had a classical education and was familiar with Ovid's *Metamorphoses*, the source of much familiar mythology. This is where he found the story of Theseus, who fought the Amazons and married their queen, Hippolyta. Also from the *Metamorphoses* comes the story of Pyramus and Thisbe, which the mechanicals dramatize at the triple wedding in act V. Oberon first appeared in a medieval romance called *Huon of Bordeaux*, and Titania's name comes from the Greek Titans.

The play's themes were important to Elizabethan audiences: order (Athens) versus chaos (the forest), the proper place and duties of the new middle class (Hermia's father's preference for Demetrius over Lysander), the definition of a proper marriage, the condescending attitude that nobles had toward the theater (which they nevertheless adored), the power of the fairies to bless or curse, the power of dreams. Four hundred years later, we're still looking at the same issues.

Reader, celebrate this magical solstice by renting one of the movie versions of this play. When you go to bed tonight, see what your own midsummer night's dream may be.

Summer Solstice

Celebrate midsummer by dancing and making a joyful noise unto the Goddess. Make a solar rattle. First, get two paper plates, a stapler, a handful of Indian corn or beads, magic markers, and yellow and orange crepe paper or ribbon. Now draw a big solar face with big round eyes and a big smile in the center of the back of each paper plate. Add solar rays all around, fat triangles and wavy lines. The idea is to make the faces jolly and friendly.

Staple the two paper plates together around the edges, leaving an opening big enough to slip in the corn or beads, then staple the opening closed. Staple the orange and yellow crepe paper or ribbon in streamers around the plate, making the streamers—the rays of your sun—as long as you want them. Double-check that when you shake the rattle the insides don't come flying out. If you know how to do wheat-weaving, add a wheat charm to dangle under the rattle. You can also add *milagros*, charms, ribbons, and bells.

If you do this with a group, you can give prizes to the most colorful, the cheeriest, the brightest, and so on, but don't be majorly competitive. Have fun.

Go outside with your friends and shake your solar rattles and dance under the sun. Let the sound of your rattle and the movement of its streamers be as radiant sunlight that touches and blesses our Mother Earth and all of her children. Add a little loop of ribbon at the top and hang your rattle on the wall. Six months from now, when you look at your rattle, you will remember the warmth of a midsummer day, the joyful sounds, the dancing, and the ever-shining light of our golden mother sun.

Covenant of the Goddess

On the summer solstice in 1975, members of several Wiccan traditions, including Feri, Gardnerian, and Feminist Wicca, came together at
Allison Harlow's home in northern California to establish an umbrella
organization to which both covens and solitaries could belong. This group,
which became the Covenant of the Goddess, was incorporated on October
31, 1975. CoG's purpose is "to increase cooperation among Witches and to
secure for Witches and covens the legal protection enjoyed by members of
other religions." As a nonprofit religious organization, CoG issues ministerial
credentials to qualified persons. (The qualifications are given on the CoG
Web site.)

CoG encourages networking through and among local councils and at
its annual Merry Meet. Along with representatives of world religions large
and small, members of CoG have also attended the Parliaments of World's
Religions.

I've been a member of CoG for some years and have served on the
board of our local council. We hold quarterly meetings at which any
pagan is welcome and present an annual public ritual. We also participate
in the local AIDS walk, and we've collected enough clothing to fill two
cars to take for distribution among the victims of southern California fires.
One of our young mothers organized a children's group that meets on or
near the sabbats for crafts and fun. In July, 2004, while I was writing this
book, I designed and facilitated a summer ritual that featured four sun goddesses, one sun god, a living tarot reading, and orange balloons.

Reader, we can find ads for pagan organizations in our magazines. It
seems to me that even the crustiest solitary needs to get out occasionally,
and getting out with our friends is good for us. What do you see as the
benefits of belonging to large, multi-tradition, pagan groups?

Sun in Cancer

Here we are in my natal sign—one, as I like to say, of the Top Twelve. (Would you believe not everyone gets the joke? People pause, then go, "Oh.") Cancer, Lilith the astrologer says, "IS feelings. Lives and breathes them. Watch a crab walk. Always sideways or backwards. . . . That's how Cancer deals with feelings—indirectly, but always with them in mind."

Although I've been known to fog up at Hallmark commercials, and if someone criticizes my writing I'll sulk for three days, in graduate school I pretended I didn't have feelings. It was camouflage. Graduate school is a cerebral venue filled with politics that would make Machiavelli hide under a desk, plus (in English departments) literary criticism arid enough to dry out the Gobi Desert. This double Cancer developed a hard shell and depended on her Moon in Gemini to succeed.

Reader, I'm wondering about the place of feelings in our culture. The official position is that we live rational lives. If we can't measure something, hold it in our hands, and examine it (with our mechanical eyes), it has no value. Psychic phenomena? Phooey. Intuition? Phony. Imagination and dreams? Only for fools. We're tough. We take our action-adventure movies and soulless computer games straight up.

At the same time, it's obvious that advertising plays on our emotions and ignores any rational faculty we may have. Does this mean there are useful emotions (useful to whom?) and useless emotions?

As pagans, we understand that psychic phenomena, intuition, imagination, and dreams are vital elements of our daily lives. It seems to me that these issues of feelings and emotions are going mainstream. Hard-core skeptics aside, people are acknowledging that something else is out there . . . or *in here*. What can the pagan community do to promote emotional balance in our larger, nonpagan community?

First UFO Sighting

In 1947, Kenneth Arnold, a pilot from Boise, Idaho, reported seeing nine unusual objects in the sky near Mt. Rainier. In what is said to be the first sighting of unidentified flying objects (UFOs), he described the mysterious objects as "bright" and said they were flying "at tremendous speed." The famous Roswell Incident—wherein an alien spaceship is said to have crashed and extraterrestrial artifacts were scattered across land in New Mexico owned by Mac Brazel—occurred less than a month later. In 1952, Arnold wrote and self-published *The Coming of the Saucers*, the first UFO book.

Ufology, the study of UFO evidence, was invented during the late 1970s when investigators interviewed people who worked at or near Roswell. Ufology is now part of our popular culture. An episode of one of the *Star Trek*s proposes that what crashed at Roswell was a Ferengi ship from the future, while in DC Comics, it was a Dominator scoutship. The Sci-Fi Channel seems to produce a UFO program every other month. And we all know that "the truth is out there."

What is the truth of UFOs? The thirty-year-old Committee for the Scientific Investigation of the Paranormal (CSICOP) opines that UFO sightings are hallucinations.

UFOs are major components of some new religions, including Unarius, the Aetherians, the Order of the Solar Temple (whose believers wanted to move to Sirius), Heaven's Gate (whose believers wanted to be carried away by the Hale-Bopp comet), the Raelians, and Scientology (whose mythos tells of a galactic emperor who brought billions of people to earth and killed them). The UFO religions, which tend to be apocalyptic, profess a belief in superior beings (the old gods?) who will come down from the sky and save the true believers.

Sonnenwenda

The German word *Sonnenwenda* means "solstice." *Solstice* comes from two Latin words: *sol*, "sun," and *sistit*, "stands." On the day of the solstice, the sun seems to 'stand still, not as it crosses the sky, but as it rises in the same place for a few days.

The solstices were tracked by ancient civilizations. About 2200 B.C.E., astronomers in China calculated the summer solstice, which they said marked the earth's yin energy. The precise moment of the solstice is often marked by the appearance of the rising sun shining upon a ceremonial structure like Stonehenge or illuminating a marker like the Sun Dagger in Chaco Canyon, New Mexico. As Europe became Christianized, St. John's Day (the birthday of John the Baptist, June 24) was added to the calendar so the people could celebrate without seeming to follow pagan customs. Among the Germanic tribes, the summer solstice was celebrated on June 25.

A proclamation of 1653 given by the town council of Nuremberg, Germany, says that "wood hath been gathered by young folk, and thereupon the so-called *sonnenwendt* or *zimmet* fire kindled and thereat wine-bibbing, dancing about said fire, leaping over the same . . . and all manner of superstitious work [is] carried on." Recognizing that they're outnumbered by merrymakers, the town fathers conclude that they "neither can nor ought to forbear or do away with all such unbecoming superstition, paganism, and peril of fire on this coming day."

Reader, if you haven't already done so, light your midsummer fire or roll your sun-wheel down a hill. In earlier times, the sun-wheel was lit from the fire, but let us not burn any hillsides. Just as the sun can scorch the earth, so can fire, sun's substitute, burn us. Leap over the fire carefully. Let no one be burnt, today or any other day.

Pied Piper Day

> Rats!
> Grave old plodders, gay young friskers,
> Fathers, mothers, uncles, cousins,
> Cocking tails and pricking whiskers,
> Families by tens and dozens,
> Brothers, sisters, husbands, wives—
> Followed the Piper for their lives.
> —Robert Browning, *The Pied Piper of Hamelin*

Deserved or not, rats have always had bad press. One reason the Egyptians had a cat goddess was because her feline children ate the rodents that ate Egyptian grain. We remember Dick Whittington and his cat because the cat saved London from an invasion of rats. Rats carried the fleas that gave Europe the Black Death in the Middle Ages.

I've found only one goddess whose animal is the rat. The Malekulans, who live on the island of Vanatu in the South Pacific, had a goddess named Le-Hev-Hev, whose name translates as "she who smiles so we can draw near and she can eat us." They offered her boars so she wouldn't eat human corpses.

The best rat story concerns the Pied Piper, that magical fellow who lived in early thirteenth-century Germany and had a magic flute whose tune attracted rats. He traveled about the countryside offering to drive the rats out of towns and into a cave under a mountain—for a fee. When he visited Hamelin, the good burghers hired him, and he whistled the rats away. But the burghers neglected to pay him. So the Pied Piper changed his tune and whistled the town's children under the mountain.

Browning's poem is a rollicking tale with a Victorian moral: Keep your promises and pay your debts. We can also interpret the story as a lesson in karma, at least in the popular sense of karma as repayment for good or bad acts.

Fan Clubs

Michael Ball is a musical theater tenor and one of the U.K.'s most popular entertainers. His 1999 concert at the Royal Albert Hall was broadcast on PBS, and I was present at his first two concerts in the United States, where he had two thousand people standing up and screaming for him to keep singing encores. In 2005, I flew to New York to see him star in Gilbert and Sullivan's *Patience* at the New York City Opera. Today is his birthday.

I'm a member of the Michael Ball Fan Club, and it's enormous fun. In 2003, when members of the club flew to Los Angeles for a Ballfest, they brought a life-size cardboard Michael and took it everywhere, even to the famous Chinese Theater on Hollywood Boulevard.

It occurs to me that gods and goddesses might enjoy having fan clubs. A fan club would be different from a circle or a coven, whose main business is holding rituals. Most circles and covens invoke different goddesses and gods at their various rituals. A fan club, however, would be faithful to one goddess or god, hold rituals to praise the deity, and perhaps travel to sites associated with her or him.

Some deities already have fan clubs. Dionysus and Bacchus, for example, seem to have a great many fan clubs that meet every weekend. These fan clubs also worship Terpsichore, the muse of dance, and (on bad nights) Cloacina, goddess of sewers. Are sports fans who attend track meets convening in honor of fleet-footed Mercury? Do quilters and weavers gather to honor Arachne? Are psychic fairs held to honor the Sybils?

Reader, if you were to establish a fan club for a god or goddess, how would you organize it? What would you do at your fan-club meetings? How fan-atical would you be?

Feast Day of St. Irenaeus

St. Irenaeus (ca. 130–202), bishop of Lugdunum in Gaul (now Lyons, France), is most famous for his five-volume work *On the Detection and Overthrow of the So-Called Gnosis,* or *Adversus Haereses* (*Against Heresies*). Until the discovery of the Nag Hammadi scrolls in 1945, this was the best surviving description of Gnosticism.

As we know from the work of Elaine Pagels, Tobias Churton, and other scholars, Gnosticism was a major competitor to Christianity. Whereas Christianity posits "One True God," Gnosticism divides the divine persona into Aeons and distinguishes between the High God, who is good, and the Demiurge, who is the evil creator of the world we live in and us. The Cathars, who were French Gnostics, taught that we should live chaste, vegetarian lives so we can overcome the influence of the Demiurge and become pure beings while we live in his defiled world.

Irenaeus argues for the unity of God and says that everything that has happened, could happen, or will happen is part of God's plan to refine humanity. God, he says, made the world a hard place to live in. People are forced to make moral decisions. Death and suffering lead us to better know God. Salvation comes through the incarnation of God in man. Irenaeus is also the first Father of the Church to draw a comparison between Eve and Mary.

The work of Irenaeus gives pagans much to think about. We don't believe in the One True God, but in whole pantheons of gods, and some pagans hold beliefs that come close to being Gnostic. To some today who rigorously believe in the One True God, we are heretics. The word *heretic* comes from the Greek *hairesis,* which means "to take counsel for oneself, to choose." Every pagan I know chose this path. Reader, how do you feel about being a heretic? How important is it for people to choose for themselves what they believe?

Zoos and Aquariums

When I was young, the St. Louis Zoo was one of the most famous zoos in the world. Several times a year, my family would pile into the station wagon and drive to Forest Park, where we would gaze at the fountains built for the 1904 Louisiana Purchase Exposition. At the zoo, we'd start at the Flight Cage, an oval aviary as big as a football field. It was commissioned by the Smithsonian Institution for the World's Fair and purchased by the City of St. Louis. After marveling at the birds in the Flight Cage, we'd go to the bear pits and the primate house and hurry through a building full of scary reptiles. The zoo also presented animal shows, where I got my first (and only) elephant ride.

Another memory, less happy: the big cats. I can still see the tiger. All he had in the world were a concrete floor, bars all around, and a big food dish. He paced. Back and forth, around and around, up to the bars and back again. Pacing was all he had to do. Even at age five or six, I wondered, what kind of life can a caged tiger have?

Today, zoos are "wild animal parks," and few animals are caged. Instead, they live in habitats that are as much like home as possible. Aquariums are likewise as natural as possible. Birds, four-footed animals, and fish that are endangered or nearly extinct in the wild are studied, protected, and cherished in zoos. If it weren't for zoos, some species might already be gone from the earth forever. And yet . . . and yet I still remember the tiger in the cage. I still have mixed feelings about zoos.

Reader, are zoos and aquariums fancy jails? Or are they sanctuaries where animals, birds, and fish can live safely and not go extinct?

The Tunguska Event

On June 30, 1908, an explosion at or above the Tunguska River in Siberia felled sixty million trees. When the Soviet government funded an investigation in the 1920s, Leonid Kulik and his associates interviewed eyewitnesses who said they had seen a huge fireball crossing the sky. The blast was estimated to be between ten and fifteen megatons and left an enormous butterfly-shaped region of scorched and flattened trees.

What was it? The explosion of an extraterrestrial body? In 1930, a British astronomer proposed that it was the impact of a small comet, but in 1983 an astronomer at the Jet Propulsion Laboratory wrote that comets are made of ice and dust and could not have flown so close to the earth without disintegrating. Expeditions sent to the region in the 1950s and 1960s found microscopic glass spheres containing nickel and iridium, which are found in meteorites, and in 2001, investigators suggested a meteorite from the asteroid belt. But there's no typical meteorite crater there.

Other theories suggest that a small black hole was passing through the earth, a piece of antimatter exploded, or a nuclear-powered UFO blew up. Some blame Nikola Tesla. In an article written in 1908, Tesla claimed that he could direct electromagnetic wave energy to any point on earth from his transformer at Wardenclyffe Tower in Shoreham, New York. One of Tesla's associates reported that during one test the Wardenclyffe Tower glowed and an owl flying nearby disintegrated. That's when Tesla stopped talking about projecting electromagnetic force.

To this day, no one knows for sure. *Star Trek*'s explanation is as good as any: An alien race saved humanity by exploding and deflecting an incoming meteor that would have struck Europe. The remnants hit Siberia.

Julius Caesar

❖

Shakespeare had it right. Gaius Julius Caesar (100–44 B.C.E.) was ambitious. Although his *gens*, or clan, traced itself back to Iulus Ascanius, son of Aeneas, son of Venus, by the time Julius was born the family was impoverished. He wanted to be an author, but joined the army. Politics in the late Republic were complex and deadly, and Julius was in it up to his neck, which he nearly lost several times. He served in important civil offices in Rome, used the spoils of some of his military campaigns to pay his personal debts, married several times, and seduced many women, among them Cleopatra of Egypt. (She was in Rome when he was assassinated.)

Generations of students taking high-school Latin have known Caesar as the author of *De Bello Gallico* (*The Gallic War*). As governor of northern Italy and southern France, he assumed the responsibility of "liberating" Gaul (though not from Roman occupation) and invaded Germany and Britain. Gaul remained a Roman province for more than three hundred years. When Caesar returned to Rome, he gained fame and fortune as an administrator and historian. Among other things, he reformed the calendar, renaming *Quintilus* (the fifth month) as *Iulius* for himself.

The Republic exploded into civil wars. Caesar raised an army. The senate demanded that he disband it, but he refused to obey, believing (with good reason) that without his legions he might be killed. In January of 49 B.C.E., he led a legion across the Rubicon, a small river in southern Gaul. "The die is cast," he said. He battled his way back to Rome. He wanted to be king but was assassinated by Roman Republicans.

When someone "crosses the Rubicon," they make an irrevocable decision. Let's use the river as our starting point for talking about water this month.

Adonis

❖

In the *Metamorphoses*, Ovid tells the story of Adonis, whose name simply means "lord." Adonis is a beautiful young man whose mother, Myrrha, is impregnated by her own father. In her shame, she begs to be transformed into a tree (which becomes either the myrrh or the myrtle); and her wish is granted. Nine months later, Adonis emerges. Venus is attracted to him, but so is Persephone. When they threaten bloodshed over him, Zeus decides that the lad will spend four months of the year with each goddess and four on his own. Adonis prefers hunting to making love. One day, in spite of warnings from Venus, he goes hunting and is killed by a boar. Outraged and bereaved, the goddess sprinkles the nectar of the gods on his body, his blood fizzes and foams, and a flower springs up. This is the blood-red anemone, which, like Adonis, has a short lifespan.

Like many other stories, this one is commonly read as a vegetation myth. Delicate plants, like sweet boys, wither and die when it gets too hot. In Rome, the Adonia was celebrated all month. Women would go up on their rooftops and plant "gardens of Adonis"—fennel, lettuce, wheat, or barley, all of which grow fast. The women tended their gardens for a week, during which the plants germinated and began to grow, but on the eighth day, they left the plants untended. Scorched by the hot July sun, the gardens died, and the women went into elaborate mourning rituals. They also constructed little Adonis poppets, which they buried in tiny coffins.

Reader, if you're up to it, read Shakespeare's sexy poem *Venus and Adonis*, which was enormously popular. Read Ovid. If it's too hot to read, find a cool way to celebrate your own private Adonia.

The Dog Days of Summer

❖

It gets so hot in July that my mother used to say, "The dogs are laying in the streets and the heat's just coming off them." She was joking about blaming the neighborhood dogs, but she was correct in the association. The dog days of summer, those sweat-inducing days from early July through August or September, are named after the "dog star," Sirius. Starting about July 3, Sirius rises and sets in conjunction with the sun. Astronomers call this "helical" (from Helios) rising and setting.

In Egypt, Sirius was the Nile Star or Star of Isis. Five thousand years ago, the helical rising of the star signaled the flooding of the Nile (back then it was late June). It's said there was a jewel in the forehead of the statue of Isis at the temple of Dendera. When the light of Sirius struck this jewel, it signaled the beginning of the innundation.

The star's name has two possible origins. It may come from the Egyptian *sihor*, "Nile," or from the Greek, *seirios*, "scorching." The star is located in the constellation *Canis major* (the big dog), which is about 8.7 light years away. The Romans called Sirius *Canicula*. Believing it drove men and dogs mad, they sacrificed a brown dog to pacify it and called the blazing hot days *caniculares*. This Latin word was translated into English in the sixteenth century as "dog days."

One of the brightest stars in the sky, Sirius can be seen with the naked eye. The Norse called it "Loki's Brand." African people also knew this star. The Bushmen celebrated its appearance with a ritual, and the Dogon said that Sirius B (the smaller companion of the brighter Sirius A) was the navel of the universe and home of a mysterious race called the Nommo.

Libertas, Lady Liberty

❖

Libertas (Freedom) is another of the Roman civic goddesses, a sister to Concordia and Pax. Although the Romans hardly ever experienced freedom, civic harmony, or peace, they always kept their eyes on the possibilities. Libertas was sometimes merged with Jupiter, sometimes with Feronia, who was originally an Etruscan or Sabine goddess of agriculture or fire. In Rome, Feronia became the goddess of freed slaves.

On Roman coins and other artifacts, Libertas is shown as a matron wearing flowing dress and either a wreath of laurel leaves or a tall *pilleus*, which is a "liberty cap" that looks like a witch hat without the brim. She holds either a liberty pole (*vindicta*) or a spear, and sometimes a cat sits at her feet.

Libertas became Lady Liberty during the American and French Revolutions and is the subject of numerous nineteenth-century paintings. To celebrate the repeal of the Stamp Act in 1766, Paul Revere created an obelisk with an image of Libertas on it. A short time later, Tom Paine addressed Lady Liberty in his poem *The Liberty Tree*. Soon the goddess took her place alongside the eagle, the Liberty Bell, and various Masonic symbols in the iconography of the New World.

An enormous bronze statue of Lady Liberty was commissioned in 1855 for the top of the Capitol Building in Washington, D.C., and in 1863 she was hoisted up there, where she stands, hardly visible, to this day. During the War Between the States, both sides claimed Lady Liberty and used her image. Among abolitionists, she was shown freeing slaves, while states' rights advocates showed her freeing mankind from the tyranny of centralized government.

The civil liberties of pagans are still being violated.

Lady Liberty (Continued)

❦

Observe good faith and justice
toward all nations. Cultivate
peace and harmony with all. . . .
—George Washington

Let every sluice of knowledge be
opened and set a-flowing.
—John Adams

"Liberty Enlightening the World," which we commonly call the Statue
of Liberty, was a gift from France to the United States on the occasion
of America's centennial. Designed by Frederic-Auguste Bartoldi and
Alexandre Eiffel, Liberty holds a book in one arm and with her other hand
raises a torch, a common symbol of truth and purification through illumi-
nation. She wears a crown of solar rays similar to the crown worn by the
Colossus of Rhodes, one of the seven wonders of the ancient world. One
hundred thousand people in France, who had their eyes on liberty, contributed money to the creation of Liberty, and people in the United States
helped finance the construction of the pedestal she stands on.

In May, 1989, Lady Liberty found a new incarnation as the Goddess of
Democracy, a styrofoam and plaster statue built by Chinese students and
carried in Beijing's Tiananmen Square in their demonstrations for academic
freedom. She became such a powerful rallying symbol that the Chinese
government sent tanks into Tiananmen Square. Liberty was crushed by
those tanks. To this day, we don't know how many protestors were shot,
because the old men who rule China refuse to even acknowledge that the
demonstrations occurred.

Reader, if you don't have Lady Liberty in your collection of goddesses,
it's time to get her in your home. My Liberty is an Avon perfume bottle
(all those busy Avon ladies personify Liberty in their own way). Since the
repairs to the Statue of Liberty in the 1980s, numerous replicas have
become available.

Apollo and the Cumaean Sibyl

❖

The Romans brought Apollo home when they conquered Greece in the third and second centuries B.C.E. The Games of Apollo became so popular that they filled seven days in July.

The ancient world had ten Sibyls—prophetesses who channeled divine energy—who lived in Persia, Libya, Samos, Cimmeria, Erythraea, Tibur, Marpessus, Phrygia, Delphi, and Cumae. The last two are the best known. Delphi, in central Greece, was ruled by Apollo.

The Cumaean Sibyl lived near Naples in the fifth century B.C.E. Her cave, which was said to lead directly to the underworld, was rediscovered in 1932; the passageway is 375 feet long. Like the priestess at Delphi, the Cumaean Sibyl gained her prophetic powers through her association with Apollo, who offered her anything if she would spend a night with him. She asked for eternal life, but as she neglected to ask for eternal youth, she shriveled away into a shadow.

She wrote her prophecies on leaves that she placed at the mouth of her cave. If no one came to pick them up, she let the wind scatter them. *The Sibylline Verses*, which told the Romans how to gain favor with foreign gods, were eventually bound into nine volumes, which the Sibyl tried to sell to the Latin king, Tarquin. He scoffed at the exorbitant price, so she burned three books and came back. The price was still too high, he scoffed again, she burned three more books. When she returned with the three last books, the king decided maybe there was something he ought to know, so he bought them. They were kept in the Capitol and consulted until some were destroyed in a fire in 83 B.C.E. The rest survived until another fire in 405 C.E., at which time enterprising Romans began writing pseudo-Sibylline prophecies.

Tanabata Festival

❖

Once upon a time, so the Chinese legend goes, Orihime (the star Vega), who was a weaving girl, and Kengyu (the star Altair), who was a cowherd, loved each other. Because of the jealousy of another star, they were separated and could only meet once a year in the Milky Way.

When the legend traveled from China to Japan, the day when the lovers met became the Tanabata Festival, which is celebrated primarily by children, who write wishes on *tanzaku* (strips of colored paper) and hang them on bamboo branches decorated with paper stars and other ornaments. At the end of the celebration, these branches are thrown into the river to dispel bad fortune.

Until recently, we seldom saw children at pagan events, but the time has come, as it should, for raising our children as pagans. Now we have excellent books that retell the myths for children, explain the wheel of the year, and give suggestions for celebrating sabbats with children. There are even magazines, like *The Blessed Bee*, for families with young children.

Reader, if the members of your circle or coven have children, this is a good day for your own Tanabata celebration. Gather your children—and maybe the whole neighborhood's children—and tell the story of Orihime and Kengyu. Give the jealous star a name and a bad attitude. Add peril and adventures and a joyous ending. Bring a star map and show where these two stars are in the sky. Decorate bamboo or other sacred trees with every kind of paper decoration—not only wishes, but also stars, moons, animals, and birds. Teach the children to fold origami peace cranes and add those to the branches. Let every child take a decorated branch home to commemorate a happy day.

The Pleiades

❖

A cluster of seven stars in the constellation Taurus, the Pleiades are about 380 light years away. In the second week of July, they appear at the east-northeast horizon, just ahead of the sun. They're relatively new stars, having formed only 100 million years ago—during the age when dinosaurs walked on earth—from a collapsing cloud of interstellar gas.

The Greeks called the Pleiades the Seven Sisters. Born in Arcadia, their names are Asterope, Dryope (or Merope or Aero), Electra, Maia, Taygete, Celaeno, and Alcyone. As Oreads (mountain nymphs), they were the daughters of the nymph Pleione and Atlas, which is why they are sometimes called Atlantides. Among their sisters were the Hyades (additional Atlantides who made it rain), Dione (a daughter of the ocean), and Calypso (another Oceanid who entertained Odysseus on her island for seven years). The Pleiades followed Artemis until the Hyades were killed, at which time they turned into stars.

In some lands, their helical rising signified the beginning of a new year. To the Vikings, the Pleiades were known as Freya's Hens; to the Maori, they were the Mataariki; in Australia, they were the Makara; and in Japan, they were the Subaru (which is why the car company uses them as its logo). To Greeks and Native Americans, the Pleiades were also a vision test. The number of stars you could see determined your visual acuity.

Readers, go outside and look at the Pleiades tonight. How many of them can you see? What is the wisdom of the stars? Many people believe that races from far-away stars visit us. What do you think an astral visitor might say?

The Holy Order of Water

❖

> The mysteries flowing from water are with us in many ways—in
> the life surrounding us; in thoughts generated by our water-filled
> minds; the smells and rhythms of our oceans; the soothing sounds
> of gurgling streams and fountains; . . . the gift of sight from our
> watery eyes; . . . the misty fog that lightly kisses our faces; the
> sight of an awe-inspiring tornado; the vortex swirl of water disap-
> pearing down a drain—the list is endless.
> —William E. Marks, *The Holy Order of Water*

Marks, who has been devoted to water since he was a boy and helped
his father dig wells, has traveled throughout the world to investigate the
status of water on our planet.

Water is created in interstellar space. The Oort Cloud, a huge watery
cloud that surrounds our solar system, is perhaps five billion years old.
Because the Oort Cloud contains ice and gases, water was possibly present
at the creation of our solar system. Oort comets are believed to have delivered water to earth as they struck it.

Reader, consider water. First, think in intimate terms: the water in your
blood, your eyeballs, your mouth and digestive system. Ponder the moisture that keeps your brain from drying out, ponder the moisture between
your legs. How do these intimate waters serve you? Consider the circulation of water on the planet. Think of rivers, lakes, and oceans flowing into
and through each other. Remember how it feels when the clouds release
their moisture and rain falls on us, on the land. Finally, see if you can get
your imagination around the Oort Cloud. Is there a watery intelligence, a
moist starry mother, watching over us?

Lady Godiva's Ride

❖

In 1040, it is said, Leonfric, earl of Mercia and lord of Coventry, laid such onerous taxes on the people that they were starving. When Lady Godiva, his wife, begged him to be merciful, he challenged her. If she would ride naked through the town, he would rescind the taxes. Godiva ordered that all windows be covered at noon and that all townspeople stay indoors. She mounted her white stallion and rode through the town, her long hair as her only garment. Only one man dared to look at her; his name has come down to us as Peeping Tom. He was struck blind, as all who spy upon women should be.

Godiva, whose story comes from *Flores Historiarum* (ca. 1236), was not just any medieval English noblewoman. This folktale is about a goddess, possibly Epona, and the purpose of her ride is bestow blessings upon the people, their houses and work, their fields and crops. She is a symbol of beauty to be preserved in a darkening world.

Perhaps Godiva, after whom the beautiful chocolate is named, is also goddess of the beauty of summer. Hers is more than human beauty; perhaps this gentle lady embodies the beauty of the earth. In the summertime, our planet is at her most fruitful. Flowers are at full bloom and fruits and vegetables are pulling ripening sunshine into their flesh. Under the blessings of Our Mother Sun, animals born with the spring are growing up and learning whatever animals learn. In midsummer, insects are busy, and birds and fish are prospering. Beauty is walking upon the earth. She is riding among us. Unlike Tom, we have permission to gaze upon her and worship her. The eyes of our imagination will see her glory until midsummer comes again.

Feast Day of St. Olga

❖

Elizabeth I. Eleanor of Aquitaine. Catherine de Medici. Isabelle of
Castile. Catherine the Great. Tz'u Hsi of China. Mbande Nzinga of
Angola. We know these great historical queens. But do we know Olga,
princess of Kiev?

Upon the assassination of her husband, Igor I, in 954, Olga, who was
said to be of Viking stock, became regent for her son, Svyatoslav. She
promptly executed her husband's murderers and ruled for twenty years,
bringing peace and prosperity to the wild lands of the Rus. In 957, she visited Constantinople, where she received baptism as a Christian. A famous
story tells how Olga's grandson, Vladimir, interviewed representatives of
the Islamic, Jewish, Roman, and Orthodox churches and chose the latter
because its rituals were the most beautiful and its temple, Hagia Sophia
in Byzantium, the most magnificent. Whatever the truth is about how
Orthodox Christianity came to Russia, the people adored Olga, who died
in 969. Although her son was still a pagan, he gave her a Christian burial.
She was soon elevated to sainthood.

After the revolution of 1917, religion was banished from Russia. Stalin
and his successors behaved like proletarian czars, however, and accepted
worship of themselves and of the state. When the Soviet empire dissolved,
churches were permitted to be reborn, and churches and cathedrals that
the Soviets had turned into stables or museums are now again houses of
worship.

Reader, midsummer is a good time to sit in the shade and read a good
book like Antonia Frazer's *The Warrior Queens*. Some people believe that if
we could roust all the men out of their supreme offices and let women rule
instead, the world would be a better place. Maybe. What about female
rulers who act like men? How can we bring ethics, honesty, and morality
back into our governments?

Water Everywhere

In my imagination, I see the Cosmic Cook standing in Her kitchen at
the beginning of time. She has decided to create an earth. The recipe is on
the counter in front of Her. *Take one cup each, earth, air, water, fire, and spirit.*
Mix well. (This "mixing well" might look like the scene in *Close Encounters of*
the Third Kind, where the character played by Richard Dreyfuss is building
Devil's Tower in his mashed potatoes.)

Where does the Cook get the ingredients? That's a good question.
(Reader, bear with me. This is not a comprehensive cosmogony. I can't
account for the kitchen or the counter, and I don't know who the Cook is,
though we can guess.) Earth comes from mountains, which are built by
drifting tectonic plates and then worn down into big rocks, little rocks,
and sand. Perhaps air swims in from outer space, which is why outer space
is airless. Like the Qabalistic lightning bolt, fire shoots out from the divine
spark of creativity, and spirit arises out of the process of mixing the other
four elements.

The water arrives from interstellar space. But answer me this: Did
someone plant a cup of water in the earth? Did that modest cup of new
water arise in magical wells and fantastical geysers and fill the oceans
and rivers?

Earth, air, and fire are not everywhere, at least not so we can see them.
But everywhere there is life, there is water. Water pulses through the planet
in its underground rivers as blood pulses through our bodies in our veins.
It's sometimes called the mother element, and it seems to me that spirit
rides on water's shoulders to touch deserts and mountaintops . . . and our
dreams. Our Mother Water and Her Child, Spirit, bless and bathe the
whole earth.

... JULY 13 ...
Bear's Day (Karuspäev)

❖

The pagan calendar of the old Baltic lands divided the year into quarters: Künnipäev (Plough Day, April 14), Karuspäev (Bear's Day), Kolletamisepäev (Withering Day, October 14), and Korjusep (Collection Day, January 14). Bear's Day is the midsummer festival.

The lands around the Baltic Sea used to be called the *Balticum* and included Lithuania, Latvia, Estonia, Finland, East Prussia, Livonia, and the Kaliningrad Oblast (the part of Russia between Poland and Lithuania). Königsberg ("King's Mountain") was established in the thirteenth century by the Teutonic Knights during their so-called northern crusade, in which they conquered and Christanized Prussia.

Tribal lands are not well known in the West. As early as the fifth century B.C.E., Herodotus described the Scythians, who lived between the rivers Don and Dneiper, as ferocious and barbaric; for two thousand years, the ferocity of the tribes of Russia and northern and middle Europe was not mitigated. Although their lands were conquered by the Holy Roman Empire and their kings and generals were nominally Christian, the people remained pagan. The popes sent bishops and armies, but not even the Teutonic Knights could persuade the Goths, Saxons, Curonians, Samogytians, Estonians, Wends, and Balts to give up their old gods. Even into the Middle Ages, they were barely "civilized" and they still lived as raiders, much as the Celts had done. Marija Gimbutas has written about her childhood in Lithuania, where they kept to the old ways; today, there are thriving neopagan communities there.

Reader, find an air-conditioned library and look at maps of medieval Europe. You'll find the kingdoms, margravates, duchies, counties, bishoprics, principalities, and palatinates you may have only read about in historical novels. You'll find lands long gone, lands now as mythical as Oz.

Discworld

❖

The wind howled. Lightning stabbed at the earth erratically,
like an inefficient assassin. . . . The night was as black as the inside
of a cat . . . . As the cauldron bubbled an eldritch voice shrieked:
"When shall we three meet again?"

There was a pause.

Finally, another voice said . . . "Well, I can do next Tuesday."
—Terry Pratchett, *Wyrd Sisters*

It's mid-July. We need an attitude adjustment. It's time to reread
Pratchett's series of Discworld novels and revisit a multiverse where witches,
wizards, humans, dwarves, vampires, assassins, barbarians, Death, and even
small gods coexist.

Nothing is sacred to Pratchett, and that includes *us*. The coven that
appears in several Discworld novels consists of three witches. The Maiden
is Magrat (her mother had problems with spelling), who wears every New
Age crystal and charm you can think of and keeps trying to work with
herbs. After Magrat's marriage, a new Maiden appears. This is Agnes Nitt,
who gets a job singing in the chorus at an opera house haunted by a
masked, deranged composer.

The Mother is Nanny Ogg. Having had several husbands, she's mother
to nearly the whole town. The Other One (we do *not* call her a Crone)
is Granny Weatherwax, who lives alone in a cottage in the woods, wears
stout boots, prefers "headology" to magic because it works better, and frequently has to jump-start her broom. She does this by running with her
broom and jumping on it to get it started.

The Great God Om is currently a very small god. He looks like a tor-
toise and *really* needs someone to believe in him.

Meditation for a Dog Day Afternoon

❖

Now there tended to be only a few very important [gods]—local
gods of thunder and love, for example, tended to run together
like pools of mercury as the small primitive tribes joined up and
became huge, powerful primitive tribes with more sophisticated
weapons. But any god could join. Any god could start small. Any
god could grow in stature as its believers increased. And dwindle
as they decreased. It was like a great big game of ladders and
snakes. Gods liked games, provided they were winning.
—Terry Pratchett, *Small Gods*

Adonis is Aphrodite's favorite. Tammuz is Inanna's. Attis is Cybele's.
They're good boys. They get sacrificed. Over and over again. Zeus rapes
Europa, Io, Danae, Leda, Antiope, Calyce, Lamia, Alcmene . . . well, it
would take two days to list all the girls who receive his unwanted attentions.

Tithonis is beloved of Eos. She asks Zeus to make him immortal. She
neglects to ask for eternal youth to go with the immortality, so Tithonis
dwindles into a cicada.

Instead of asking Actaeon to just go away, Diana turns him into a stag,
whereupon he is torn to pieces by his own hounds.

When Arachne weaves a more beautiful pattern than Athena, the goddess turns the girl into a spider. This is the same goddess who votes to
acquit Orestes, who murdered his mother.

The gods are so disinterested in human affairs that they wander off
among the rosy clouds of Olympus, ignoring us. . . . We must tempt
them [and] sing songs to them . . . and still they care little if we
live or die. Our petty fears strike them as absurd. And who can
blame them? They are immortal. We are not. We pass before their
all-seeing eyes like mayflies.
—Erica Jong, *Sappho's Leap*

And these are the divine ones we're worshipping?

Hegira of the Prophet Mohammed

❖

Before the Prophet Mohammed (570–632) received and preached the words of the Angel Gabriel, the Arabs were pantheists who personified the sun, moon, stars, and desert. Scholars of the esoteric tell us that the Kaaba ("cube") has been built ten times—first by the angels, next by Adam and Seth, the fourth time by Abraham and Ishmael, and the remaining times by Islamic kings. Lodged in one of the inner walls of the Kaaba is the sacred Black Stone, a meteor said to be a visitor (or messenger) from the heavens.

Even before the coming of Islam to Mecca, the Kaaba was a temple of Allah. Allah's name, which means "space-filling god," is the Arabic version of the Canaanite El, or Baal. In the temple were altars not only to the god, but also to his eight wives and daughters, who represented the seven known planets and the earth. Al-Uzza, "the mighty one," was the sun; she was worshipped by the clan of Mohammed's mother. Al-Manat, the moon, was a triple-faced goddess. The earth goddess was Al-Lat.

At one point in his life, Mohammed lived in the city of al-Taif, the center of Al-Uzza's "cult." It was here that the so-called Satanic Verses of the Koran were received. They are so called because they seem to endorse Goddess worship. When Mohammed returned to Mecca from Al-Taif, he cleaned out the Kaaba and threw out the altars to the goddesses.

There are temples, cathedrals, and churches in every country on the planet. Many of them occupy sites that were holy before the present occupant-god arrived. Some were built over caves or in groves that were holy precincts. No matter what god or goddess an altar was built to honor, every altar deserves our respect. Every altar is sacred space.

Festival of Amaterasu

❀

Amaterasu Omikami—Great August Spirit Shining in Heaven—is the supreme deity of the Shinto religion, queen of all the *kami*, the forces of nature. Nothing grows without her shining power. She is the ancestor of the Japanese royal family, but, as her stories show, her true roots lie in Siberian shamanism.

When the Chinese arrived in Japan in the second century C.E., they found so many female shaman-rulers there that they called the country the Land of Queens. The most powerful shaman-queen was Himiko, Sun's Daughter, who died in 247. Unmarried, chaste, and reclusive, Himiko performed magical ceremonies while the work of the government was done by her brother.

Confucianism, which arrived in Japan about 400, decreed that women were inherently unfit to rule. The shaman-queens were overthrown. A century and a half later, when Buddhism arrived, the status of women fell still lower. Among other things, it was said that a woman must be reborn as a man to be liberated from the wheel of life. As the Great Sun Buddha gained popularity in Japan, even the great sun goddess underwent a sex change. The people were told that Amaterasu was really a male god named Roshana.

But the native Shinto beliefs did not die, and it was an empress, Gemmyo, who in 712 first published the old Shinto myths of Amaterasu in the *Kojiki*, or "Record of Ancient Matters." One folktale tells how, like a shaman, Amaterasu climbs up a pillar to the heavens, creating the first sunrise. In the most famous story, she is insulted by her brother and hides in a cave until another shaman-goddess, Uzume, hangs a mirror in a tree, dances, and reveals her yoni. Amaterasu peers out, sees her glorious beauty in the mirror, laughs at Uzume's performance, and emerges from the cave.

Unintended Consequences of Damming Rivers

❖

I love it when native-born southern Californians travel east of the Rockies and see rivers with water in them *all the time*. It's that water in rivers "all the time" that can be troublesome. I have seen the Mississippi in flood. In spite of dams all along its length, it turns into an inland sea a thousand miles long. Flood control is useful and necessary.

Nevertheless, I wonder about the unintended consequences of building dams. In south-central Illinois, there used to be a beautiful little river whose water was clear and full of nice little fish that glided in the dappled shade of the trees along its banks. The river drained into the Mississippi. It occasionally flooded. So the U.S. Army Corps of Engineers was called upon to fix it. The last time I saw it, the river looked like the Los Angeles River. It was a ditch with concrete banks. No trees. Probably no birds or fish, either.

The Aswan High Dam was begun in Egypt in 1960 by President Gamal Abdel Nasser to create a reservoir. The Nubians who lived in the area were relocated, and the Great Temple of Abu Simbel was broken down, moved, and rebuilt elsewhere. The dam was inaugurated by President Anwar Sadat in 1970. Now, according to news reports, the Nile, whose floods had nourished Egypt since time out of mind and ruled the Egyptian calendar from the age of the first kings, isn't flooding anymore. And the delta is silting up.

China is building the Three Gorges Dam, the largest dam in the world, across the Yangtze River. The project is already over budget, and engineers have already had to relocate thousands of villages that were thousands of years old. What will be the unintended consequences of the construction of this dam?

Moon Gods

❖

We're always told that the sun is a god and the moon is a goddess. The sun's energy is projective. Daytime is more important than nighttime. Sun gods are strong and creative, moon goddesses are mystical and mysterious. It's the way it's always been.

But everyone has heard of the man in the moon. He first appeared in a Saxon folk tale with his wife, the woman in the sun. To our European ancestors, the sun was female and the moon was male. Earlier, the Sumerian city Ur (we use this name to indicate the oldest anything, like an ur-belief) was named after the moon god Hur. He's an ur-god. The Babylonian moon god, Sin, was the Father of Time. His name is a contraction of the Sumerian words *Su-En*, "the crescent moon." Also called Nanna ("the full moon"), Sin was the father of Ishtar. Why do we know this god? He was the voice of the famous burning bush, divine presence on Mt. Sinai and the carver of commandments. In Iran, 4,500 years ago, the moon was worshipped as the Great Man, who incarnated on earth as a divine ruler. Even the great thirteenth-century Mongol emperor, Genghis Khan, traced his ancestry back to a moon god.

The moon gods were overthrown by the sun and sky gods. Solar gods married solar goddesses and usurped their mythologies. Conquering tribal chiefs married female shamans and stole their powers. Men mastered the horse, fire, metallurgy, cities, and temples. It is said that they came to fear what they couldn't see in broad daylight, under the blazing sun, so they relegated the mysteries of the night to something else they feared—woman.

Go out tonight and look up at the moon. Ask the man in the moon what he's seeing as he looks down at us.

"Tranquility Base here. The Eagle has landed."

❖

My son swears he remembers being lifted out of his playpen and held in front of the television to watch Apollo 11's landing on the moon and Neil Armstrong's "one giant leap for mankind." July 20, 1969, is one of those days that grab hold of our memory and never let go. Where were you on December 7, 1941? On November 22, 1963? On September 11, 2001?

In the 1950s, when the Cold War was driving American policy, President John F. Kennedy worried that the United States was falling behind the Soviet Union, which launched Sputnik in 1957, in technology and prestige. In a speech on May 25, 1961, the president challenged the nation to put a man on the moon before the end of the decade. The National Aeronautics and Space Administration (NASA, established in 1958) promptly got to work and issued monumental contracts to design the program and build the hardware. On July 16, 1969, Apollo 11 was launched from the Kennedy Space Center. The members of the crew were Armstrong, Michael Collins, and Edwin E. Aldrin, Jr., pilot of the lunar module, Eagle.

I think it's interesting that the vehicles for this *lunar* project were given *solar* names. Apollo is a sun god, the eagle is a solar bird. Perhaps this is another, unconscious, example of the mastery of the sun over the moon?

It has been suggested that NASA faked it. Some conspiracy theorists assert that in 1969 NASA's technology was not sufficiently advanced to put a man on the moon and bring him home alive. Maybe Apollo really landed in Nevada. Maybe in Area 51?

Sun Enters Leo

Leo, says Lilith the astrologer, wants everyone to know what he's doing and how he's feeling. Leo wants to be always the center of attention. Leo overflows with the ever-blazing fires of inspiration, creativity, and passion. On the other hand, Leo can also be pompous and bossy. Leo is ruled by the sun.

Thirty years ago, I met an artist, every one of whose planets, I'm convinced, was in Leo. Reader, you know when you meet someone for the first time whom you know you've known forever? It was like that with R'becca and me. We met at a consciousness-raising group in southern Illinois. We were friends immediately. It was she who invited me to move to California.

If R'becca hadn't died so young, you'd recognize her name and be seeing her work in museums and galleries. She worked in nearly every medium, from fiber art to bronze sculpture to pen and ink so fine it looked like an etching to paintings in oils or acrylic. I remember her telling me about her art lessons where she had to draw people at a party, but every person in the drawing was bones and muscles only. She knew how a hand worked, what a lower back really looked like, the details of the musculature of a face. I'm proud to own three of her works.

But she was also the world's foremost Leo drama queen, and her life lurched from one melodrama to the next. It was impossible not to adore her, for she was generous and warm-hearted, but it was equally impossible to live with her (as both of her ex-husbands would also tell you). She became the sun of any room she entered, and everyone else was a pale planet, glad to be bathed in her solar wind.

Mary Magdalen

❖

As a friend inelegantly remarked the other day, "Mary's the major babe of the Bible." She's the First Lady of the New Testament. The true mystery of Christianity is not the birth or death of its god, but his resurrection. Who was present during the crucifixion when the male disciples were hiding? The Maries. Who was there when Jesus came out of that tomb? Mary Magdalen. Their reunion was not, however, happy. "Don't touch me," he said. "Don't hug me because I'm half-way between life and death." Mary's the one who informed the boys that their rabbi had risen. But, Reader, think about this: Was the resurrection real? Or was it a vision Mary had?

Mary Magdalen has had major press during the last twenty-five years, including appearances in novels and news magazines. All but the most conservative churchmen have finally figured out that she wasn't a prostitute, but perhaps the sister of Martha and Lazarus. Noncanonical gospels say she was Jesus' most beloved disciple and the only one who really understood his parables. Margaret Starbird and others say that Mary and Jesus were married (the wedding at Cana was theirs), and many believe that Leonardo da Vinci's *Last Supper* shows Mary, not the disciple John, sitting to Jesus' right. Some believe that Mary went to France and gave birth to a daughter, and that it's Magdalen who really is the holy mother to whom all the Notre Dame cathedrals were dedicated.

Susan Haskins, whose *Mary Magdalen: Myth and Metaphor* may be the most complete study of history and art devoted to Mary, says that her story is interpreted according to the biases of the authors who write about her. Elizabeth Cunningham's novel, *The Passion of Mary Magdalen*, is the best Goddess-oriented retelling of the Synoptic Gospels.

Ras Tafari

❖

The Rastafarian religion (which is not pagan) was developed in Jamaica in the 1930s and is based on the Back to Africa movement of Marcus Garvey, an early twentieth-century Jamaican author. Garvey's philosophy was that African-Americans should be able to go home to Africa and live peacefully in their own nations. Ethiopia had been seen as a mystical homeland of freed slaves in the Caribbean since an American Baptist minister named George Liele founded the Ethiopian Baptist Church in Jamaica in 1784.

Haile Selassie (1892–1975), whose name means "Power of Trinity," was the direct descendant of Menelik, the son of the Queen of Sheba and King Solomon. It was Menelik who brought the Ark of the Covenant to Ethiopia. In 1916, Ethiopian nobles and the Ethiopian Orthodox Church deposed Emperor Lij Iyasuin, whom they suspected of converting to Islam, and crowned Selassie, whose birth name was Tafari Makonnen, as Ras ("Duke") Tafari ("Fearsome" in Amharic, the language of Ethiopia). In 1930, he assumed the title emperor. His full title was "His Imperial Majesty, Conquering Lion of the Tribe of Judah, Elect of God, King of Kings of Ethiopia." At the time of his coronation, residents of Harlem and the Caribbean islands believed that deliverance was at hand for all downtrodden peoples. Selassie abolished slavery, modernized his country, secured its admission into the League of Nations; when Fascist Italy invaded Ethiopia in 1935 he went to exile. In 1974, he was deposed by a military and/or communist coup led by radical Islamic Africans and murdered.

Rastafarians believe that Haile Selassie is still alive. They see him as their messiah, the emperor who will lead all people of African descent to the Day of Liberation. He is the Living God of Abraham and Isaac, He Whose Name Should Not Be Spoken.

Neith

❖

In *Black Athena: The Afroasiatic Roots of Classical Civilization*, Martin Bernal asserts that European scholars saw Greek culture as a white culture. They ignored Egyptian and Phoenician influences on Greece and, subsequently, all of Western civilization. In other words, he says that European history is racist and anti-Semitic and that the Egyptian gods and culture were largely black African. (I've greatly oversimplified an enormously complex thesis.)

Neith is one of the eldest Egyptian goddesses. Originally a tribal goddess of the city of Saïs, she was worshipped as early as the First Dynasty (ca. 3000 B.C.E.). She was both virgin and self-created, and her icon was two crossed arrows and a mottled animal skin. As Egypt grew, this goddess absorbed the deities of conquered tribes. Plutarch records an inscription on her temple: "I am all that has been, that is, that will be, and no mortal has yet been able to lift the veil that covers me."

Neith may be Athena's many-times great-grandmother. She may be a black Athena. Like the familiar Greek goddess, Neith was the mistress of handicrafts. In the beginning, it is said, Neith strung the sky on her loom and wove the world. She then pulled people and other creatures out of the primordial waters and, in the shape of a cow, gave birth to Ra, who grew up to be the longest lived and most powerful of the sun gods. This makes her the mother of the sun itself. If the Egyptians had known our modern Big Bang theory of the origin of the universe, might Neith have embodied the exploding energy that brought all things into being?

Reader, we pagans like to "borrow" practices, rituals, folklore, and beliefs from every possible source. Sometimes it's useful to search out the true origin, the ur-source, of things we think we know.

Furrinalia, Neptunalia

The Furrinalia is sacred to Furrina, a goddess of springs, wells, and the fresh water that visitors can still see flowing near her sanctuary on the Janiculum Hill in Rome. Furrina was such an ancient goddess that the Roman authors forgot who she was and simply remarked that prayers and sacrifices had always been made to her.

Two other pre-Roman water goddesses are Venilia, an otherwise unknown goddess of coastal waters, and Salacia, a goddess of wells. While it's possible that Salacia's name lives on in our word *salacious* through her connection with Aphrodite, who was born in the sea from the castrated genitals of Uranus, I wonder if she might also have been a sea goddess and if her name holds "salt." Salt, *salis*, was a source of wealth in many ancient cultures. We still see it in *salary*; Roman soldiers were paid partly with salt.

These three archaic goddesses of water were likely related to Neptunus, an ancient god of water who protected against drought. He also protected waterways and was later conflated with Poseidon. Another god, Vertumnus, changed the course of the Tiber River. Offerings and prayers were made to these divine watery ones in July to ensure a steady supply of water during the hot summer months.

Reader, this is a good time to build your own water altar, indoors or out. If indoors, set up a small tabletop fountain or aquarium with living fish. Set a figure of a water god or goddess (I have a pink satin mermaid) or some beautiful shells on an altar. If you add a recirculating fountain to your garden, you can install a larger god or goddess and add river pebbles or shells. Let these things remind you to be thankful for fresh water every day of your life.

St. Anne

❖

The medieval Christian church had as much mythology as we do, but they called it history. Learned men created long catalogues of saints, some of whom were pagan gods and goddesses renamed and re-biographied. The *Golden Legend*, compiled in 1275 by Jacobus de Voraigne, told tabloid-true stories of the lives of saints and the childhood of Jesus. It was medieval Europe's most popular book. Two apocryphal gospels were the *Pseudo-Matthew* and the *Protoevangelium* of James.

It is from these three works that we get the story of St. Anne, also known as Hannah, which means "grace" in Hebrew. Anne is the traditional name of the mother of the Blessed Virgin Mary. Anne and her husband, Joachim, were a rich and pious couple. Childless for twenty years, they prayed to God that if he would take away their curse of sterility, they would dedicate the child to his service. He did and they did.

In 1579, John of Eck of Ingolstadt said that Anne's parents were Stollanus and Emerentia (whose name seems to be related to "hermit"). John further tells us that after Joachim died, Anne married Cleophas, by whom she had another daughter, Mary Cleophas, mother of three apostles. She was one of the Maries who sailed to Marseilles with Mary Magdalen after the crucifixion. A Greek Orthodox scholar says that Salome and Elizabeth (mother of John the Baptist) were daughters of Anne's sisters. In the sixteenth century, there arose a great dispute over Anne's marriages, wherein scholars vigorously defended her serial monogamy. Reader, notice their fascination with the *female* line of the Holy Family.

A cult of St. Anne arose in Byzantium, where July 25 became her official feast day. On this day in 710, her official relics arrived in Constantinople.

Hatshepsut

✤

Hatshepsut, who was born about 1503 B.C.E. and reigned from 1473 to 1458 B.C.E., was the daughter of Thutmose I and his chief wife, Ahmose. Upon her father's death, she married her half-brother, Thutmose II. Because Thutmose III (son of Thutmose I by another wife) was still a minor when Thutmose II died, Hatshepsut declared herself regent, then king. She dressed in the traditional garb of kings and wore the headdress with its uraeus and headcloth. She even wore a false beard. Calling herself the female Horus, she said that her *true* father was Amun-Ra. The "true story" of her divine birth was painted on the walls of her funerary temple at Deir el-Bahri.

During her reign, King Hatshepsut chose to pursue not war but trade. Two of her most famous trading expeditions were to Byblos for turquoise and to the fabled Land of Punt (thought to be Eritrea) for incense. As the fifth ruler of the Eighteenth Dynasty of the New Kingdom, she also had great interest in the history of Egypt and embarked on a major building program to restore sanctuaries that had been destroyed during the Hyksos invasions (ca. 1674–1567 B.C.E.). She built a temple to Amun-Ra at Karnak and began her own temple at Deir el-Bahri. The temple still stands but, like her other works, it was left incomplete when Thutmose III proclaimed that a female could not be king. He led a revolt against Hatshepsut and probably murdered her. Her architects and courtiers were also murdered. Thutmose promptly had her name and image hacked out of every monument in the kingdom. He became Egypt's foremost warrior-king and through numerous wars and conquests created an empire that lasted until Egypt was conquered by Alexander the Great and his generals a thousand years later.

Pythias

❖

Today is traditionally dedicated to Pythias, who is said to have served at Delphi. If this is so, we don't know her true name, for Pythia is the title used by the female mediums starting about 1400 B.C.E., when Delphi first became the setting for an oracle. Given that her son, Pythagoras, was born about 569 B.C.E., she would have been at Delphi about the same time the poet Sappho was alive.

When the first temple of Apollo was built in 650, Delphi was already becoming wealthy and famous. The temple was destroyed by fire about 558 and rebuilt with contributions from Croesus, the richest king of the ancient world (you've heard the phrase "rich as Croesus"). In 480, a Persian army invaded Delphi but was, it is said, driven off by the god himself. A hundred years later, the second temple of Apollo was destroyed by an earthquake and rebuilt soon after. By 300, Delphi was falling on hard times. Celts plundered the temple in 279, a Roman general plundered it in 86, and barbarians from Thrace plundered it in 83. Although the Roman emperor Hadrian did some rebuilding in the second century C.E., the Constantine's conversion to Christianity furthered the oracle's decline.

At last, about 364 C.E., the emperor Julian, who was endeavoring to revive paganism in the Roman Empire, consulted the oracle at Delphi.

> Tell to the king that the carven hall is fallen in decay;
> Apollo has no chapel left, no prophesying bay,
> No talking spring. The stream is dry that had so much to say.

This is said to be the oracle's reply to Julian. It is also the last recorded reply, although I've found Web sites of people who say they're channeling the oracle and, like the olden days, offer advice for a price.

St. Martha

The Gospels tell the story of Mary and Martha. Mary ignored the cooking and the housework and sat outside in the shade at the feet of the teacher.

Nobody paid any attention to Martha. The housewife of Magdala is, in fact, sometimes admonished for cooking and serving dinner instead of hanging out with the scholars and listening to the teacher's parables. In the story of Jesus' visit to Bethany, where he calls Lazarus out of the grave, she almost becomes invisible.

But hospitality was important in the Middle East two thousand years ago and still is today. Even though Martha is grieving the death of her brother, Lazarus, she goes out to greet Jesus and the other guests, but then she goes back inside to prepare their dinner. Martha understands service on the most practical level. This is why she became the patron saint of servants.

Honoring service is an important lesson we modern pagans need to learn. We like to dress up and run fancy rituals . . . but who brings all the stuff? Who schleps the altar decorations to the ritual? The candles, the oils, the magical tools, the ritual props, the cakes and ale? Who are our, so to speak, bag ladies?

And who cleans up after the ritual? Who scrapes candle wax off the floor, sweeps up the incense crumbs, and makes sure everyone gets their tools or jewelry or tokens back? I've been to rituals where the priestess lounges in the center of her circle of admirers and explains to us lesser mortals how the ritual should really have worked. I've also been to rituals where the priestess changes out of her ritual garb, picks up a scraper, and goes after the wax on the floor. She's the last one to leave.

Blue Moon

As I write this, we're having a blue moon. Lunar power is magnified. One definition of a blue moon says it is the third full moon in a season that has four full moons. In order to set Easter properly, the medieval ecclesiastic calendar required a maximum of twelve full moons during the year; by calling the occasional thirteenth full moon a blue moon (which didn't really "count"), they kept the calendar on track. A modern definition says the blue moon is the second full moon in a calendar month. There will be blue moons on June 30, 2007; December 31, 2009; and August 31, 2012.

Saying the moon is blue, serious people tell us, is like saying it is made of green cheese. But with air pollution, clouds, and ice crystals in the atmosphere, the moon does occasionally appear to be blue. If we can believe in a blue moon, they also tell us, we're credulous enough to believe in any kind of nonsense. If something happens "once in a blue moon," they say, it ain't gonna happen.

Who cares what they say? Gather your circle or coven and have a blue-moon ritual tonight. Prepare tokens that symbolize good fortune. If you plan far enough ahead, you can collect wishbones and paint them with blue glitter. Ask your priestess du jour to dress up like the Blue Fairy from Disney's *Pinocchio* and lead everyone in a meditation to find out what wish their heart makes. At the end of the meditation, the Blue Fairy can give everyone a glittery wishbone or a piece of blue lace agate or a magical verse written in blue ink on palest blue paper:

On this night when the moon is blue,
I hear your wish and make it true!
XOXOX,
The Blue Fairy

British Witches Stop Hitler's Army

❖

Because Adolf Hitler, believed to be the modern world's most famous black magician, planned to invade England, British Prime Minister Neville Chamberlain went to Munich in September, 1938, and returned with a treaty declaring there would be "peace in our time." Widely accused of appeasing the Nazis, he was voted out of office. A year later, when Hitler invaded Poland, World War II began.

In May and June, 1940, the British Expeditionary Force was crushed by the Nazi army. What saved them was what Winston Churchill called a "miracle of deliverance." Three hundred thousand men were rescued by English civilians in every kind of boat—yachts, fishing boats, pleasure boats, even rowboats. The men were brought home to Dunkirk, on the south coast of England. Was England about to be invaded for the first time since William the Conqueror arrived in 1066?

On July 31, 1940, it is said, English witches gathered in the New Forest and raised a monumental cone of power to stop Hitler's forces. It is also said that Gerald Gardner's coven joined this grand coven. Five of Gardner's coveners died a few days later, and Gardner reported that he had been weakened by the energy.

Lammas Night, by Katherine Kurtz, is a magical-adventure novel that tells the story of the grand coven. A colonel in British intelligence must "stop the onslaught of evil." Drawing on the idea, popularized by Margaret Murray, that English kings since William Rufus, William the Conqueror's son who was mysteriously killed while hunting in the New Forest in 1100, have been sacrificial kings in time of need, Kurtz's hero appeals to a fictitious brother of King George VI. After much suspense and ceremonial magic on both sides of the English Channel, this brother becomes the sacrificed king, and England is saved.

Motherpeace Tarot Deck

> As a guide to telling stories about our lives together and as an
> illustration of these stories, the Motherpeace images can lead us
> toward the creation of a new mythology, a "creative visualization"
> for the future, as well as toward an account of our evolution that
> is no longer biased by the distortions of the Patriarchy.
> —Vicki Noble

Karen Vogel and Vicki Noble were living in Berkeley, California, in
1978, when they were given a tarot deck. One night soon after, their world
readjusted itself. Karen felt the room tilt, and Vicki had a life-changing
vision of the Goddess. After subsequently researching thirty thousand
years of art and goddesses throughout the world, they began drawing the
first Motherpeace images—the Six of Wands and Athene's Chariot. "All
this knowledge," the Motherpeace Web site says, "pours through the . . .
images, whether or not a person ever reads any of our books or studies the
tarot." Vicki and Karen self-published the Motherpeace deck on August 1,
1981. Two years later, U.S. Games picked it up.

Unlike most other tarot decks, Vicki says, the Motherpeace cards
"are multi-cultural and multi-racial. . . . We had a vision of a rainbow tribe
(before people were calling it that). We made the cards psychologically
up to date, while keeping true to the ancient structure of the tarot (also
unlike many newer decks)." The Motherpeace Tarot is one of only two
round decks. The other is Daughters of the Moon, created by Ffiona
Morgan and others in 1983.

Vicki, who believes that the first shamans were female, also created a
quarterly journal called *Snake Power;* it was censored by the post office. Her
book *The Double Goddess* (2003), is the result of years of research. Images of
two linked goddesses—mother and daughter, sisters, lovers—are found in
cultures throughout the world.

First Harvest

❋

Bright sun and warm days have brought our crops to the zenith of their growth. Now we begin harvesting what we planted last spring. In the olden days, when we were still agricultural people, we offered the best part of our harvest to a god or goddess as a sacrifice to make it holy. We were celebrating the fruitfulness and generosity of Mother Nature.

The OED offers several definitions of *sacrifice*, most of which come from Judeo-Christian sources. Theology that pagans might accept is "the destruction or surrender of something valued or desired for the sake of something having, or regarding as having, a higher or more pressing claim."

Two of the best-known biblical stories of sacrifice concern Cain and Abel and Abraham. In the earlier story (Genesis 4), Abel is a shepherd, Cain a farmer. Their god happily receives the burnt animal sacrifice from Abel, but rejects the sacrifice of harvested grain from Cain. In the second story (Genesis 22), the Lord says to Abraham, "Take thy only son [and] get thee into the land of Moriah and offer him there for a burnt offering." It's a parable of the change from human sacrifice to animal sacrifice.

When modern pagans go to a Lammas ritual, we seldom take along a sheaf of wheat to offer to Lugh. When we're asked what we want to harvest, we write something we've finished with in our lives on a little piece of paper and burn it in the cauldron.

Reader, do we have to destroy something in order to make it sacred? If our harvest becomes our sacrifice, are we harvesting or sacrificing something we've already used up? We're not growing wheat in the city. We're not raising cows or horses or sheep. In our modern urban lives, what do we harvest? What do we sacrifice?

1492

On the very day that Christopher Columbus set sail for the New
World, the queen and king of Spain banished Jews from the country.
Purging the land of every kind of infidel, the pious Isabella of Castile
and Ferdinand of Aragon sanctioned the work of the Inquisition.

The newest research on Columbus says he might not have been from
Genoa, Italy. In the 1480s, he developed a plan to sail to the Indies, which
at that time meant southeastern Asia. He presented his plan to the king of
Portugal in 1485; after being rejected, he went to Spain, where he spent
several years at court lobbying. It's a myth that he's the only one who
thought the earth was round. Objections to his plan were based on how
long—and how expensive—such a voyage might be, not that he might
sail off the edge of the earth.

Columbus is seen as either a mighty hero or a mighty villain. Hero
worship reached its peak about 1892, the four hundredth anniversary of
his first voyage, when he became a model of that good old American
"can-do" attitude. He had a plan, he persisted, he succeeded. The five
hundredth anniversary of his voyage was less celebratory, for by 1992,
we were equating conquest with atrocity, exploitation, slavery, and genocide. President Hugo Chavez of Venezuela has signed a decree changing
Columbus Day to the "Day of Indigenous Resistance."

In 1492, Spain had been under Muslim rule for several centuries.
While the rest of Europe was struggling through the Dark Ages, Muslim
Spain had a civilization that preached tolerance and literacy. It was only
after the Cid had driven the Arabs out that the Catholic Church assumed
power and began burning unbelievers.

Hans Christian Andersen

Hans Christian Andersen (1805–1875) wanted to be a serious author. In his own time, he was. What do we remember him for? Fairy tales.

After his father died young, Andersen quit school, built himself a toy theater, and read every book and play that he could find, including the plays of Shakespeare. Before he was twenty, he moved to Copenhagen, and somehow attracted the interest of the king, who sent him to school. Andersen later wrote that these years were the bitterest of his life.

It wasn't until 1835 that he found fame as a novelist, but by that time he'd already published his first volume of fairy tales. A second volume followed in 1838, a third in 1845. He was celebrated throughout Europe, partly for his poetry and plays, but primarily for *The Emperor's New Clothes*, *The Ugly Duckling*, *The Snow Queen*, *The Little Match Girl*, *The Red Shoes*, *The Little Mermaid*, and a hundred other stories. We love their sentimentality and their moral lessons.

Reader, nearly every pagan I know is an Ugly Duckling. We all hatch into ordinary families. We go to school and learn the basics, but family and teachers alike fail to recognize or appreciate our sterling qualities of creativity and nonconformity. We grow up, we get jobs, we get our electronic toys, we get along. As the little girls in *Annie* sing, it's a hard-knock life.

And one day we meet a Swan! We pick up a book of mythology or metaphysics that turns our life upside down. We meet a Real Witch, a teacher. Someone drags us to a ritual, and there we Feel At Home. No longer are we drab, gray ducklings. We've found our True Kin. We balance our chakras and find our spirit guides and become Wise and Wonderful Swans.

Tree-Month of Hazel

The Celtic tree calendar was made famous by Robert Graves in *The White Goddess*, where he says it predates Julius Caesar's calendar by at least three thousand years. Graves drew not only from his own vast scholarship but also from other sources to show that in the Celtic languages trees correspond to letters. The calendar comes from various sources. One is a thirteenth-century "riddling poem," *Câd Goddeu*, or *The Battle of the Trees*, which is part of the Welsh *Romance of Taliesin*. The tree alphabet and calendar are also found in the *Song of Amergin*, which tells the journey of the sun god through the thirteen stages of his life.

The thirteen tree months are Birch, Rowan, Ash, Alder, Willow, Hawthorn, Oak, Holly, Hazel, Vine, Ivy, Reed, and Elder. The month of Hazel, which is also Apple (these two trees are interchangeable), runs from August 5 or 6 to September 1. Its Irish tree names are *coll* and *quirt*, its birds are the crane and hen, its colors are brown and mouse colored, and its jewel is red agate. Hazel also belongs to Wednesday. Other correspondences for Wednesday are wisdom and the creation of heavenly bodies and seasons (Genesis 1:14–19). Wotan, Apollo, and Hermes rule Wednesday.

The Hebrew substitute for hazel is the almond, which was the tree of Aaron's magic rod. The story of Aaron is told in Exodus, where he and his brother, Moses, do magic tricks to make the pharaoh release the Hebrew tribes. While the tribes are wandering in the desert, Aaron becomes their chief high priest.

Reader, do you have a wand? A hazel wand would aid in setting verbal charms and in meditation. Dowsers use hazel to find water and things that are hidden or lost.

Rulers of the Days of the Week

❋

> In the beginning, Eurynome, the Goddess of All Things, rose
> naked from Chaos, but found nothing substantial for her feet to
> rest upon, and therefore divided the sea from the sky. . . .
> —Robert Graves, *The Greek Myths*

And so begins the pre-Olympian story of creation, as told in Homer's
Iliad, Apollonius Rhodius' *Argonautica*, and Hesiod's *Theogony*. Eurynome
mates with the great serpent, Ophion, then with Boreas, the north wind.
Assuming the form of a dove and "brooding on the waves," she lays the
universal egg, out of which, Graves writes, "tumble all things that exist,
her children: sun, moon, planets, stars, the earth with its mountains and
rivers, its trees, herbs, and living creatures." The goddess's next move is to
Mt. Olympus. But Ophion vexes her, so she kicks out his teeth and banishes him to the dark caves below the earth. Next, the goddess creates the
planetary powers. These are the elder powers, the Titanesses and Titans
that rule the days of the week:

Sunday: Theia ("Divine") and Hyperion ("Moon-man on high")

Monday: Phoebe ("Bright moon") and Atlas ("He who dares or suffers")

Tuesday: Dione ("Divine queen") and Crius ("Ram")

Wednesday: Metis ("Counsel") and Coeus ("Intelligence")

Thursday: Themis ("Order") and Eurymedon ("Wide rule")

Friday: Tethys ("Disposer") and Oceanus ("Of the swift queen")

Saturday: Rhea ("Earth") and Cronus ("Crow/Raven")

When I'm planning a ritual or a spell, I like to know not just which
Olympian rules the day of my working but also which of the earlier
powers I can invoke for greater energy. If I need help with my writing,
for example, I can do my working on a Wednesday and maybe get an
intellectual jump-start.

Birth of Hathor

❋

One of the eldest goddesses, Hathor was originally a local deity of Dendera in southern Egypt. She was incorporated into the cults of Ra and Horus as Ra's mother or daughter or Horus's mother. Hathor is her Greek name. First, she was *Het-hert*, or "Sky-house" or "My House in the Sky." Then worshippers of Horus renamed her *Het-heru*, or "House of Horus," meaning she was the sky through which the hawk flew. Hathor also become the solar eye, the cow of the sky whose right eye is the sun and left eye is the moon.

Like Isis, Hathor corresponds to "golden Aphrodite" and is the goddess to invoke when you're "in sexual need." She's the goddess of singers, dancers, artists, cosmetics, and intoxicating drinks. Early inscriptions also identify her as the goddess of the date palm and the sycamore tree. On New Year's Day, Hathor's image was brought out of the temple to be bathed in the first rays of the rising sun.

In an early Egyptian story, we learn of the Seven Hathors, goddesses of fate to whom a childless king prays. When his wife gives birth to a son, the Hathors arrive and pronounce his destiny: he will die by means of a crocodile, a snake, or a dog. In another story, the Seven Hathors tell a beautiful young woman that she will die by the knife. Hathor not only foretells the fates of humans, but also receives them when they arrive in the Underworld, which makes her a goddess of regeneration.

Sometimes, however, Hathor causes the untimely ends of those whom the gods decide must die. As the Eye of Ra, she was once set upon blasphemers. She turned into the lion-headed goddess, Sekhmet, and as Sekhmet, she "prevails over humanity" with such *joie de mort* that the gods have to pacify her.

Traveling Tribes

*

On August 8, 1844, in Nauvoo, Illinois, Brigham Young was named leader of the Mormon Church's Quorum of Twelve Apostles. Young was the second prophet of the Church of Jesus Christ of Latter-day Saints; the church was founded by Joseph Smith, Jr., discoverer, translator, or author of the *Book of Mormon*, first published in 1830.

The *Book of Mormon*, like other holy books, sets forth history and dogma. It begins with an account of the journey of Lehi and his family to America around 600 B.C.E. and describes the visit of the resurrected Jesus Christ to the Americas, where he gives many of the same teachings that appear in the New Testament. Numerous opinions exist regarding the possibly mythical origin of the *Book of Mormon*.

The story of the Mormons and their journey across the plains to their new home in Salt Lake City, Utah, reminds me (in concept, if not in details) of the Lost Tribes of Israel. During the age of David and Solomon, the twelve Hebrew tribes constituted a "mighty kingdom." Upon the death of Solomon, the kingdom fell apart, and only Benjamin and Judah remained loyal to the Davidic line. In 722–721 B.C.E., the ten northern tribes were captured by the Assyrians, carried into exile, and disappeared from history. Although they were probably absorbed by the people who lived wherever the Assyrians dumped them, the legend of the Lost Tribes arose. It became especially popular in medieval Europe, and the Lost Tribes were spotted in many lands, including Persia, Zimbabwe, and the Americas. My favorite theory is the British Israelites. It is said that the Lost Tribes of Israel migrated across Europe, ended up in the British Isles, and founded England.

Today there is a thriving pagan community in Salt Lake City that includes the Order of Lady of Salt. I've met them.

The Elemental Salamander

I just found one—marginally—trustworthy source that asserts that "today was the ancient Greek salamander festival." I don't believe it for a moment, but because I want to talk about fire in August, I'll use this make-believe festival as my hook.

I dug into *The Secret Teachings* and learned what Manly P. Hall has to say about salamanders, which are spirits of fire.

> [They] live in that attenuated, spiritual ether which is the invisible fire element of Nature. Without them material fire cannot exist; a match cannot be struck nor will flint and steel give off their spark without the assistance of a salamander, who immediately appears (so the medieval mystics believed), evoked by friction. *Man is unable to communicate successfully with the salamanders* [emphasis mine]. . . .[15]

I don't know much about magical salamanders, having never met one personally, and I have trouble keeping candles lit. But I recognize the importance of fire, both real and metaphorical.

Readers, nearly every "expert" says that the elemental spirits are untamable, mischievous, and not much interested in petty human concerns. They should be invoked with enormous care. When I cast a circle, I invite the powers of the four directions and elements to bring their *gifts* to the circle. The gifts of air include discernment; of water, compassion; of earth, growth; of fire, creativity. If we can draw these gifts into our lives and our consciousness, I believe, we will live more magical and more productive lives.

Do you invoke elemental spirits into your circles? What kinds of manifestations have you had? The next few times you cast a circle, experiment with asking the elemental powers to bring their gifts to your magical work. See if there are any changes in your magical work.

Creativity

Fire, said Heraclitus, is "the agent of transmutation." All things arise from fire and all things return to fire. It is the seed of life (and libido), the sun's rays that stimulate the growth of our fields, our animals, and ourselves. Fire is the energy that is creative and destructive and re-creative.

Mainstream metaphysicians like to talk about becoming "co-creators with God" and creating their own reality. Reader, is this different from what our pagan or Wiccan teachers say? How does an affirmation differ from a spell? We manipulate energy, which is what we call doing magic. In *The Spiral Dance*, Starhawk describes "starlight vision," the creative mode that "sees the universe as a dance of swirling energies."

Reader, what have you learned about creativity? How do the powers of fire—creativity—manifest themselves in your life? Some people use the words *passion* and *fire in the belly* for the creative urge that we must not resist. My passion for words is why I sit at my keyboard all day. What's your passion? What do you absolutely have to do for your life to be worth staying on the planet?

In *The Artist's Way*, Julia Cameron writes, "Creativity is the natural order of life. Life is energy: pure creative energy. There is an underlying, in-dwelling creative force infusing all of life—including ourselves."[16] She advises us to write "morning pages." We must diligently produce three pages of longhand stream-of-consciousness writing every morning. These pages are not art. They don't have to make sense or sound smart. They're just whatever's on your mind. This writing helps you find and remove the blocks to your creativity that may be buried deep within you because someone laughed at a piece of art you produced when you were seven years old. How else can you draw creativity into your life?

Isis

Isis, Great Lady, Queen of Heaven, mother goddess of Egypt, is mentioned in papyri that date back to 1500 B.C.E. We know that the Romans brought her worship to Italy in the second century B.C.E. Some years later, as she later became associated with the Ptolemaic god, Serapis, she became the foremost Hellenistic goddess and was soon as popular in Greece and Rome as in Egypt. Thanks to the Romans, the "cult" of Isis found its way north and west into Europe, where she was often identified with local goddesses and is probably the original of Europe's many Black Virgins. She was likewise carried east by the Romans into Asia Minor.

Temples to Isis, called *isea*, were built in nearly every land. There are *isea*, for example, in the ruins of Pompeii, and her likeness appears on Roman coins as late as the fourth century. In 188 C.E., an *iseum* was built at Szombathely, Hungary; it was enlarged in the third century. This same *iseum* was rebuilt in the 1950s and now hosts an annual Mozart festival.

The popular worship of Isis thus endured from the fourth century B.C.E. until early in the fifth century C.E.. The Serapeum in Alexandria was destroyed in 391, the last official festivals of Isis and Magna Mater took place in 394, and the last mention of an Isis festival in classical literature dates to 416. Although her worship gave way to Christianity, we know that her iconography endured in the images of the young mother nursing her holy son.

Our major literary sources of information on Isis are Plutarch's *Of Isis and Osiris*, which was read by Shakespeare and countless other poets, and *The Golden Ass*, a novel by Lucius Apuleius, in which the goddess says "I am Nature, the universal Mother, mistress of all the elements, . . . sovereign of all things spiritual. . . ."[17] The first is Greek, the second, Roman; both were written in the first century C.E.

Feast of St. Clare

We are familiar with the Hindu concept that a god needs a goddess to animate his male energy. The goddesses are called *shakti*, "activating female energy," and transmission of energy is often sexual.

Don't look for sexual imagery with St. Clare and St. Francis, though. The founder of the Franciscan Order was born in the town of Assisi in 1181 or 1182. One day at Mass, he heard that disciples of Christ were to possess neither gold nor silver, nor two coats, nor shoes, nor even a staff. Feeling that these teachings applied to him personally, Francis gave away everything he owned and set out preaching. He gathered twelve disciples of his own and, with the permission of Pope Innocent III, founded the Order of Friars Minor in 1209.

Clare, a nobleman's daughter, was eighteen years old when the preaching of Francis "kindled a flame in her heart." After Francis recognized her as a chosen soul, she secretly left her father's house and met him in a "humble chapel." There she laid aside her rich clothing, he cut her hair, and she took vows of poverty. He placed her in a monastery. Two weeks later, her sister joined her, and they founded the Order of Poor Ladies, or Poor Clares, which became the second Franciscan order.

The daily life of the Poor Clares, the Catholic Encyclopedia tells us, is "a life of penance and contemplation" occupied with work and prayer. They never eat meat and maintain silence at all times. Some people assert that St. Clare was the *shakti* of St. Francis, and that the power of her prayers helped him maintain the energy he needed for his preaching, which included attempts to convert the Saracens. If she is his *shakti*, however, it is only in the most holy, abstract, virginal sense.

Aradia

In *Aradia, or, The Gospel of the Witches*, published in 1899, Charles Godfrey Leland writes that "this little work sets forth how [Aradia] was born, came down to earth, established witches and witchcraft, and then returned to heaven." Diana "greatly loves" her brother, Lucifer, proud god of light and splendor, and gives birth to Aradia, "the female Messiah." Diana instructs her daughter "to be a teacher unto women and men. . . . And thou shalt be the first of witches known." Aradia is directed to teach civil disobedience to the poor. It's pretty incendiary stuff—"the art of poisoning those who are great lords," how to ruin rich peasants' crops "with tempests dire," and how to return double the harm to any priest who does injury to her.[18]

La Bella Pelegrina (the Beautiful Pilgrim), whom tradition names Aradia of Tuscany, is said to have been born on August 13, 1313. (Notice those three thirteens. Roman women had performed rituals to Diana on August 13.) As the traditional founder of Strega and rabble-rouser among the peasantry, Aradia was accused of heresy, arrested by the Inquisition, and imprisoned. When the priests went to preach to her, they found her cell empty. She was pursued and arrested again, and again she escaped, possibly into the East.

There are questions about the authenticity of Leland's work. Does it record a genuine tradition or did Leland's friend, Maddelena, make it up? Or did Leland write it himself? Reader, how cautious should we be when someone presents us with "traditional wisdom"? I have friends who head a Dianic order devoted to Aradia. Every year, they present a lovely ritual on Aradia's birthday that takes participants on a "mystical pilgrimage." What kind of ritual should we devise to honor a figure whose historicity is questionable? Does historicity matter? Do we read—and believe—selectively?

Bon Festival

During the mid-August festival of Obon, or Bon, the Japanese honor the souls of their ancestors with special foods and folk dancing. Prayers are said at the family altar for those who have died during the past year, as it is believed they need guidance to find their way safely through the other world. Red lanterns are hung throughout the festival area to guide the spirits, and there may also be fireworks and bonfires.

Some Japanese sources say that Obon is a shortened form of the Sanskrit word *Urabonna*, which means "hanging upside down in hell and suffering." The festival is said to have originated when a monk saw an image of his dead mother suffering in hell. He asked Shaka (the Buddha) for advice and was told to hold a feast for seven generations of dead souls. He did so, and his mother's suffering was relieved.

Westerners are familiar with the Christian purgatory and hell with its demons and eternal fires. Medieval art is full of demons torturing damned souls. Half of the Sistine Chapel illustrates hell. We may be familiar with *Paradise Lost*, which describes hell as "pandemonium" and demonizes gods and goddesses. We've also heard of the Puritan preachers Cotton Mather and Jonathan Edwards, whose most famous sermon was "Sinners in the Hands of an Angry God." This cultural background is one reason many of us choose to become pagans.

Sometimes we take up Buddhist meditation. Buddhism seems so appealing in so many of its teachings that we forget about the Buddhist hells, which are full of demons. Look at Tibetan Buddhist art. If we know what we're looking at, it's scary.

Reader, I don't know anyone who knows *for sure* what the other world is like. I'd rather go to Summerland when I'm finished with this life.

Ten Occasions for Celebration

❋

Numerous events that are of interest to pagans occurred on this day.
Pick one. Celebrate it or contemplate its meaning.

1. In 778, the Frankish hero Roland, nephew of Charlemagne, died in
   battle against the Saracens at Roncesvalles, Spain. His story is told
   in the *Chanson de Roland*, which dates from the eleventh century and
   is probably the most famous medieval *chanson de geste*.

2. In 1517, seven Portuguese vessels commanded by Fernao Pires de
   Andrade met with Chinese officals at the Pearl River estuary. This
   was the first meeting of Europeans and Chinese and the beginning
   of Western exposure to Far Eastern culture.

3. In 1620, the Mayflower departed from Southampton, England.

4. In 1824, Charles Godfrey Leland, author of *Aradia or The Gospel of
   the Witches*, was born.

5. In 1872, Sri Aurobindo was born. An Indian nationalist, he meditated on the *Bhagavad Gita* while he was in jail and developed the
   idea of passive resistance (usually attributed to Gandhi). Aurobindo's
   philosophy is that human beings are not currently at the top of the
   evolutionary ladder.

6. In 1888, Thomas Edward Lawrence (Lawrence of Arabia) was
   born. Read his biography, *The Seven Pillars of Wisdom*.

7. In 1939, *The Wizard of Oz* was released. This movie has its own
   mythology.

8. In 1950, Pope Pius XII declared the bodily assumption of the
   Virgin Mary into heaven. She slept through it, which is why the
   Greek Orthodox Church calls the holiday the *Dormition of the
   Theotokos*.

9. In 1969, the Woodstock Music and Art Festival opened. Some
   people who were there may actually remember it.

10. In Latvia, today is the festival of Marae Mara goddess of the land.
    "God made the table," it is said, but "Mara makes the bread."

The Ring of the Nibelungen

❧

A century before today's Asatru and heathens began to study the mythology of northern Europe, anyone interested in the gods and heroes of Valhalla had to go to the opera.

Richard Wagner (pronounced *VAHG-ner*, 1813–1883) based his operas on Germanic mythology and folklore. Because he had the emotional stability of a six-year-old, was a ferocious anti-Semite, and seduced the wife of another man and had four children with her before they married, his personal reputation was terrible. He was also admired by Adolf Hitler, who sought justification of Aryan supremacy in Germanic mythology. For these reasons, American music critic Deems Taylor called him "Wagner the monster." At the same time, Taylor admitted, the music Wagner wrote is sublime.

Reader, this is a good day to find CDs of Wagner's *Ring Cycle*. The *Ring Cycle* is the short name for four connected operas with a total playing time of about fifteen hours. The story revolves around the ring forged by the Nibelung dwarf Alberich from gold he stole from the Rhine Maidens. Alberich sets the plot in motion by placing a curse on love; doomed love is the theme that drives all that follows. The first opera, *Das Rheingold*, is based on the Norse *Eddas*. The second opera, in which we hear the famous "Ride of the Valkyries," is *Die Valküre*; its source is the *Volsunga Saga*, and its story is the disobedience and punishment of Brunhilde. The third opera, *Siegfried*, comes from the same source, though Wagner changed the hero's name. The fourth opera, *Die Götterdämmerung*, is based on the twelfth-century High German epic, the *Nibelungenlied*, and dramatizes the end of the world.

The first complete performance of *Ring Cycle* took place from August 13 to 17, 1876, at the Bayreuth Festspielhaus, the theater Wagner designed and built in Bavaria.

Odin's Ordeal (Nine Days and Nights)

❋

Odin is not the only shaman to climb the world tree to gain knowledge. The *axis mundi*, the tree growing out of our roots and rising into the heavens, is a common symbol around the world.

Reader, when you were young did you climb trees? In your imagination, go back to your childhood and find your favorite climbing tree. Like another famous shaman, Jack, whose *axis mundi* was a bean stalk, start climbing your tree. You're going to climb for nine days and nights—three for your youth, three for your maturity, three for old age.

As you climb, notice that when you began you were a child and that as you move up the tree you age. You pass through not only the nine worlds but also the stages of your life. Look around at the other branches. There you are in elementary school, in high school, in college. You can see yourself meeting your partner and falling in love. At your first and succeeding jobs, perhaps in the military. Traveling wherever your life takes you. Can you reach out and adjust any of these scenes to make changes in your life? Give it a try.

As "wounded healers," shamans are ritually wounded (and become "differently abled"). Some die and are reborn. You are making your journey, however, without injury. As you climb, think about Odin. How did Odin get those runes? Did someone (a goddess?) ride up and deliver them? Did a hand reach down and give them to him? Did he just invent them himself?

You are near the top of your tree. No giants here, though maybe you'll hear singing. A hand reaches out from a cloud and hands you one rune. What is the symbol that has lured you to climb the world tree for nine days and nights?

A Walk on a Sunny Day

❋

Yesterday we took an imaginary vertical journey. Today, let's travel horizontally in the real world. It's time to take a late-summer walk.

Reader, do you walk in the sun? If you do, I hope you use sunblock. Let's remember that too much of a good thing ceases to be good. When Phaeton, the son of Helios and Clymene, decided to go joy-riding in his father's sun-chariot, he couldn't control the sun horses, which scorched the earth and turned northern Africa into desert. Zeus had to kill the boy to stop fire from spreading across the world. (The tears of Phaeton's sisters turned into amber.) When golden Hathor turned into Sekhmet the lioness, her anger likewise burned the earth.

Don't walk when the summer sun is high. One of the sun's least welcome gifts is melanoma. Instead, go out close to dawn or dusk and follow your customary route through your neighborhood.

It's half-past August. Can you discern any changes in the light? How is sunlight today different than it was February or May? One of the gifts of light is shadow. As you walk, look at the shadows around you. What do they reveal? Look at the shadow you cast yourself. Do you cast a long shadow, either literally or metaphorically?

Look at the trees and plants along your route. What are deciduous trees doing in late summer? Are the fruit trees rich with summer decorations? How about the flowers? Which have wilted and died back and which are sun worshipers? As I walk, I see a number of plants I thought were strong, but now they're dry and gray, and their flowers are long gone. Is there a lesson for us humans in the fact that some of Gaia's green children thrive better in full sun whereas others prefer the shade?

Vinalia Rustica

❋

In Rome, the year's first wine festival was held in April. Eight days before the new moon, the wine from the previous year was opened, offerings were made to Jupiter and Venus, and the wine was tasted.

The second wine festival, the Vinalia Rustica, was held in August in the countryside. (We get our word "rustic" from *rustica*.) Rituals were performed to protect the growing grapes, and auguries were sought for the coming vintage. Offerings to Venus included myrtle and mint. On this day, she was seen not as the goddess of love, but as the earlier goddess of kitchen gardens and other enclosed gardens. Strawberries and herbs were sacred to her. Gardeners and farmers were permitted to rest on this festival day.

The god honored today was Jupiter, not Bacchus, the wild god of intoxication and fertility who is said to have brought viniculture to many lands. Bacchus had festivals of his own: the Liberalia in March, when a (presumably sculpted) phallus was carried around the fields on a cart; the Ambaravalia in late May, when Ceres and Bacchus were invoked to promote growth; the Lesser Quinquatrus in July, when hymns were sung to Bacchus, Apollo, and Aesculapius; and the Meditrinalia of mid-October, when toasts were drunk to Bacchus and Jupiter.

Jupiter wasn't always the king of the gods. Before he was conflated with Zeus, he was Tinia, an Etruscan thunder god. Wherever Tinia's thunderbolts struck the earth, it was declared sacred ground. The Roman Jupiter (sometimes spelled Juppiter) was thus originally a weather god who was propitiated to keep the growing season friendly. It was later that he became, as Virgil calls him, "the omnipotent king of Olympus." He was also the father god to whom gods, goddesses, and humans appealed for help in difficult situations. His response usually took the form of a miracle.

Consualia

※

Rome held three festivals to honor Consus, the god of the grain storage bin. Because nearly all grain was imported from Egypt, the never-ending possibility of famine and the need for safe storage of grain made the worship of Consus vital.

The altar to Consus and the storage bin said to lie under the southeastern turn of the Circus Maximus were first dug up by the chief priest and the Vestal Virgins early in July The altar and storage bin were opened again late in August, when Consus was honored with burnt offerings from the first harvest, and farmers hung garlands around the necks of their farm animals. At the third Consualia, December 15, there were chariot races.

We tend to forget how important secure food storage is. Before there was the refrigerator-freezer with its handy faucets in the door, there were chest freezers in which it was possible to store enough food to last all year. Refrigerators and freezers used to need regular defrosting. You'd spend all day with pans of hot water and your portable hair dryer blowing hot air at the ice. Before that, we had iceboxes, to which the ice man would deliver blocks of ice every morning. Before that, there were cold rooms and cellars, and before that vegetables and fruits were canned or pickled and meats were salted and dried. Before that . . . well, we just ate as much as we could as fast as we could and hoped the hunters would get lucky again real soon.

Reader, open your refrigerator and marvel at the steady temperature. Open your cabinets and look at your staples. If you live in an older house, you may still have a cellar or a large pantry where you line up cans and jars. Whoever said preservatives were such a bad thing?

Sun Enters Virgo

❋

The sixt was August, being rich arrayd
In garment all of gold downe to the ground . . .
[He leads] the righteous virgin which of old
Liv'd here on earth, and plenty made abound . . .
—Edmund Spenser, *The Faerie Queene*

As Spenser reveals in the final two lines of the stanza above, that righteous virgin, who is holding stalks of wheat, is Astraea. But, he continues, "after wrong was lov'd and justice solde, / She left th' unrighteous world and was to heaven extold." During the Golden Age, the deities lived among us. As the ages declined, however, and mankind became increasingly violent, the deities departed. Astraea, a goddess of justice and daughter of Themis and Zeus, was the last to leave. She is now the constellation Virgo.

Spenser (1552–1599), an older contemporary of Shakespeare, is considered the greatest Elizabethan poet. *The Fairie Queene* (1590) is dedicated to Elizabeth I. Book VII, Canto VII, presents a masque (think of the Rose Parade on stage in Radio City Music Hall with singing, dancing, and acting) before the "great goddesse, Great Dame Nature, great grandmother of creatures bred."

First to appear is Mutabilitie, who reigns in all things and to whom all things are subject. As the four elements enter, we learn that Vesta and Vulcan rule fire, Ops rules earth, Juno rules "ayre," and Neptune rules the seas. Next are the seasons—"lusty Spring," "jolly Summer," Autumne "in his plentious store," and "Winter cloathed all in frize." Then come the "Monthes," Day and Night, the "Howers," and, finally, Mercury, Venus, Phoebus, Mars, Sir Saturne, and Dan Jove. Thus we see an Elizabethan version of pagan mythology.

We all know Virgos. They're the folks who pay attention to the details.

Fire Magic

It's a common conceit to say that fire is alive. It eats. It dances and leaps, gives light and warmth, is fecund and reproduces itself. The alchemists saw fire as a symbol of transformation and regeneration. We see fire's relations in lightning, gold, spirit, and passion.

Here's a bit of exceedingly modest fire magic. First close the blinds, lower the shades, and draw the curtains to keep the blast-furnace August sun out. We're visiting a smaller fire today.

Next, lay a square of aluminum foil over a cookie sheet or some other fireproof surface and lay it on a trivet on your portable altar or coffee table. Do not use a candleholder for this working. Get out a candle, preferably a beeswax taper, of any color. Unless you want to sit all day with this candle, use your chef's knife to cut off a three-inch piece.

Sitting comfortably before your makeshift altar, empty your mind of intention and monkey chatter. Light the three-inch candle, drip some wax on the aluminum foil, and set the candle in it.

Watch the candle burn. Just watch it. Don't do anything else. Simply observe the flame. If there's any kind of breeze, the flame will dance. Why is the little bit of flame around the wick blue? Don't try to answer. Just watch the flame. Watch the wax drip down the sides of the candle and puddle around it. Do not read anything into the formations of the wax puddle.

Be present with fire. As the candle burns down completely, watch the dying flame dance as it seizes the last little bit of wick, the last little bit of wax. When the flame expires, reflect on what's been happening here. How has this working been magical for you?

Vertumnalia, Nemesis, the Moirai

Like most Roman gods, Vertumnus was originally Etruscan. A shape-changer whose name comes from *vertere*, "to change," he's in charge of the transformation of flowers to fruits and the harvesting of every delicious, nourishing thing—the grains, the fruits, the vegetables and herbs. We can give thanks today for the bounty of our harvest.

Today is also the feast day of Nemesis, daughter of Erebus and Nyx. Also called Adrasteia ("the Inevitable One") and originally from Asia Minor, she's the defender of divine law and the voice of divine anger against those who break it. If you've had too much good luck, they say, look out. Maybe you should sacrifice something to Nemesis . . . just in case. She also defends the relics and memory of the dead from insult.

Also honored today are the three Moirai. Like the Norns and the Lamia, the Moirai represent youth, maturity, and old age. They may be the fairies who come and speak charms over our cradles. They may also be the hags who judge us as we weave the threads of our lives. No one can overrule the Moirai, and we never know for sure when they are present.

Reader, it's time for another feast. Make it a barbeque. Go to your local farmers' market and buy every vegetable and fruit that appeals to you. Invite your friends. As you eat, talk about how much easier it is these days, when we don't have to harvest the wheat and slaughter the animals ourselves. At the end of your meal, rise and give thanks four times. First to Vertumnus, who transformed plantings into harvest. Second to a god or goddess of fire for cooking your dinner. Third, to Nemesis, may she preserve your good fortune. Fourth to the Moirai for bringing friends into your life.

Fire + Earth = Volcano

✤

Although Pele is the most famous fire/volcano goddess, we also know of Italy's Aetna, Japan's Fuji, Mexico's Iztaccihuatl, and half a dozen others. The best known volcano god is Vulcan, who gave his name to the fiery mountain.

Vulcan, Robert Graves tells us, was originally a fire god from Crete, a volcanic island. Early on, he was conflated with Hephaestus, the metal-worker and blacksmith originally from Asia Minor. Maybe the people thought the dance of flames and lava in a volcanic eruption looked like the blacksmith's forge. There's a definite resemblance to a modern steel mill, though I'm not aware of any altars to Vulcan at Bethlehem Steel. (Maybe if they'd invoked him, they'd still be in business.)

On August 24, 79 C.E., Mt. Vesuvius erupted and buried Pompeii and Herculaneum. Pompeii was a large commercial town, Herculaneum a smaller town where wealthy Romans built their vacation villas. One rich Roman was Julius Caesar's father-in-law, Lucius Calpurnius Piso, whose wealth has been compared to that of Bill Gates. In the 1970s millionaire J. Paul Getty built a reproduction of Piso's villa in Malibu, California, to house his collections of art and antiquities.

We know a great deal about the eruption of Vesuvius because Pliny the Younger, an eyewitness, described it in letters to Tacitus. Earthquakes preceded the eruption, and both Pliny the Elder (who died in Pompeii) and his nephew observed the cloud of ash above the mountain. Pliny the Younger says the explosive column looked like a pine tree that "went high and expanded in different branches." Red-hot stones and pumice fell on the land and on ships in the Bay of Naples. There were earthquakes and a tsunami, and black clouds filled the sky. Dio Cassius reports that ash from the eruption crossed the Mediterranean and caused widespread pestilence.

Dirty Dancing

You think watching this movie isn't a spiritual experience? Just ask the members of the Patrick Swayze Fan Club. Ask the thousands of women who regularly visit *Dirty Dancing* Web sites. Some of them say they've seen the movie a hundred times; like *Rocky Horror* fans, they can recite the liturgy . . . uh . . . the lines along with the characters. When you watch Johnny Castle and Baby Houseman's midnight dance in Johnny's "great room," then, omigod, you'll have a Majorly Spiritual Experience. (Some women say it's orgasmic. The first time my friend Sandra, whose birthday is today, saw the movie, she gasped, "That's *foreplay*.")

Hey, we're pagans. When the Goddess says, "All acts of love and pleasure are My rituals," we believe her. If we're pantheists, we find god or goddess in *all things*. If we're panentheists, we believe that *all is god or goddess*. "All" can include movies, right? If we're chiliasts—I've just learned this Gnostic term, which means we come into a new spiritual reality full of light (and what is a movie if not light?) after the end of the world—then maybe we can find a new spiritual reality at Kellerman's resort.

We worship the ground we walk on. In the classical Greek theater, where drama was invented, the dance floor (the *orchestra*, where the chorus danced) was holy ground. Maybe we should worship the ground we (dirty) dance on. Maybe we should worship the dancer and the dance, which are identical, and dance with the Lord of the Dance, who in the movie happens to be a kind-hearted young man from the wrong side of the tracks.

Dirty Dancing was released on August 25, 1987. Some people like movies with messages. Other people like film noir. Just let me take dancing lessons from Johnny Castle.

Ilmatar

Ilmatar ("Mother of the Waters"), sometimes also called Luonnotar
("Nature's Daughter"), is the Finno-Ugric creation goddess and daughter of
Ilma, the god of air. For seven centuries she floated on the sea until she
was impregnated by the East Wind and gave birth to the first human, the
Finnish bard, Vainamoinen. Alternatively, a duck or an eagle laid eggs on
her knee, which the bird mistook for an island. The eggs rolled into an
abyss and became the earth, the heavens, the sun, the moon, and the stars.

Although most of the languages of Europe derive from Indo-European
roots, the Baltic languages (Finnish, Saami, Estonian, Livonian, and
Karelian) have a different linguistic base, Finno-Ugric. Not only did the
Baltic lands not become part of the Roman Empire, but they also didn't
speak a language related to Latin. There was, however, considerable trade
with Rome along the amber routes, which reached as far as Delphi. Amber
was sacred to Apollo. When the sun faded in winter, he was said to be visiting the Hyperboreans, who lived beyond the north wind, Boreas. Amber
was also sacred to the sun goddess and, out of respect to her, maidens carrying amber were given safe passage across Europe.

The people who lived north of the north wind were considered to be
magical by southern peoples. Some Arctic peoples are pagan to this day,
and many tribes close to the Arctic Circle have leaders who are shamans.

As nearly every modern pagan knows, Santa Claus is a shaman. He
travels between the worlds in a magical sleigh drawn by magical reindeer
(pregnant females—the males don't have antlers in the winter). When he
goes up and down our chimneys, he's traveling up and down the world
tree. He knows all things and brings us gifts appropriate to our behavior.

Mother Teresa

I was at a local Goddess gathering in 1997 when Mother Teresa died, and someone sidled up to me and whispered in my ear, "Teresa was one of the Fatima children, you know. The Vatican done her in so she wouldn't reveal the third secret. It's the date of the end of the world!"

Another conspiracy theory. Ya gotta love it.

Mother Teresa was born Agnes Gonxha Bojaxhiu in Skopje, Macedonia, on August 27, 1910. Her family was Albanian. At age eighteen she joined the Sisters of Loreto, an Irish community in India. Teaching in a high school in Calcutta, she looked out the window one day and saw, as if for the first time, that people were suffering from poverty and hunger. She left the convent and gathered volunteers to serve the poorest of the poor. In 1950, she received permission from the Holy See to form her own order, the Missionaries of Charity. This order now works throughout the world to help people no one else will help.

Our Lady of Fatima appeared six times to three shepherd children in Fatima, Portugal, between May 13 and October 13, 1917. She proclaimed that God had chosen Russia (whose revolution occurred in 1917) as the instrument of chastisement for the world. It is said that one of the shepherd children became a nun and delivered other teachings from Mary to the Vatican, where they are still kept.

Why am I writing about a Catholic nun in a book for pagans? Because of the work she did. She cared about people and took care of them. She didn't merely pray for the poor; she got out on the streets and worked on their behalf. People of any religion can do better than sitting around and discussing theology and thealogy all the time. Reader, what can *you* do?

Nephthys

❊

Nephthys (or Nebhet, "Lady of the House") is the sister of Isis. After Isis married Osiris, Nephthys married Set, but he was sterile. Nephthys wanted a baby, so she got Osiris drunk and conceived Anubis by him. When Set tried to murder Anubis, Isis adopted him. When Set murdered Osiris, Nephthys left him and set out with Isis to collect his parts and restore some parts of him to life. Henceforward, though she also attended births, Nephthys was a guardian and mourner of the dead. A papyrus survives with the text of her lamentations for Osiris.

One scholar says that Nephthys, whom Plutarch called Aphrodite and Nike, did not have her own cult or temples in Egypt until the Ptolemaic period (after 300 B.C.E.) and that her name may actually be a title that was given to the eldest woman of any household.

Pagans deal pretty well with death. Maybe this is because we aren't stuck in the "God took him" or "God sent him to hell" paradigms. Like everyone else, though, we're not so good with dying and grieving. Possibly because of our "higher understanding" of death, we tend to go all philosophical. Or maybe we don't grieve well because our culture expects us to get over it and not embarrass anybody. When someone close to us dies, our philosophies go right out the window. Mourning is hard work. We hold enormous emotions that we need to process, for, like caregivers, we feel burdened, guilty, alone, relieved, angry, sad, cheated . . . just name an emotion. We also need to establish a whole new set of habit patterns.

Perhaps the pagan community needs to establish a Nephthys group. We have excellent books on death and dying, but an organized group of caring grandmothers would also give us the personal support we need.

Emperor Augustus Caesar

❋

Caius Julius Caesar Octavianus (63 B.C.E.– 14 C.E.), called Octavian,
was the adopted son of Julius Caesar. Although his ancestors were of
plebian stock, he was living in Caesar's palace at the time of Caesar's assassination. In the chaos that followed, Octavian and Mark Antony set themselves up with another general as the Second Triumvirate, then embarked
on a bloody civil war that ended when Octavian defeated Antony and
Cleopatra at Actium in 31 B.C.E. A year later, he assumed the title *Augustus*
and became the first Roman emperor.

After twenty years of civil war, the Italian peninsula was in ruins. Farms
were neglected, property values declined, trade and investment fell off,
taxes were killing everybody, and Rome was an enormous slum surrounding the villas of a few rich senators. Exhausted and dispirited, the Romans
decided they'd rather have security than freedom. They gave Augustus all
the power he wanted. He was devious, patient, and puritanical.

Augustus Caesar ruled from 30 B.C.E. to 14 C.E. He sponsored literature
we still read and began the rebuilding program that replaced the city's
shabby, red-brick tenements with the great marble edifices whose ruins we
admire. But absolute power corrupted the empire absolutely, and barbarians, greedy for the good life, invaded the world's greatest city. Rome
became dissolute and weak and the empire finally lurched out of business
in 476, when Romulus Augustus was deposed by Odoacer, a German.

The Western Roman Empire lasted only five hundred years, though
the Byzantine Empire (which called itself Roman) went on until 1453.
Islam and the major European powers built empires in what we now call
the Third World. All those empires, and the Soviet Empire, too, are gone
now. I've heard pundits on TV talk about "the American empire." Perhaps
they should read more history.

Thoth

Thoth, "lord of the holy words," is the ibis-headed god's Greco-Roman name. In Egypt, he was called Tehuti or Djehuti. The patron of science and literature, wisdom and inventions, he is said to have invented arithmetic, astronomy, geometry, hieroglyphics, magic, medicine, music, soothsaying, surgery, surveying, wind and string instruments, and writing. His principal spouse is Seshat, "lady of the house of books," who may also have invented writing.

When Thoth arrived in Greece—or, more likely, when Greek scholars settled in Alexandria, site of the great library and museum—the Greeks identified him with Hermes. Because he invented nearly all elements of learning and wisdom, this amalgam of the two gods became Thrice-Great Hermes, or Hermes Trismegistus. By the Middle Ages, he was being called the father of alchemy and was given authorship of the Emerald Tablet, where we learn that "that which is above is like that which is below."

The blending of Egyptian and Greek mythology produces a number of interesting stories that "explain" things. Another reason Thoth was identified with Hermes was because the crane, cousin to the ibis, was sacred to Hermes, and the patterns of cranes' feet as they danced created the original sacred alphabet. The Greeks also said that when Typhon, the biggest monster ever born, came to avenge the killing of the Titans by the Olympians, the latter fled to Egypt, where they lived disguised as animals—Zeus as a ram; Apollo, a crow; Dionysus, a goat; Hera, a white cow; Artemis, a cat; Aphrodite, a fish; Ares, a boar; and Hermes, an ibis. Robert Graves says this is "why the Egyptians worshipped animals."[19] This exodus, he adds, may reflect the historical flight of Greek priests and priestesses after the volcanic eruption of Thera, which engulfed much of the Mediterranean around 2000 B.C.E.

Alan Jay Lerner

❃

We don't normally expect to see magic, mythology, and metaphysics in Broadway musicals, but that's what Alan Jay Lerner (1918–1986) gave us with *Brigadoon, Camelot,* and *On a Clear Day You Can See Forever.* Lerner, who also wrote the book and lyrics for *My Fair Lady*, worked during what is called the Golden Age of Musical Theater.

Brigadoon (1947) is the story of a Scottish town that, to save it from outsiders, is magically put to sleep in the 1700s by its preacher. It wakes up every hundred years to live for a single day. When it wakes up in the 1940s, two American hunters wander inside the magic circle around it and one of them—Gene Kelly in the 1954 movie—falls in love. Back in New York, he is disheartened by the rat race and returns to Scotland. His love and faith are so great that he wakes up the town off schedule, marries the girl, and (presumably) enters into Brigadoon's shadow life between centuries.

In *Camelot* (1960), the Arthurian mythos is set to music, and the presidency of John F. Kennedy gets its own myth. (Lerner and Kennedy were classmates at Harvard.) We may have more scholarly studies of Arthur's court by John and Caitlin Matthews, and Marion Zimmer Bradley has given us a look at the court through the eyes of the women, but we can't sing along with the books.

On a Clear Day You Can See Forever (1965) deals with reincarnation. Daisy Gamble (played by Barbra Steisand in the 1970 movie) is a chain-smoker who seeks psychotherapy to get rid of her addiction. One day, she suddenly flips into past lives, and her therapist (Yves Montand in the movie) falls in love with one of her earlier selves. They don't get together in this life, but we're given clues that they will meet in a future life.

Haligmonath

The Venerable Bede (673–735), a Christian scholar and historian of Anglo-Saxon England who lived two hundred years before *Beowulf* was written, describes the heathen beliefs and customs of his time. Because his interest is in converting the pagans, however, he says that Haligmonath is called "holy month" because that's when "the heathens pay tribute to their devil." The real reason the month is holy probably lies in the harvest and the thanksgiving feasts celebrated in honor of the gods and goddesses of the earth. Harvest Home was celebrated in September.

The Angles, Saxons, and Jutes came from northern Germany and the Baltic lands. The most famous leaders of the Jutes were Hengist and Horsa, whose names roughly translate as "horse" and "mare." These Germanic tribes were settling in England about the time King Arthur (or the tribal chief who was amalgamated into the medieval legends of Arthur) might have lived. This was the fifth and sixth centuries, about the same time as the Merovingians (of *Holy Blood, Holy Grail* fame) were ruling the Franks, and St. Brigid was founding her abbey in Cill Dara.

The Anglo-Saxon calendar is based on an agricultural year. Our information comes not only from Bede but also from Tacitus and from Norse and Germanic literature and customs. The month names are:

Æfterra or Geola = January	Æfterra or Litha = July
Solmonath = February	Weodmonath = August
Hrethmonath = March	Haligmonath = September
Eostremonath = April	Winterfylleth = October
Thrimilci = May	Blotmonath = November
Ærra or Litha = June	Ærra or Geola = December

There are numerous modern groups who follow the paths of the old Norse and Germanic pantheons. The Troth of Berkeley, California, publishes an "Old Heathen's Almanac" with much useful information.

The Lord of the Rings

Not all of our myths and legends come from historical sources. Sometimes pop culture rises to the status of mythology. Examples are the Oz books by L. Frank Baum and J. R. R. Tolkien's *Lord of the Rings* (LOTR) oeuvre.

Tolkien (1892–1973) was a lexicographer, expert in Anglo-Saxon and Old Norse, professor at Oxford University, and friend of C. S. Lewis, another creator of myth (the Narnia stories). When the first LOTR movie, produced and directed by Peter Jackson, was released in 2001, I sat down and reread the whole book, which is properly not a trilogy but a long book published in three parts. I also reread the Harvard Lampoon's *Bored of the Rings*, which is sophomoric and hilarious with all its double-entendre names.

Curiously, at least to me, while there are kings and elves and hobbits and dwarves and wizards and ents (my favorites), and I think I saw an obscure mention of a witch, I don't remember hearing anyone in LOTR mention or pray to gods or goddesses. Is Middle Earth a wholly secular mythos? Or is the idea of deity so basic that it goes without mentioning? Is Tom Bombadil a nature god? Is Gandalf resurrected or reincarnated? Does Aragorn remind anyone else of Theseus or Aeneas? Are the elves really deities in disguise? Would Tolkien, an Oxford Christian, have sympathized with pagan beliefs? Although Frodo is not a god or even a godlet, I remember the "FRODO LIVES" bumperstickers on the bumpers of Beetles throughout the sixties.

I have pagan friends who own *everything* LOTR and teach seminars on aspects of the mythos. Reader, what do you think? Have elements of LOTR become part of our pagan religion? How is our philosophy/theology/thealogy changed by modern myths and legends?

Akwambo Festival

This path-clearing festival is celebrated in Ghana in late August or early September. According to Ghanaian Web sites, festivals maintain the link between the living and the dead and focus on purification, thanksgiving, dedication, and reunion. To celebrate Akwambo, paths to streams, rivers, shrines, and other places important to the community are swept clean. When people assemble at the shrine the next day, the chief pours libations to the ancestral spirits to give thanks for their protection during the last year and to ask for good harvest during the next year. The people then dance and hold vigils at the shrines. If you go to Ghana as a tourist, you can witness tribal rituals, many of which were suppressed in colonial times but have been restored.

Ghana, which used to be called the Gold Coast, was a major slave depot, starting with the Portuguese, who built the infamous Elmina Castle in 1482. Other European powers soon invaded western Africa and came away with fortunes in gold, ivory, and kidnapped people. Ghana became a British colony in 1874, gained independence in 1957, and became a republic in 1960. It is the home of Kente cloth and Pan-Africanist W. E. B. Du Bois.

Reader, I think it's disrespectful when New Agers and neopagans read about a ritual that sounds interesting and just pick it up and do it however they want to. Doing this takes a ritual—and a belief system—entirely out of its proper context. But we're all guilty, aren't we?

The idea of path-clearing and giving thanks to our ancestors is a good one, but let's not engage in cultural piracy. We can do our own kind of path-clearing. When you walk, carry a trash bag and pick up some trash. At home, neaten up your sidewalk or front yard.

Changing Woman

When an Apache girl comes of age, she "becomes" Changing Woman. The women of the tribe prepare the girl for her ceremony, her father showers her with corn and candy so that she will never be hungry, and she dances under a teepee frame so she will always have a home.

According to Apache myth, Changing Woman (*Asdzáá nádleeché*) is a personification of the earth itself. Her parents are First Man and First Woman, who may be the sky and the earth. Each dawn, First Man repeatedly holds up his medicine bag toward a certain mountaintop, and from this gesture Changing Woman is born. She grows from infancy to puberty in four days. Now comes the first puberty ceremony, in which she is dressed in white shell, turquoise, abalone, and jet and blessed with pollen. She is instructed to run toward the dawn for four days, and the jewels on her dress jingle as she runs. When she isn't running, she is kept busy planning the future of the earth. It is from this story that the elements of the modern ceremony are derived.

Reader, again, let us not engage in cultural piracy by trying to replicate this ceremony. It's like holding a sweat lodge for wealthy, middle-aged white people. That's just not right. Let us respect these First Peoples' ceremonies.

But we can—and must—honor our girls as they experience their first blood. Menstruation used to be called "the Curse." Let's make it a blessing. Plan a ritual for your daughter or granddaughter. Give her a party! Instead of blowing out candles, let each person present light a candle and pronounce a blessing. Give her red gifts to symbolize blood. Eat red food (bake a scarlet chocolate cake). Tell stories about how adolescence used to be. Talk about how things have improved.

Louis XIV of France

Le Roi soleil (1638–1715) reigned for seventy-two years, the longest reign in European history. Like Charles I of England, Louis XIV seriously believed in the divine right of kings. He could quote from scripture to prove that his power as king derived directly from God and that he was responsible only to God. Whereas Charles had the Puritan army to contend with, however, Louis was unchallenged. As the "new Apollo," he was the patron of the arts and dispensed his royal bounty to dramatists, painters, musicians, sculptors, and scientists. His grand palace at Versailles was filled with images and symbols of Apollo, the plays and operas of his era were based on classical themes, and his courtiers were required to attend the daily rising and setting (*levée* and *couchée*) of the "royal sun."

I once met a woman who had visited Versailles and seen the multitude of paintings of Apollo and the other Olympians. She concluded that Louis was a closet pagan. Even though I explained that he was the king of a Catholic country, had cardinals as advisors, and went to Mass regularly, I could not disabuse her of her opinion. If someone says he's Apollo, she insisted, and if he's surrounded by paintings of gods and goddesses . . . well, then, he's just got to be "one of us."

I got tired of arguing with her. But, Reader, that makes me wonder about identifying people in history as closeted pagans. If we say that Joan of Arc was really the Maiden of a secret French coven, upon what evidence do we base this claim? When Margaret Murray and other "authorities" write that the kings of England were pagans, some were sacrificial kings, and the Order of the Garter is a pagan lodge, I enjoy the stories, but I'm still skeptical.

Mutable Earth

Because Virgo is an earth sign, let's talk about earth this month. We worship the ground we walk on. We ground, or earth, ourselves after rituals. Our religion is called a nature, or earth, religion.

Reader, let's think about what's really under our feet. I remember a wonderful article by Richard Ely, "The Nine Layers of Gaia," in *PanGaia*, in which he suggested that we investigate the deep geology of our neighborhood. It's important, he said, to find out precisely what's down there so we know what ground we're grounding ourselves in.

Let's make a simple hands-on survey for ourselves. Dig up a handful of dirt from your yard. Hold this dirt, this bit of Mother Earth, in your hands. Notice, first, that it's not the same as potting soil. Feel its texture. Is it solid? Sandy? Poke around in it. Are there little bits of compost in it? Tiny rocks? Insects or worms? (If there are, let them go.) What color is your earth? In the southeastern United States, the soil is red. In other areas, it's loamy and black, and in some places it is, alas, worn out and pale.

I remember a ritual on the beach. We were sitting around the fire pit and doing our invocations, and when we came to north, the priestess picked up a handful of very dirty sand and said, "Here is mutable earth." She let it trickle out through her fingers. We like to think of the earth as unchanging, but that's not true. Geological changes come slowly, but change does happen.

Put your handful of earth in a bowl and set it on your altar. Let this real earth represent elemental earth. Does having real earth from right where you live trigger any changes in your ritual or magic? What makes earth mutable?

The Theosophical Society

The Theosophical Society was founded in New York in 1875 by Madame Helena Petrovna Blavatsky and Colonel Henry Steele Olcott. Madame Blavatsky (known to her admirers as HPB) was born in Russia in 1831 and married at sixteen. She promptly left her husband and, after a varied career as a circus horseback rider and factory manager, discovered the occult. First, she worked as an assistant to Daniel Douglas Home, a Scot who was the nineteenth century's greatest medium, then she became a world traveler and may even have reached Tibet. She became famous for her outrageous habits, which included swearing and smoking marijuana.

Blavatsky is the author of *Isis Unveiled* and *The Secret Doctrine*, complex and voluminous works that reveal the ancient mysteries to the modern world. The "perennial wisdom" that the Theosophical Society brought to the West includes the practices of meditation and yoga, the notions of reincarnation and karma, and vegetarianism. The Theosophical Society is headquartered in Wheaton, Illinois, and publishes *Quest Magazine*.

Madame Blavatsky's greatest legacy is the Mahatmas ("great souls"), or Masters, whom she claimed were the Society's inner guides. She channeled correspondence from invisible Tibetans named Morya and Koot Hoomi and other members of the Great White Lodge that rules the planet. Following Blavatsky, famous occultists including Charles W. Leadbeater, Annie Besant, Alice Bailey, and Elizabeth Clare Prophet corresponded with these Masters. At the same time, Rudolf Steiner's Anthroposophical Society, the Hermetic Society of the Golden Dawn, various Masonic and Rosicrucian groups, and Aleister Crowley's Ordo Templi Orientis (OTO) also claimed to have secret founders and inner chiefs. More recently, we have met invisible adepts like Seth and Lazaris. Reader, are the invisibles really smarter than the rest of us?

Xena, Warrior Princess

Riding out of a quasi-Greco-Roman-barbarian land of long, long ago (well, 1995 in TV time) comes Xena, warrior princess. The rest, as they say, is history. And romance. Played by actor Lucy Lawless, Xena captured the hearts and souls of millions of fans.

As those fans know, Xena's first appearance was in episode 9 of the first season of *Hercules: The Legendary Journeys.* After Hercules kills the family of King Eurystheus in a fit of madness, the Delphic Oracle gives him twelve famous labors, success at which will expiate his great sin. The fantasy TV series seems to have been very loosely inspired by the Labors of Hercules. Actually, it ventures far beyond them.

In episode 9, "The Warrior Princess," Xena schemes to seduce Hercules's best friend, Iolaus, and kill Hercules himself. The scheme doesn't work, of course, and Xena rides off . . . —into her own series, at the beginning of which she decides to give up her life as a warrior. She buries her sword and other warrior equipment. But within minutes she learns that the girls of her village are being attacked by an outlaw band. She defeats the men single-handed, and zounds! She's back in business.

The Xena stories, which are great fun, follow the common theme of good against evil. The writers use plots and concepts from mythology, and the names of some characters also come from recognizable myth and legend. In the first season, for example, Pandora's box—with a timelock—appears, along with Pandora's granddaughter. In another episode, the Titans appear, though they're not quite the Titans that Thomas Bulfinch, Edith Hamilton, or Robert Graves might recognize.

People have always told stories. We've always loved our brave and beautiful warriors. Setting the technology aside, how are TV's Xena and Hercules different from the earliest mythological heros?

Atar

In ancient Persia, the ninth day of the ninth month was sacred to Atar or Adhur, a fire god. Persia was one of the greatest empires of the ancient world. The Persians started out as Aryan nomads from the Central Asian steppes and arrived in Asia Minor about 1000 B.C.E., when they inherited the land and the language from the Medes, an older Aryan tribe. The Persian Empire, founded by Cyrus the Great (559–530 B.C.E.), stretched at its height from the Mediterranean Sea to the Oxus River in Central Asia and Indus River in modern Pakistan. Persian armies conquered Babylonia and Assyria, and it was Cyrus who let the Jews go home from their Babylonian Captivity. Cyrus and his successors also invaded Greece. The marathons we run today commemorate the famous battle at which the Greeks defeated the larger Persian army in 490 B.C.E.

Some time before the time of Cyrus, a priest (*zaotar*) whom the Greeks called Zoroaster reformed the traditional tribal religion. Like Judaism and Christianity, Zoroastrianism calls itself monotheistic while it preaches dualism—the great god of good and light, Ahura Mazda, is forever doing battle against the equally powerful god of evil and darkness, Ahriman. Some scholars believe that Zoroaster invented the devil as a political tool to hold down the masses and that the devil was imported by the Judeo-Christian mythmakers for the same purpose.

The Persian cult of fire is said to be as old as the oldest Aryan nomadic religions. Atar personifies fire, of which there are five types: *Atah Bahram*, the temple and hearth fire; *Vohufryana*, the fiery human life-principle; *Urazista*, the fiery life-principle of plants; and *Vazista*, lightning; *Spanishta*, the pure fire that burns in paradise with royal glory.

The Zoroastrians called their homeland *Airyama-vaejo*. Roman historian Strabo called the land Ariana. Today it's Iran.

...SEPTEMBER 10...

T'Wan Yuan Chieh

Buddhism, Taoism, and Confucianism have long coexisted in China. Lao-Tsu and Confucius both lived in the sixth century B.C.E.; Taoism and Confucianism arose to prominence during the "age of a hundred philosophers" (550–250 B.C.E.), which was about the same time as the Age of Pericles and the rise of the Roman Republic. Although Buddhism arrived in China in the second century, Confucianism became the state religion under Emperor Wu Ti (156–87 B.C.E.) and was China's official religion until the Maoist Revolution of 1949, which turned Chairman Mao into a sort of god. None of these religions call themselves pagan.

Chinese mythology is rooted in fragmentary oral traditions written down by Confucian philosophers. There is no single source, no Chinese Homer or Virgil. Like Egypt, China has numerous creation myths. In one, insects on the body of the giant, Pan Gu, turn into people. In other myths, ancestral goddesses give birth to dynasties, or Woman Gua, the creator goddess, kneads yellow clay to create humankind. Like some western mythologies, Chinese myth tells of a golden age, world catastrophes (including a flood), and savior gods and superheroes. One scholar says that the Chinese pantheon looks suspiciously like the Confucian bureaucracy with its hierarchies and departments.

The lunar goddess, Chang-O, who is always shown as a beautiful young woman, is the wife of the Excellent Archer, who shot nine suns with his bow and arrows. The T'Wan Yuan Chieh festival honoring Chang-O takes place at the full moon nearest the fall equinox. It is a festival for women and children only—men are not permitted to attend. Sacrifices are offered to the moon. The offerings are fruit, cakes, sprigs of red amaranth, and paper hares to honor the hare that lives in the moon and makes the drug of immortality.

Terrorism

As nearly everybody in the world must know, on September 11, 2001, a gang of Islamic fundamentalist terrorists hijacked two jet airliners and crashed them into the World Trade Center in New York City. At the same time, another hijacked plane crashed into the Pentagon in Washington, D.C. The passengers on a fourth hijacked plane fought back, and that plane (possibly headed for the U.S. Capitol) crashed in Pennsylvania. More than three thousand people were killed that day.

Lest we forget—two days later, the Reverend Jerry Falwell appeared on *The 700 Club*, which is broadcast on national television and hosted by the Reverend Pat Robertson. Falwell said:

> I really believe that the pagans, and the abortionists, and the feminists, and the gays and lesbians who are actively trying to make that an alternative lifestyle, the ACLU, People for the American Way—all of them who have tried to secularize America—I point the finger in their face and say, "You helped this happen."

Robertson concurred, saying, "The problem is we have adopted their agenda at the highest levels of our government."

The attack on September 11 led to a war of reprisal in Afghanistan and war in Iraq.

I have a T-shirt with a drawing of the fierce Hindu goddess Durga riding on her tiger and carrying both weapons and flowers in her twelve arms. Above the goddess, it says, "What Would Durga Do?" Below her it says, "She brings liberty and justice to all." It's obvious that there are widely divergent definitions of liberty and justice in the world today. Everybody thinks they've got the truth.

Reader, *what would Durga do today?*

Margaret Hamilton

Margaret Hamilton (1902–1985), a former kindergarten teacher, is best remembered as the green-skinned Wicked Witch of the West in the 1939 film *The Wizard of Oz*. Her performance ranks fourth on the American Film Institute's list of the Greatest Screen Heroes and Villains.

We're always meeting people who announce, "Oh, I'm a *white* witch," implying that *the other kind* are "black" witches. In the series of Oz books by L. Frank Baum and in the famous movie, there are wicked witches and good witches. Life is less simplistically dualistic in Gregory Maguire's 1996 novel *Wicked*, which is the basis of a Broadway musical. Here, the wizard is no bluff and hearty fellow. A failure in our world, he somehow arrives in Oz via balloon; overthrows Ozma, the hereditary ruler; and sets up a police state. The "wicked witch" is Elphaba, whose father and sister are bigots. Elphaba, mysteriously born with emerald green skin, sharp teeth, and an allergy to water, attends the University of Shiz, where she meets Galinda, a socialite. Her experiences at the university lead her to "wicked" acts of civil disobedience. "Wicked" depends on context.

Reader, if all you know about Oz is from the movie, it's time to read Baum's original books and Maguire's novel. You'll get a whole new picture of a complex, varied mythological land full of fantastical creatures and adventures.

Today is not only Margaret Hamilton's birthday. It's also the birthday of Bilbo and Frodo Baggins. Baum, Maguire, and J. R. R. Tolkien created full, realistic other worlds that could very well be aspects of our world.

In *Wicked*, Elphaba is born with green skin. In Isabel Allende's *House of the Spirits*, the character Rosa is born with green hair. Are these new outcroppings of *veriditas*?

Silent Spring

Rachel Carson's *Silent Spring* was published on September 14, 1962.
That means September 13 was the last day we could claim to be unaware
of what "mankind" is doing to our planet.

Carson was born in 1907 and attended Pennsylvania College for
Women, where she majored in English and zoology. Her work at the
Woods Hole Oceanographic Institute and the Bureau of Fisheries led her
to see the harm pesticides do, especially DDT, which was extremely
popular at the time. From 1941 until her death in 1964, she wrote about
nature and the sea.

Since the Renaissance and, especially, the Industrial Revolution, science has been our secular religion and scientists have been our gods on
earth. For two hundred years, we have believed that if there's anything
wrong in the world, science and technology can make it all better. This is
partly true. Science has cured smallpox and polio and improved our lives
in innumerable ways. But it's not quite the panacea we imagine. There are
always unintended consequences. While pesticides, for example, kill insects that eat our crops and invade our homes, they also poison our land
and water. We also know that when birds and animals higher on the food
chain eat poisoned insects, the pesticides kill them, too. As *Silent Spring*
says, "As crude a weapon as the cave man's club, the chemical barrage has
been hurled against the fabric of life."

The publication of *Silent Spring* inspired enormous controversy. The
chemical industry accused Carson of being (among other things) a hysteri-
cal woman. Other industries denied they were doing anything that could
possibly be harmful. Even today, her work remains controversial. As the
Ecology Hall of Fame writes, however, "Thanks to [Rachel Carson], the
destruction of nature can no longer be called progress."

Reforming the Calendar

When Julius Caesar decided to reform the Roman lunar calendar, the year was ninety days out of joint. To correct the seasons, he made the calendar solar and fixed the mean length of the year at 365 ¼ days. To shove the spring equinox back where it belonged, he and his advisor, Sosigenes, inserted two months between November and December, which made the year 46 B.C.E. 445 days long. People called it the Year of Confusion.

The reformed year began on January 1, the Kalends of January, and months alternated between thirty and thirty-one days. The names of half the months got changed, but after Julius named a month after himself, Augustus demanded a month, too, which also had to be thirty-one days long. Somehow they forgot to rename September through December, whose names still mean "seventh" through "tenth."

In 525, Dionysius Exiguus proposed the *anno Domini* ("year of our Lord," or A.D.) system in which years were henceforward numbered from the birth of Christ, which Johannes Kepler tried to correct to 4 B.C.E. Our modern system of C.E. ("common era") and B.C.E. ("before the common era") aims at being less parochial.

Julius's calendar was not, alas, quite perfect. The equinoxes still kept slipping backward. The problem was that if the equinox was wrong, so was the date of Easter, the most important holy day in the ecclesiastical calendar. Several popes tried to reform the calendar, and finally a papal commission got the job done. In 1582, Pope Gregory XIII officially re-formed the Julian calendar. But reform came hard. While Catholic countries changed immediately, the Protestant countries suspected a papist plot. England didn't yield until 1752. In Great Britain and the American colonies, Wednesday, September 2, was followed by Thursday, September 14. There were riots in the streets. Did people really lose twelve days out of their lives?

Feast of Ma'at

We know Ma'at by the feather on her head. This is the ostrich plume she lays in one pan of the scale of justice when we come before her. She lays our heart in the other pan. If in our life we endeavored to live in accordance with Ma'at's principles of justice, truth, and law, then our heart is light and the scale of justice will balance. Osiris will say to us, "Depart in victory. Go and mingle with the spirits of the gods and the dead."

If the scale doesn't balance, and our heart is weighed down by injustices, lies, and law-breaking, then we're in big trouble. The monster Ahemait will devour our heart. It's a good thing reincarnation gives us more lives in which to learn the lessons of divine order.

Ma'at didn't have temples of her own, and rituals to her seem to have been modest. Let's invent our own Ma'at ritual. Get out all your tarot decks and pick out all the Justice cards. Sit comfortably on the floor and, if you have enough Justice cards, lay them in a circle around you. You can also lay four cards around you in the four directions or put one before and one behind you. Take a few deep, easy breaths and enter a meditative state.

We're approaching the fall equinox, a harvest festival. How has your life been since the summer solstice? Ponder truth and untruth in your life. What have you done that you're proud of? Is there anything you'd rather hide? Remember, it's not possible to hide from Ma'at. But we can nearly always correct our mistakes. What change will you make? Do a tarot reading with Justice as the central card. Your question is this: *What do I need to set right?*

After your ritual, put your words into action. Set things right. Make amends. Forgive where you need to forgive.

Rosh Hashanah

Rosh Hashanah, the Jewish spiritual New Year, begins at nightfall on the twenty-ninth day of Elul. Part of a period called *Yamim Noraim* ("Days of Awe") Rosh Hashanah occurs 162 days after the first day of Passover, which puts it in September or October in the Gregorian calendar.

The Jewish lunar year has twelve months of 29 ½ or 30 days. To keep the holidays in their proper seasons, so the spring festivals don't wander back into harvest season, a "leap month" called Adar II is added seven times in a nineteen-year cycle.

Traditionally, a month begins when the new moon is sighted by two witnesses. People gather in the open air where the moon is visible, greet each other, and dance. This blessing of the new moon is Rosh Hodesh. I have attended beautiful Rosh Hodesh services led by women who called themselves "Jewitches."

There is also a service to bless the sun and thank it for being set into motion on the fourth day of creation. This celebration occurs once every twenty-eight years. (The next one will be in 2009.)

Elements of Judaism resonate in pagan hearts. We have all, for example, been persecuted (though let us *not* play games of "my persecution was worse than your persecution") and in one voice we cry out, "Never again." Celebration and observance of the moon is another common theme, and many Jews say that in blessing the moon they are also invoking Shekinah. But while women are highly respected at home in Orthodox Judaism, they have to sit behind a wall in the synagogue. And what kind of god is it that is shamed by the sight of a woman's hair? The issues are complex, and a number of rabbis, both male and female, are working to bring greater equality into their religion today.

Bewitched

The ABC series *Bewitched* ran from 1964 to 1972. Starring Elizabeth Montgomery as Samantha, a modern witch who makes magic by wiggling her nose, it's alive and well in reruns and has been revived in a 2005 movie starring Nicole Kidman as the world's stupidest "witch." Mattel has a Samantha doll.

The TV show was based on a 1942 movie, *I Married a Witch*, starring Veronica Lake and Fredric March. When a seventeenth-century ancestor of Wallace Wooley (March) burned Jennifer, the witch (Lake), she cursed his family: the sons would always marry the wrong woman. In 1942, she reincarnates and falls in love with Wallace. Plot complications follow.

Hollywood likes witch movies wherein gorgeous witches are forced by love to forswear their magical powers. In *Bell, Book and Candle* (1958), Kim Novak falls for James Stewart and can't cry until she forsakes witchcraft. The really cool witch in this movie is Jack Lemmon, who does tricks with streetlights.

In *Practical Magic* (1998), another seventeenth-century witch curses another family, this time her own, the result being that beloved husbands die unnaturally. Starring Sandra Bullock and Nicole Kidman as witches looking for love and Stockard Channing and Dianne Wiest as their aunts, this movie's happy ending shows the formerly scornful townspeople accepting the witches, who fly off the roof of the ancestral mansion. *Practical Magic* is based on one episode of the novel by Alice Hoffman.

Reader, although these movies are more or less witch-friendly (unlike some disgusting horror movies), how do you feel about the way they portray us? I know many happily married Wiccan and pagan couples. I object to the idea that a witch has to give up her powers for love. How do we get Hollywood to lose the stereotypes and keep the witches?

National Public Lands Day

On National Public Lands Day (NPLD), volunteers throughout the United States clear trails, make repairs, pick up trash, and engage in a hundred more activities in public parks, forests, grasslands, reservoirs, wildlife refuges, cultural and historic sites, playgrounds, and recreational areas. The idea is to inspire us to take better care of the land we use collectively. As a program of the National Environmental Education and Training Foundation (NEETF), NPLD has been going on for twelve years.

NEETF was chartered by Congress in 1990 as a private nonprofit organization dedicated, the NPLD Web site says, to advancing environmental education in its many forms. Since its establishment, NEETF has become "a leader in the development of new policies, grant-making approaches, and direct programming to advance environmental literacy in America." Its goals are to link environmental education to "society's core goals," including health, education, "environmentally sound and profitable business," and volunteerism. NEETF also focuses on the needs of "under-resourced people in American society."

NPLD is a day I'm sure every pagan from Maine to California can get into. Not only do we worship the ground we walk—and camp and dance and play—on, but we also sometimes hold our public festivals and rituals on public lands. We always clean up after ourselves, but sometimes, alas, we also need to clean up after everyone else.

Reader, what does your ideal public land look like? Do you dream of an Arcadian wilderness? The enclosed gardens of medieval art? The gorgeous landscapes of the Hudson River School? The stark wilderness in the photographs of Ansel Adams, the deserts of Georgia O'Keeffe? It seems to me that our planet has room for every kind of landscape and that people should cherish them all.

Greater Eleusinian Mysteries

For more than two thousand years, beginning about 1500 B.C.E., the Greater Eleusinian Mysteries were held in Eleusis, a small town north of Athens. During the rule of Pisistratus, tyrant of Athens (ca. 550 B.C.E.), the mysteries became a Pan-Hellenic event, and about two hundred years later the state took control. More and more pilgrims came to Eleusis seeking initiation, the only requirements for which were that the person speak Greek and never have committed murder. The Christian Roman emperor Theodosius I closed the Eleusinian sanctuaries in 392 C.E., and the mysteries disappeared forever in 396 when Alaric, king of the Goths, arrived and, with other Christians, desecrated the site.

We know that the Greater Eleusinian Mysteries ran for nine or ten days in mid-September. Here's what may have happened. On days one and two, young men escorted the sacred objects from Eleusis to Athens. On day three, people gathered in the *agora* in Athens to declare their intention. On day four, they marched to the sea to wash themselves and their sacrificial piglets. On day five, sacrifices were offered to Demeter and Persephone. Days six and seven saw the procession to Eleusis. Carrying torches and swinging myrtle branches, the people walked along the Sacred Way behind the sacred objects. On day eight, the final phase of initiation occurred in the Telesterion, a large, windowless building. Here the initiates viewed the sacred relics and learned the inner mystery. Day nine was devoted to feasting, celebration, and honoring the dead.

This much we know. The Mysteries dramatized the story of Persephone's descent into the underworld, Demeter's anger and grief, and how the gods yielded to the grain mother and restored her daughter. We don't know what the inner mystery was. No initiate ever violated the oath to keep the mystery hidden.

Jacob Grimm

The fairy tales collected and/or written by the Grimm brothers, H. C. Andersen, Andrew Lang, and others are almost never about real fairies. Our "fairy" tales are really folktales, nursery tales, anecdotes, beast fables, wonder tales, extended jokes, parables, allegories, cautionary tales, social satires, and romances. They're called fairy tales because Charles Perrault's *Histoires ou Contes du temps passé* ("Tales from Days Gone By," 1697) and the Comtesse d'Aulnoy's *Contes Nouveaux* ("New Stories") were gathered into a multivolume anthology called *Le Cabinet des Fées* ("The Fairy Closet"), which was published between 1785 and 1789. These stories were written not for children but for bored and sophisticated courtiers. On the cover of Perrault's book was a drawing of a grandmotherly woman telling stories at the fireside; she became Mother Goose.

Children's verses (some of which predated Shakespeare), moralized stories, and various streams of make-believe literature came together during the nineteenth century and somehow fairies got the credit. Occasionally fairies do show up in the stories. There is a christening in the kingdom and the local fairies are invited. The young girl with the ugly stepsisters wants to go to the ball and her godmother, who just happens to be a fairy, says that if she's a good girl she'll arrange it.

But the context of the fairy godmothers—and of most of the stories— is not pagan. Jacob and Wilhelm Grimm collected folk and household tales because they wanted to establish a Germanic literary tradition dating back to the pagan tribes. The stories they collectedy were intended to teach children lessons of Christian virtue and growing up in Christian society.

As we mine the legends of Egypt, Greece, Rome, and Northern Europe, we can also turn to fairy tales for dramas to reenact in our rituals.

Blessed Bee, Inc.'s Magazines

SageWoman: Celebrating the Goddess in Every Woman was created in 1986 under the editorship of Carol SheBear. By issue 5, Lunaea Weatherstone became publisher and editor, and the current publisher, Anne Newkirk Niven, bought the magazine in time for issue 23. Although feature articles in *SageWoman* are written by the magazine's readers, regular columns are by professional writers. These include Diana Paxon's scholarly and entertaining "One of Ten Thousand" columns about goddesses, "Herbal Adventures" by Susun Weed, and others. *SageWoman* also serves the Goddess community with book and product reviews; "The Rattle," letters to the editor and replies from other readers; and "Weaving the Web," networking resources.

SageWoman's son was *The Green Man* (first published in 1993), which in 1997 became *PanGaia: A Pagan Journal for Thinking People*. If *SageWoman* is soft and feminine, *PanGaia* is edgier and more intellectual. Not only does this magazine talk about gods, but it also features the occasional "Toe to Toe" readers' debate on controversial topics.

In 1999, realizing that pagan families needed their own magazine, Anne began *The Blessed Bee: A Pagan Family Newsletter*. It gives advice to parents ("Creative Spellcasting for Desperate Parents"), suggests activities for the kids, including songs and lessons in the wheel of the year, and prints reviews of books for pagan children and about raising pagan children.

In 2001, Anne saw a need for a magazine with attitude, so she launched *newWitch: Not Your Mother's Broomstick*. Its target reader is the intelligent teen or post-teen witch who has questions about how to live a pagan life in a nonpagan world. I am *so* not a part of that demographic that I think the advice column is hilarious, but its readers love the magazine.

Sun in Libra

I look at the pans of Libra's scale and sigh. How nice it would be to achieve balance. Libras, Lilith the astrologer tells me, have to think *and* feel. In fact, they have to think before they know what they're feeling. That's air signs for you: always up in their heads.

The scale, which is the only inanimate object among the sun signs, is said to have originally been Scorpio's pincers. It is also said to be held in the right hand of Astraea, the Virgin.

Balance is generally a good thing. The seasons of the year achieve a natural balance; our bodies seek homeostasis. As above, so below. Reader, let's think about our lives. What do we need to balance? Our chakras. Our mind and our heart. Work and play. Cleanliness and creative messiness. What can you add to this list?

Early Libra is a good time to look at balance in our lives. Think about three elements of your life that you think are out of balance. How can you bring these into balance?

But we don't want to be too balanced. That would be *unbalanced*, right? If we were in perfect balance, we'd never move, and how boring would that be. Every time we take a step, we are temporarily off-balance.

What elements of your life are out of balance and that's exactly the way you want it? For example, when I'm leading a public ritual, I put on my public persona and entertain the folks. I'm an extrovert. But I'm home more than I'm out, and some days, I don't even get out the door. I sit right here all day, writing and editing. I'm a happy introvert, and I'm not gonna change that.

How about you? Think about three unbalanced aspects of your life that satisfy you.

Lewis and Clark
Return From Their Expedition

When President Thomas Jefferson made the Louisiana Purchase in 1804, he wanted to know what the land looked like, so he asked Congress to appropriate $2,500 "to send intelligent officers" to travel from the Mississippi River to the Pacific Ocean and back again. The mission of the Corps of Discovery was to study Indian tribes, geology, and flora and fauna.

Jefferson appointed Captain Meriwether Lewis to lead the expedition, and Lewis appointed William Clark as his partner. On May 14, 1804, thirty-three men set out from St. Charles, Missouri. They followed the Missouri River westward. During the winter of 1804–1805, the Shoshone/Hidatsa woman, Sacagawea, joined them as their chief guide. They reached the Pacific Ocean in the summer of 1805, spent the next winter in what became the Oregon Territory, and arrived home with journals and souvenirs on September 23, 1806. In the 1997 Ken Burns documentary about Lewis and Clark, historian Stephen Ambrose compares their expedition with NASA's trips to the moon. In each case, the men faced unknown dangers, and they saw things no one they knew had ever seen before.

I'm especially impressed by Sacagawea. Ginger Rogers is said to have done everything Fred Astaire did, but backwards and in high heels; Sacagawea did everything the men of the Corps of Discovery did, but with a baby on her back.

Although there have always been explorers, if anyone had asked me to lead such an expedition, the United States would still end at the Appalachian Mountains. Reader, if you were asked to go with a real or metaphysical Corps of Discovery, where would you go? Would you rather do inner or outer traveling?

The Dinner Party

In its review of Judy Chicago's *The Dinner Party*, the *New York Times* compared it to Norman Rockwell, Walt Disney, the WPA murals, and the AIDS Quilt. The project made its debut in September, 1979, in San Francisco and has been exhibited on three continents. When I first saw it, as when I first saw the AIDS Quilt, I was struck speechless. It was more beautiful and more detailed than I'd imagined. I wanted to stay all day.

The Dinner Party is a an exhibition of feminist art on an open triangular table. The three table wings are spread with place settings, each of which is an embroidered runner that celebrates traditional women's crafts. Upon the runners rest symbolic ceramic plates (lots of vulva images), chalices, flatware, and napkins. How many of us have wished we could invite a goddess or a great woman to dinner? How many of us have set the table for a more modest dinner party? How many of us have arranged every element on the table with painstaking care? *The Dinner Party* is domestic and provocative at the same time. Some people love it, others hate it.

The first wing, which begins in prehistory, is dedicated to the Primordial Goddess, the Fertile Goddess, and five more. The eighth place setting is for Hatshepsut, who "straddles the mythological and real worlds." The next wing is a sequence of place settings that chronicle early Judaism, early Greece, Rome, and medieval and Renaissance Europe. The third wing begins with Anne Hutchinson, a Puritan poet, and moves "from the American Revolution to the Women's Revolution." Embroidered at each place setting are symbols associated with the goddesses and women, and on white tiles on the floor beneath each place setting are written the names of other women, some famous, some unknown.

Yom Kippur

Yom Kippur, the last of the ten days of *Yamim Noraim*, occurs at night-fall on the ninth day of Tishri. The rites for Yom Kippur are set forth in Leviticus 16.

The *Jewish Catalog* describes a custom called *kapparot*, which "entails swinging a chicken around one's head as a . . . symbol of expiating sins. The chicken is then slaughtered and given to the poor. . . ." Most people these days, the *Catalog* adds, tie money in a handkerchief and swing that around their head, saying, "This is my change, this is my compensation, this is my redemption."[20]

No matter which or how many gods we believe in, thinking about what we've done wrong and how we can set it straight is useful. The Day of Atonement, the Talmud says, "absolves from sins against God, but not from sins against a fellow man unless the pardon of the offended person is secured." People seeking recovery in Twelve-Step programs likewise turn their lives over to the care of "God as they understand him" (step three), make a list of people they have harmed and become "willing to make amends" (step eight), and then actually make amends (step nine).

Pagans can make amends before Samhain. We want to have a clean emotional field in which to rest over the winter and plant fresh seeds in when spring comes. Let's revive that old Jewish custom. (But not swinging the chicken! That's cruelty to swinger and swingee.) Tie crystals, red corn, or other symbolic items in a clean white handkerchief and swing it around your head, reciting the blessing quoted above. Then go around and see the people you need to see. Speak heart to heart with them. Give them something blessed from your handkerchief. Get on with your lives, as friends or no longer as friends, but not as enemies.

George Gershwin and Genius

George Gershwin (1898–1937) wrote *Rhapsody in Blue* in only three weeks at the age of twenty-five. As I was listening to it last night, I began thinking about genius. Where did Gershwin get the talent to write all the different kinds of music he wrote?

Consider Gershwin. Consider Wolfgang Amadeus Mozart. Both wrote music that will knock your socks off. Both were gregarious and admired by their peers. Both died before they were forty.

Where does genius come from? Some say it has to be born in you. Twenty years ago, I worked as an editor of aerospace proposals. Sitting at the desk next to mine was John, a Religious Science minister who had studied with Earnest Holmes. John and I talked a lot and shared our love for music. One day he told me that he believed he'd been Tchaikovsky in his last life. In this life, he added, he was only a mediocre pianist and had no talent for composition. So what good did it do him *now*, I wondered, to have been Tchaikovsky *then*?

When people like Gershwin and Mozart start composing fully realized music at a young age—or when geniuses in other fields begin their life work as children and outshine their adult teachers—people sometimes use this as evidence of reincarnation. Is reincarnation a satisfactory explanation for the genesis of genius? Many people also believe that a passion we have in this life is carried over from an earlier life. Does this mean George and Wolfgang have reincarnated as musicians? If so, where might they be performing now?

Reader, what's your passion? What do you totally and besottedly love that you have little talent for? If you believe in reincarnation, what do you want to do when you come back?

Miss Piggy

The Goddess Of Everything hurled herself into the world in the first episode of *The Muppet Show*, September 27, 1976. She had a supporting role at first, as an astronaut (porkonaut?) in "Pigs in Space," but then . . . well . . . she and Kermit the Frog fell in love. She demanded more lines, and bullied the guest stars. Soon we witnessed a satined, sequined theophany. Excuse me. *Thea*phany. Starring in five seasons of *The Muppet Show* and five Muppet movies, she ascended in purple-gloved glory to the heavens of the Muppet pantheon. Who can forget the Busby Berkeleyesque underwater ballet sequence in *The Great Muppet Caper* where The Pig rises in perfect balance atop the fountain of life? It's a porcine apotheosis.

Then she ventured into epigraphy: she wrote a book. Like the oracles and sibyls of old, The Pig pronounces words of wisdom. Her *Guide to Life* tells us everything we will ever need to know about beauty, fashion, finance, manners, romance, success, and other vital topics. Do we think we're ugly? "Not everyone can be a superstar," Miss Piggy says, "but anyone can be a semistar, a starette, or a teensyweensystar."

Our goddesses attend to our emotional needs. Henson knows, life in the twenty-first century is not easy. "Misery loves timpani," The Pig writes. "If your depression is particularly acute, you may be able to deglumify things a bit with some upbeat music. But if you like classical music— as moi does—do be careful: even the most sprightly, toe-tapping symphonies have at least one grouchy movement filled with oboes, doldrums, and bassinets."[21]

There's no one like The Pig. Aggressive and winsome at the same time, she loves her Kermie. Maybe she's the reason it's not easy being green. . . .

Zisa

Zisa is one of those goddesses whose name we have but nothing else about her remains. I found her name in several sources, along with the statement that she was honored on September 28 by "festivities," but the festivities are not described, and no one says anything about her biography or attributes. She is not described by any Roman or other source, and there are no temples or other archaeological remains identified with her. Tacitus names her in his description of a Germanic tribe who worshipped a goddess he called Isis, but Zisa may or may not have been the Greco-Roman Isis. (Several Web sites say Zisa is a transliteration of Isis.) We know that the Romans thrust the names of their gods and goddesses upon the deities of the barbarians.

Jacob Grimm connected Isis and Isa (or Zisa or Cisa), who was the tutelary deity of Augsburg (originally Zizarim) in the medieval German duchy of Swabia. He found an etymological connection between Zisa and Teiwaz (Tyr, called Ziu by the southern Germans) and speculated that she might have been his consort, which makes her a goddess of Tuesday. One Web site I read says that a weathervane in the shape of Zisa "holding her sacred pinecone" was erected in 1615 above a temple that later became a church of St. Peter am Perlach and that the goddess later became identified with the Virgin Mary.

What is the lesson to be learned in all this speculation? We don't really know anything about Cernunnos, either, or about a number of other "gods" and "goddesses." Sometimes we build our myths and rituals on spiderwebs of mystery and turn old names into projection holders. Reader, let us honor the unknown gods and goddesses of the world whose believers all died long ago.

The Temple of Sekhmet

As we approach the end of our "earth month," let's visit the Temple of Goddess Spirituality, built in 1992 by Genevieve Vaughan in Indian Springs, Nevada, near the nuclear test site.

As *Atomictourist.com* informs us, the Nevada Test Site was established in 1950 as the nation's "on-continent nuclear weapons testing area." The first bomb to be tested was a one-kiloton warhead dropped from an airplane on January 27, 1951. Between 1951 and 1962, 126 atmospheric tests of atomic weapons were conducted at the test site, which features a "doom town" (where they studied the effects of atomic bombs on buildings and animals), Mercury (the main base camp), Frenchman Flat, and the Hazardous Material Spill Center.

Visitors are advised not to take soil, rocks, plants, or pieces of metal from the site. Reader, I can't help it; I'm skeptical about *atomic tourism*. Does the Department of Energy know about the half-life of radiation? During the 1950s, monster movies showed giant ants and other mutant beings that were created by atomic radiation. How do we know, only fifty years later, that the radiation's gone?

This burned and wounded land is where Sekhmet now dwells. Her temple, built of straw bales and stucco, is open to all of the elements of nature. The entrances are archways, and the open-roof dome, made of seven interlocking copper rings, is a gateway to the sun, moon, and stars. It is unbelievably beautiful. "Peace and reverence live within the temple," its Web site tells us, "along with a quiet sense of self-empowerment." The temple houses statues by Marsha Gomez and Madre del Mundo, and there is a full schedule of ceremonies to honor the goddess.

Reader, spill some holy water on the ground today. In your imagination, see this healing water flow into burned and cratered lands and heal them.

Themis

Themis, daughter of Gaia and Uranus, is a Titaness who survived in full power into the era of the Olympians. The Greeks saw her as the embodiment of absolute justice, which is perhaps the law of karma or the psychological principle of meeting the natural consequences of our actions. Themis is shown blindfolded and holding the scale of justice in one hand and a sword in the other.

Jane Ellen Harrison traces her history and position as an adviser to Zeus, whom she married before Hera arrived on Olympus. Their daughters include Dike (Justice), who carries the sword but not the scale, and/or Astraea, who holds the scale but not the sword. Dike's sisters are Eirene (Peace) and Eunomia (Order). Some sources say that Themis is also the mother of the Moerae, or Fates, who spin, weave, and cut the threads of our lives. Themis is also said to be the inspirer of the oracles at Delphi. Her daughters are thus forces of justice and natural law.

In my first book, when I made some sweeping comment about justice, the copy editor asked if justice was the same for all people. That's a good question. As I'm writing this, justice is much in the news. The people in Rwanda are still trying to come to terms with the slaughter of 1994. The trial of Serbian president Slobodan Milosevic dragged on until he died. Israel and Palestine are still bombing each other's civilians.

People who have survived terrorist attacks, tyranny, and ethnic cleansing want justice, but when does justice tip over into revenge? In Shakespeare's *Merchant of Venice,* Shylock has reason to seek revenge. He's been cheated and his daughter has run away with a Christian. Portia pleads with him for mercy. Reader, is justice the only solution? Is mercy a better answer? Should we prefer mercy or justice?

Fides

Like Pax, Concordia, and Salus, Fides is one of Rome's abstract civic goddesses. Her name translates as Faith. We hear its echoes in *fidelity* and *infidel*. *Fides* signifies not the faith between people (as in fidelity in a marriage), but faith between the deity and humankind. The procession to the Capitol was led by the three chief *flamines* (priests), who wrapped their right hands in white cloth bands to symbolize that faith must be maintained. They offered sacrifices to Faith and Honor, and people who attended the sacrifice may also have wrapped their right hands in white bands. It is said that right hand of the statue of Fides was wrapped to remind her to keep faith with her people.

Reader, what does Fides mean to modern pagans? To whom are we faithful? Most of us abandoned one faith—usually Christianity or Judaism (I've never met any pagans who were formerly Muslim, Buddhist, or Hindu) —so why do we think we're going to be faithful pagans?

In the twenty-first century, it's not practical to walk around with white cloth wrapped around your right hand, though we can do it for a ritual or meditation. After you've cast your circle, wrap white ribbon that you've never used before around your hand three times. With each turn, speak aloud your promise of fidelity. Make a promise that you can keep, even it it's no more than to hold the god or goddess in your heart.

We lead such busy lives that it's useful to have something to remind us of Fides. Select one piece from your vast jewelry collection. Let it symbolize your fidelity. Cast your circle and declare your intention to keep the faith. Wear the jewelry. Any time you're conscious that it's touching your skin, say the name of the goddess or god. Be faithful to the path you've chosen.

HaMakom

I first learned about Rabbi Malka Drucker's work when we both wrote for a Web site called *Soufulliving.com*. I "met" her via e-mail after I reviewed her book *White Fire*, which describes the work of thirty spiritual women of all faiths.

Like many people, Malka felt a need for the comfort of family to better deal with the tragedy of 9/11, so she and her partner decided to build a new community. On Sukkot (October 2, 2001), which is, Malka told me, "a holiday of hospitality and the ingathering of all nations sitting together in peace," she ingathered friends at her home in Santa Fe, New Mexico. HaMakom, which means "The Place," is a community of "lovingkindness guided by Jewish principles."

So why is HaMakom in a book for pagans? The rabbi's intention is to build a family, a Big Family in which we are brothers and sisters and cousins. The services may be Jewish, but the teachings are inclusive. Here's a quotation from Malka's *Weekly Reader*,

> The theme of our service is family. . . . Most of us live . . .
> without physical extended family, yet we carry memory
> of our families. Elie Wiesel says that memory is our
> weapon against the despair of not belonging. We invite
> you to bring any object to the service that reminds you
> of family and who you are. . . . It needn't be associated
> to your Jewish connection, but if the object links you to
> the Big Family, that's great. If you travel light . . . then
> bring a story. Or just come to listen and offer your
> presence.

We're raising pagan children. We're gathering in public rituals and festivals and craft fairs. At your next new-moon ritual, build a Big Family. Bring mementoes of and tell stores about your families.

Durga Puja

Durga, whose name means "inaccessible," is the personification of the energy (*shakti*) of Shiva, the Hero-God, the Lord of the Dance. Here is a story of Durga's birth. Disclaimer: this is an interpretation by a Witch of the West.

Once upon a time, a big, strong, mean buffalo demon named Mahishasura paid enormous devotion to Shiva and earned the favor of the hero-god. Succumbing to flattery, as hero-gods are wont to do (praise is, so to speak, their Achilles' heel), Shiva blessed the demon and decreed that neither god nor man would be able to kill it. This was just what Mahishasura wanted. He promptly embarked upon a reign of terror so vast that the gods were driven out of heaven. Shiva, who hadn't noticed the pandemonium (has anyone noticed how heroes tend to be fairly self-involved?), suddenly opened his eyes.

As Shiva stared unwittingly at the violence wrought by his alter ego, out of his third eye a new energy began to emerge. Was it a bigger, longer weapon? No. The energy took the form of a ten-armed woman, Durga, riding a ferocious lion. Leaping from the projectile thinking of the hero-god, she attacked the demon. An epic battle followed. But the demon was almost too strong for the goddess. Out of Durga's third eye streamed a new energy. Was it heroic masculine energy? No, another goddess was manifesting. This was Kali, who redoubled the attack. We are not told what the hero-god was doing at this point. It was the goddesses who defeated the demon. Soon he was down and out. Durga wanted to make sure he wouldn't rise up again, so she transformed herself into her most ferocious form, Devi Chandika, and beheaded him. Heroes and gods were then able to attend to their proper heroic dancing.

Tara

The great mother goddess does not belong only to the people of Tibet. She is beloved throughout the world, and there are many stories about her. In one, she is present at the creation of the universe and declares that she will remain in a female body until all sentient beings are enlightened. In another, she is born male, as Avalokitsvara, then reborn female. Historical tradition tells us that her first image (a sandalwood statue) arrived in Tibet when the Nepalese princess Tr'itsun came to marry King Songtsen Gampo in the seventh century C.E. Her name can mean "Lady Star" or "Lady who Accepts the Ceremonial Scarf." It is said that her name can be discerned in the names of goddesses in cultures all around the world. Some believe that the Tibetan Tara is connected with the Hill of Tara in Ireland.

Prema Dasara and Anahata Iradah travel the world teaching the Tara Dance. As soon as I found out they were coming to the Goddess Temple of Orange County, I sent them an e-mail: could I bring some of my Tara figures to set on the altar? Prema said yes. It's a small world. It turns out that Dagmola Jamyang Sakya, who gave me the Green Tara initiations, is a friend of theirs. Traditionally, Tibetan women have stayed at home, and the nuns keep house for the more famous monks. Prema and Anahata have broken through the chauvinism and taught the women to dance in praise of Tara.

On Tara's birthday, October 4, I went to the temple with fifty other women. As Anahata played a twelve-string guitar, Prema told us stories of Tara and taught us the dance. Raise your eyes to the heavens, she said. See the luminous and beautiful goddess above us. Raise your arms to her and twirl. *Om Tare Tutare Ture Soha*!

Opening of the Mundus

❋

A strange rite occurred in Rome on three days of the year. On August 24, October 5, and November 8, the *mundus* ("pit") was opened. There were actually two *mundi*, one dug by Romulus, by the other, the Pit of Ceres. When the Romans opened the Pit of Ceres, they were opening the gate to the underworld so the *manes*, spirits of the dead, could visit the city. The day the pit was opened was a holy day, probably related to the harvest season, during which business transactions, battles, and marriage were forbidden. Crops from the last harvest were stored in pits, and seed for next season was preserved in underground bins. In 1914, a vaulted pit, which may be the *mundus Cereis*, was discovered on the Palatine Hill.

Reader, reinvent the opening of the *mundus* where you live. First, find out who has lived in your neighborhood through the years. Search newspaper and magazine archives to find records of the original peoples and of immigrants. Walk through your neighborhood and see if you can find where the local *mundus* might be. In the roots of a mighty tree? In the shed behind an elderly house? In the churchyard? Use your intuition or make it up.

If you can do so without being rousted by kids or cops, sit near where your neighborhood *mundus* might be. In your imagination, open the door to the underworld. Invite the people who lived on the land your neighborhood occupies to return. Who were these people? How did they live? Where did they come from? Observe them. Engage them in conversation. How do they deal with "progress"? Let them speak to a local landlord or politician. Let them visit the mall. Let them watch teenagers in action and listen to our music. When they tire, bless them and let them go home.

Transformation of the Bennu Bird

❁

Once every five hundred years, the mysterious and sacred Bennu Bird constructed a nest of myrrh, upon which it sat and promptly died. Three days later, its decaying flesh produced a worm that sprouted feathers. This new creature flew to the temple of Ra in Heliopolis, where it deposited its parent's bones and then flew away, some said, to Arabia. The Bennu Bird was associated with the flooding of the Nile and the re-creation of the fertility of the land. Its cry was said to mark the end of the innundation.

We can see drawings of the Bennu Bird, a heron wearing the crown of Osiris (the solar disk between two plumes) on its head, in Egyptian tombs. In the *Book of the Dead* are formulas to transform the soul of the dead person into the Bennu Bird.

The Bennu Bird has been a popular symbol of rebirth and immortality, not only in Egyptian myth but also among medieval alchemists, who called the bird a phoenix, which perished in its own flames, which nourished its single egg, from which hatched the new phoenix. This transformation was a form of the much sought-after alchemical transmutation. An Islamic Web site relates the Bennu Bird to the Egyptian date palm (and "everything sweet") and cites the Greek botanist Theophrastus as saying that both ripe dates and the royal purple of the murex shellfish were called "phoenix."

In Greece, the bird looked more like an eagle and was also called the phoenix. Its five-hundred-year cycle and Arabian genesis come from Herodatus; its nest of myrrh comes from Pliny. Other mystery birds that share elements of the phoenix legends and symbolism are the Arabian *roc*, the Persian *simurgh*, and the Turkish *kerkés*. In China, the phoenix was the emperor of birds. We're also familiar with Professor Dumbledore's royal phoenix at Hogwarts School.

...OCTOBER 7...
Elijah Muhammad

The Nation of Islam (NOI) is a spiritual and political movement founded by Wallace Fard Muhammad (1877–1934) and built by his early disciple, Elijah Muhammad (Elijah Poole, 1897–1975). Fard Muhammad taught that only black people in America have no knowledge of their past, no control over their present, and no guidance for their future. Elijah taught that Fard Muhammad was God on earth.

In the late 1940s, the teachings of the NOI came to Malcolm Little, who was in prison at the time. Little changed his name to Malcolm X. (The X is the mathematical sign for the unknown variable that shows the rejection of "slave names.") In the 1950s, the NOI attracted actor/singer/violinist Louis Walcott. He changed his surname to Farrakhan and is currently head of the NOI.

Repudiating "white man's religions," the NOI believes the teachings of Islam are friendlier to people of color. But just as worldwide Islam split into factions, so did the Black Muslim movement. After Elijah Muhammad's death in 1975, his son, W. D. Muhammad, worked to bring the NOI closer to Sunni Islam. When Malcolm X made his *hajj*, or pilgrimage, to Mecca in 1964, he recognized the fellowship of Muslims of all colors and converted to orthodox Islam. Although W. D. Muhammad and Malcolm X (who renamed himself El-Hajj Malik El-Shabazz) promoted a message of reconciliation and possible integration, Farrakhan restored the earlier black-separatist teachings in 1981.

Islam and the NOI agree that there is one god and that there will be a resurrection of the dead. Both fast during Ramadan. Worldwide Islam disagrees with the NOI's teachings that God manifested as a human being, that blacks are the supreme race, and that Elijah Muhammad and Farrakhan are authentic prophets.

Theseia

The Theseus celebrated in Athens on the eighth day of the Greek month Pyanepsion was not Shakespeare's judicious duke of Athens in *A Midsummer Night's Dream*, but an action hero who, like his cousin Hercules, specialized in slaying monsters. The secret son of King Aegeus, Theseus traveled from Troezen to Athens, killing Procrustes (of the famous bed) and other outlaws along the way. His appearance in Athens alarmed his father and stepmother, Medea. Thinking to get him out of the way and hoping he'd be eaten by the Minotaur, Aegeus sent him to Crete, but Theseus seduced Ariadne, killed the sacred bull, and followed Ariadne's thread out of the maze. (If it had been a real labyrinth, he wouldn't have needed the thread, would he?) He sailed back to Athens with Ariadne and her sister, Phaedra.

Athens celebrated his return for centuries. Because the starving hostages had boiled and eaten all the beans on the ship, the Athenians ate boiled beans. There was a procession led by young men carrying olive branches wreathed in white wool and hung with fruits, followed by fourteen mothers who represented the fourteen hostages. Because it was harvest time, the Theseia merged with the Feast of Grapes, and honor was also paid to Dionysus and Athena, who had guided Theseus to victory in Crete. If Theseus really lived, it may have been about 1400 B.C.E. He helped make Athena the city's tutelary goddess.

The Athenians ignored their hero's less noble exploits. He participated in the murder of centaurs. He deserted Ariadne, attacked the Amazons and raped Antiope, and abducted Helen of Troy. He indirectly caused the death of his son, Hippolytus.

Reader, if we're going to honor heroes, they should be wise and merciful. Let us honor Theseus as the king who gave sanctuary to blind Oedipus and his daughters.

Germanic Winter's Day

In medieval Europe, the year was generally divided into just two major seasons, summer and winter, and Winter's Day fell in October. It makes sense to me that the cross-quarter days are the true beginnings of the seasons—spring begins with Imbolc, summer with Beltane, fall with Lammas, and winter with Samhain—and that the solstices and equinoxes are the hinges of the seasons when we can feel the energetic tides turning toward light or darkness. In October the energetic tides of the dark night of the year are getting noticeably stronger. Pagans know that, like Ebenezer Scrooge, we're going to be meeting the dead and learning lessons from them.

Reader, even if you're not doing any harvesting, you can tell that winter's approaching. Today is a good day to think about what you might do with your winter. I used to crochet afghans during the winter, I wrote at least one of my previous books during a winter season, and when I teach, I start my classes in the late fall. What winter projects do you have lined up? What can you teach? What can you learn? What can you build or organize? What does your community need?

Rome honored Felicitas, the goddess of good fortune, on October 9. What good fortune have you recently had? What has happened in your life that is *felicitous*? Make a point to honor Felicitas by celebrating every little good thing you can think of—you found a parking place precisely where you needed it, something you've been yearning to buy was suddenly put on sale, a dinner you prepared was so delicious that everyone asked for second helpings *and* helped you clean up afterwards, your project at work not only sparked your boss's acceptance, but also wasn't stolen by any of your coworkers.

Thesmophoria

The Thesmophoria, a three-day celebration of *sporetos* ("seed time"), the autumn sowing season, was a women's festival dedicated to Demeter Thesmophoros ("law giver"), she who oversees the order of the seasons. The women camped in little huts near Demeter's hillside sanctuary, the *Thesmophorion*.

On the first day, the priestesses performed the *kathodos* ("going down and coming up") ritual in which they descended into Demeter's cave carrying piglets. The pig was sacred because it loves the earth, eats grain, and (when barbecued) provides good food. The priestesses were symbolically returning food to the goddess, source of all food. They left the piglets at the underground altar, cleaned the altar and the sacred images, and brought up the remains of last year's piglets.

On the second day, in remembrance of Demeter's refusal to eat while she was in mourning for her daughter, the women fasted. When their hunger made them cranky, they engaged in *aiskhrologia*, or abusive language, which recalled the taunting back and forth of Demeter and Iambe. Because Demeter was the law giver, the city's courts were closed on this day and prisoners were pardoned. Z. Budapest writes that the women also told the men that they would nurture them only to a certain point in their lives; eventually, men had to take care of themselves.[22]

On the third day, which began with a torchlight procession at dusk of the second day, the *thesmoi*, or sacred items, and the putrefied remains of last year's piglets were displayed in buckets on the altars. After this compost was removed, it was mixed with grain to be sown in November. What had been under the earth had been brought up into the light. What was dead and buried would be revived in new life, new grain, food for the people.

Vinalia or Meditrinalia

The Vinalia, "Feast of the Grape Vines," was dedicated to Bacchus, lord of vegetation, fertility, and inebriation. This was the day the new wine was tested. The Meditrinalia was marginally more sober. Meditrina was the goddess of healing, so the Romans' excuse for partying was that they were testing the medicinal properties of the new wine. They would pour an offering of the new wine and taste it "to be healed." Toasts were made to Meditrina, Bacchus, and Jupiter. Feasting and games took place during the next several days.

Reader, I'm not good at partying. I don't like the taste of alcohol. When I go to parties, I tend to sit and people-watch. (That's because I also write novels, and novelists are spies; we observe people interacting with each other and find ideas for plots and dialogue.) I know lots of pagans who love to party, and I've had some illuminating conversations at the edges of parties.

I'm sure we've all noticed that "cakes and ale" at rituals doesn't always mean ale anymore. There's usually a choice between wine and a nonalcoholic beverage. There are, of course, several reasons for this, one being respect for people in twelve-step programs. Just as some traditions, covens, and circles have figured out that too much incense chases people with breathing problems away, they're also figuring out that we don't need strong drink. Some people quaff mightily, some know they can no longer quaff, others decline to quaff at all.

I'm cheered to see that we're more courteous around people who are uncomfortable with smoke and alcohol. This is a sign that we're outgrowing our adolescent need to prove how wild and macho we are. Perhaps we're learning respect for each other and for nonpagans who may visit our rituals.

Fortuna Redux

Fortuna Redux was the Roman goddess of successful journeys and safe returns. I'm sure she has been invoked, if only unconsciously, by every explorer who ever set foot on unknown land. Whether we're outward bound or returning home, it's good to know there's a goddess keeping an eye on us.

Augustus erected an altar to Fortuna Redux after he returned from a long journey through Asia. Her temple was erected by the emperor Domitian, who was forever doing battle to keep the empire together and himself on the throne.

If we seek good fortune in the journeys of our lives, I'm hard pressed to think of better advice than that of Satchel Paige (1906–1982), said to be the best pitcher in the Negro Baseball League:

> Avoid fried meats which angry up the blood. . . . Keep
> the juices flowing by jangling around gently as you move.
> Go very light on the vices, such as carrying on in society.
> The social ramble ain't restful. Avoid running at all times.
> Don't look back. Something might be gaining on you.

In 1948, Paige was hired by the Cleveland Indians, who won the pennant thanks to his fastball. He also played for St. Louis and Kansas City and was elected to the Baseball Hall of Fame in 1971. Crones and sages will love his comment on getting older. "Age is a question of mind over matter," he said. "If you don't mind, it doesn't matter."

Reader, are you inward bound or outward bound? Are you jangling gently as you're moving? Have you looked back lately? Is anything gaining on you? Call on Fortuna Redux!

The Camenae

The Camenae ("foretellers") were early Italian goddesses of wells and freshwater springs who were later identified with the Greek Muses. The Vestal Virgins drew water for their rites from the spring of the Camenae, who were also worshipped at springs and wells throughout the countryside of Latium and in the Porta Capena, a sacred forest just outside the city. Their festival, the Fontinalia, was celebrated by tossing wreaths of flowers into the springs, wells, and fountains.

We know the names of some of the Camenae. Antevorta, Postvorta, and Prorsa aided expectant mothers who prayed to know the outcome of their pregnancy and the fortune of the newborn child. Carmenta was a goddess of prophecy, midwifery, and magic. Egeria ("of the black poplar") was an early Italian goddess of wisdom and prophecy who may be an earlier form of Diana.

The Porta Capena is where Egeria and Numa Pompilius, the second king of Rome, met. Egeria married him, taught him wisdom and piety, and gave the city its first laws. Numa was also favored by Mars, who was originally a god not of war but agriculture. Mars caused a shield, upon which was written a prophecy concerning the fate of Rome, to fall from the sky and land on the Palatine Hill. Recognizing the importance of this sacred shield, King Numa had eleven matching shields made. These were the *ancilia*, the sacred shields of Mars, which were carried in procession each year by the Salii priests. When Numa Pompilius died in 673 B.C.E., Egeria is said to have changed him into a well in the forest of Aricia. This well was sacred to Diana in later times.

Reader, what do you want to know about your future? Toss a flower into a spring, well, or fountain and ask for a sign.

Vinternagtsblot

They say winter is nearly upon us. I have friends in northern states who e-mail cheery notes about frost and early snow while I'm sitting here trying to breathe while the hot Santa Ana winds are blowing.

In earlier times, preparation for winter started when the birds flew south. Most travel, especially long-distance sailing, stopped, and armies put away their weapons until spring. Herds were brought down from mountain pastures, and crops were harvested. People turned to indoor tasks. One thing they did was ask the blessings of the goddesses and gods for survival through the winter. The word *blot* means "blood sacrifice" and is cognate with "blood" and "blessing."

Because we pagans know that the dark side of the year is when we do our inner work, we feel uncomfortable with the coming holiday season, with its emphasis on secularized commercialism or an overly pious "churchianity" that denies pagan antecedents to celebrations of the rebirth of the light.

Reader, it's time to start thinking about your inner winter work for this year. If you have a Book of Shadows, is it up to date? Add your newest spells to it. Do you want to write a book? Buy a three-ring binder. Print out your ideas and random thoughts and put the pages in the binder. Give each page a title and a date. When the pages are an inch thick, see if you can organize them into a coherent order. That's the beginning of your rough draft. Every time you write anything you think might go into your book, put it in the binder. The essential tasks of writing are *prewriting* and *rewriting*.

Sports writer Red Smith said, "There's nothing to writing. All you do is sit down at a typewriter and open a vein." Let your writing be your "blood sacrifice" this winter.

October Horse

Because agriculture and wars were ruled by Mars and employed horses, planting and warfare began on March 14 and ended on October 15, when the Romans celebrated the last harvest. The October Horse festival was marked by a two-day horse race in the Campus Martius. The near horse of the winning chariot was sacrificed to Mars, whose sacred spear the *flamen Martialis* (head priest) used to kill it. Its head was amputated and decorated with cakes, its genitals were cut off, and its blood was given to the Vestal Virgins. Sometimes the head was taken to the home of a great landowner and nailed to the wall; sometimes rival communities fought for it and took it home as a symbol of good luck (well, not for the horse) and fertility.

Mythology is full of horses. Helios and other solar gods and goddesses drove chariots across the sky; Saule's chariot had a hundred horses. The Buddha is said to have left home riding a white horse. In the *Bhagavad Gita*, the central dialog is between the warrior Arjuna and his charioteer, Krishna. Goddesses to whom the horse is sacred include Epona, Hecate, and Macha. Odin owned an eight-legged horse called Sleipnir.

But the horse is not always a positive symbol. One of the major Trojan gods was Poseidon, to whom the horse was sacred, so when the Trojans saw the Trojan Horse, they hauled it inside the city's walls. A "dark horse" is ill favored or unknown. The Four Horsemen of the Apocalypse symbolize famine, pestilence, death, and war.

The word *nightmare* did not originally have equine connotations. It comes from an Indo-European root, *mer*, which means "to harm," something foreboding trouble. The Old English *mer* became *maere*, then *mare*, which became an incubus or succubus "riding" one while one is asleep.

Ulysses, Air

We've discussed three elements. It's time for the fourth, air, which is associated with Libra. Reader, I don't need to tell you that we need air to live. Like me, you use breathing exercises to get yourself into a meditative state. We associate elemental air with thought, intellect, and intuition. Let's think airy thoughts this month.

> How dull it is to pause, to make an end,
> To rust unburnished, not to shine in use,
> As though to breathe were life!

Tennyson's Ulysses has long passed his prime. It's been decades since he went to Troy and engineered the Horse. He came home, slew the suitors, then settled down in his rocky island kingdom. He hasn't even heard from Athena lately. He says:

> It little profits that an idle king,
> By this still hearth, among these barren crags,
> Match'd with an aged wife, I mete and dole
> Unequal laws unto a savage race.

Ulysses is bored. He's facing death, not the glorious death of war or adventure, but the humiliating decline of old age. All he can manage these days is sitting. Breathing. Dreaming.

In Shakespeare's *Troilus and Cressida*, Ulysses is in the prime of his life. He is crafty and cunning, if not particularly admirable. But Shakespeare knew what old age brings. In our last scene on the stage of life, he writes in *As You Like It*, we reach "second childishness and mere oblivion, / Sans teeth, sans eyes, sans taste, sans everything." Tennyson knew this, too.

Reader, pick out your favorite myth. Think about the hero or hera, in all his strength, in all her majesty. Project that hero or hera forward fifty or sixty years. How are they doing?

Breathe In. Breathe Out.

Astronauts and asthmatics know it for sure—if we're still breathing, we're still alive. But pagans understand that breathing is more than just being alive. It's our best tool for meditation and magic. We use our breathing to transport ourselves into an alpha state.

Some people say that breath is the foundation of life. It is *prana* (Sanskrit), *ruach* (Hebrew), *rookha* (Aramaic), *pneuma* (Greek), *spiritus* (Latin), *chi* (Chinese), and *ki* (Japanese). When we breathe in, we are inspired, and when we breathe out, we expire. The last time we expire, we pass into another world. When what we "breathe in" is more than just the air around us, we are inspired to sing or dance or write or drum or do whatever we love to do. There's something more than molecules in the air, something else that's invisible even under a microscope, and it's that something that circulates in our souls and hearts as well as our lungs. Reader, what do you call that "something more" in the air?

All too often, alas, something else in the air is dust, smoke, and unfriendly gases. What we see as clear blue sky is not the clear blue sky our ancestors knew. Our ancestors started polluting the air as soon as they started building fires, and I've heard reports that even the air in the Himalayas and in the deserts shows signs of pollution. People seem to think that polluted air is normal air. To some, it's a sign of "progress." Reader, how's the air where you live? How's your breathing?

Today is also the feast day of St. Audrey. At medieval fairs, so many "holy relics" were sold that her name gave us the word *tawdry*. We pagans love our jewelry, tchotchkes, and all our altar stuff. Are we perhaps tawdry pagans?

Pandrosus, Athens (Part 1)

Pandrosus (the "all-dewy one") was one of the three daughters of
Cecrops, first king of Athens. When Hephaestus attempted to rape
Athena, his semen fell on the ground and impregnated Gaia. Gaia bore
the baby, Erechthonius, but didn't want him, so she gave him to Athena,
who put him in a small box. She gave the box to Pandrosus and her sisters,
Aglaulus and Herse, telling them never to open it. The sisters opened it.
The sight of Erechthonius, around whom a serpent was coiled, drove
them mad, and they jumped off the Acropolis.

Pandrosus married Hermes and had a son named Ceryx. The Pandrosion,
a small temple, was built in the west court of the Erechtheion. Beside this
temple grew the sacred olive tree, also referred to as the Pandrosion.

The story of the founding of Athens is exceedingly complex. Greece
was originally populated by the Pelasgians. The first king of Attica (central
Greece) was Actaeus. Historically, Attica was populated in the second mil-
lennium B.C.E. by Hellenes, invaders from Thrace (today's Balkans) who
later called themselves Ionians. Later, Attica was invaded by the Achaeans,
Aeolians, and Dorians, all of whom conquered and intermarried with the
Pelasgians. The classical Athenians were proud of their ancient heritage
and celebrated it in myth and drama.

Cecrops became king of Athens by marrying Aglaurus, the daughter
of Actaeus. He was an autochthonous (born from the soil of Attica) figure,
half man, half snake. During his reign, the Olympians challenged each
other to be tutelary deities of the Greek cities. When Athena and Poseidon
contested for rulership of Athens, Cecrops voted for Athena. He went on
to invent writing, the building of cities, and the burial of the dead. One of
his daughters was the grandmother of Daedalus, who built the Minoan
labyrinth.

Athens (Part 2)

After the son of Cecrops died childless, Cecrops handed the kingdom over to the city's most powerful citizen, Cranaus. The region took the name Attica from Cranaus's daughter, Atthis. Another daughter married Amphictyon, a son of Deucalion (the "Greek Noah"). Amphictyon is said to have given Athens its name.

Athena raised Erechthonius in the Parthenon. He seized the kingship from Amphictyon, introduced money and the four-horse chariot into Attica, and established the Panathenaean festival. Erechtheus, grandson of Erechthonius, had nine children whose mythic connections are numerous. While Erechtheus was king of Athens, the city went to war with Eleusis. Like Agamemnon, Erechtheus sacrificed his daughter to win his war.

Several generations later, Aegeus became king of Athens. His son, Theseus, freed the city from Cretan dominion and unified the various villages of Attica under a single government in Athens.

Historically, we know of Draco (r. ca. 620 B.C.E.), whose "draconian laws" codified criminal law, and Solon (r. 594–593 B.C.E.), who is considered the father of democracy. His legal reforms concerned land ownership, trade, industry, and personal issues like the settlement of debts and weddings and funerals. Solon also divided the citizens of Athens into four classes based on wealth. The tyrant (that was his title) Pisistratus (r. 560–527 B.C.E.) built temples and minted the first coins with owls on them. During his reign, Thespis invented drama, and the first tragedies were performed during the festivals of Dionysus.

Reader, it's useful to have an overview of how history, myth, and legend wind together, so we have a context for the mythology we study and reenact in our rituals and for the lives and exploits of the gods and goddesses we are reviving in our modern religion.

Diwali

Diwali, the Indian Festival of Lights, is the beginning of the Hindu lunar calendar's new year. The word *diwali* comes from the Sanskrit *deepavali: deepa*, "light," and *avali*, a row of lamps. Throughout India, people set out masses of *diyas*, small clay oil lamps, to welcome Lakshmi, Rama, Kali, and Krishna. The lights signify the renewal of life and herald the beginning of winter and the sowing season. People also create elaborate *rangoli*, designs drawn with colored rice flour. The origin of Diwali is said to be the celebration of Lord Rama's return to his kingdom in Ayodhya after fourteen years of war and exile.

Each day has its own significance and *puja*, or worship of a specific deity. On day one, people light the lamps and set marigolds throughout their houses. Day two is devoted to the worship of Kali. On day three, new *rangol* patterns are created to honor Lakshmi. Because Diwali is the end of the Hindu fiscal year, business owners balance their books and set up new account books. On day four, everyone dresses in new clothes and visits friends and business colleagues. This day is auspicious for shopping, business, and starting new ventures.

In southern India, Diwali is connected with the legend of Bali, a benevolent demon king who grew so powerful that the gods felt threatened by him. They sent Vishnu, disguised as a dwarf, to him, and Vishnu asked for as much land as he could cover in three steps. When Bali agreed, Vishnu revealed himself in his full splendor. His first step covered heaven, his second covered the earth. Bali surrendered. Vishnu gave him a lighted lamp of knowledge and promised that one night a year people would light millions of lamps to bring peace and harmony into the world.

Orsel and St. Ursula

Orsel was possibly a Slavic moon goddess who may have been Christian-ized as St. Ursula, an apocryphal British princess who fled to Germany with eleven thousand handmaidens to avoid marriage. When they reached Cologne, they were martyred. Although fables about Ursula and her eleven thousand virgins became popular in medieval Europe, there is no evidence that the women really lived. The *Catholic Encyclopedia* names eleven virgins of Cologne, including Ursula, all of whom may be honored on October 21. Ursuline cakes are traditionally crescent shaped, like croissants.

A careful reading of Greek or Roman literature shows that the pagans of old were as puritanical as any Father of the Church or Reforming Protestant. Pythagoras advised sexual abstinence for medical reasons, and Hippocrates wrote against sexual pleasure. While the Greeks had wives to serve as pots for their seeds and produce boy children, the men, especially the Spartans, had their fun with boys; it was part of military training. When we read of Roman orgies, we are reading of exceptions that prove the rule that Roman life was stoic and stolid. St. Paul, Thomas Aquinas, and other Christian theologians followed in the ascetic footsteps of Plato, Aristotle, Plutarch, Seneca, and Pliny. Gnosticism also preached in favor of cerebral and spiritual pleasures and against marriage, meat, and wine. Condemnation of the world, the flesh, and the devil has deep roots.

Why do we read about women saints who chose to become virgin martyrs instead of being married? Maybe it has something to do with the fact that a married woman lost all of her rights and became her hus-band's property. This may be one objection today's conservatives have (but do not voice) to same-sex marriage: when two gay men or two les-bians get married, they are equal partners. Neither becomes the property of the other.

Selket

When we look at the four golden goddesses from King Tut's tomb, we recognize Selket by the scorpion on her head. "She who increases by giving breath and food" is a daughter of Ra. She's a goddess of fertility, an underworld goddess, guardian of the bound serpent Apep, sometimes the guardian of marriage. Her husband is Nekhebkau, a serpent god with human limbs; together, they sometimes bind the dead with chains, sometimes feed them. Selket leads the dead into the underworld and back again into new life. She was known to the Babylonians as Ishhara, the female scorpion and wife of the archer.

Reader, have you been initiated? Have you ever been in some way "stung" into new consciousness? Did some small thing, a word or a gesture, suddenly "sting" you into change?

Like me, you probably know people who collect initiations like they collect tchotchkes for their altars. Some traditions make a great deal of initiation. I know one that won't let people come to its rituals until they're initiated. (Upon initiation, one becomes a low priest or priestess; it takes another year and day to be elevated and actually get to come to a ritual.) The word *initiation* comes from the Latin *initium*, "beginning"; cognate words are *initial* and *initiative*. The idea of initiation goes back into antiquity, and it's possible that Wicca got the practice from Freemasonry or ceremonial magic.

When we get our initial initiation, what are we starting? How much initiative does it take to get where we're going? Yes, we have to take a specified number of classes or study for a year and a day to reach a point where we can request initiation, and, yes, we need to hold a certain body of knowledge in our minds. But after we've been through the ritual—what comes next?

Sun in Scorpio

Scorpio, the third of the water signs, is said to be the most intense. Scorpio, Lilith the astrologer tells me, "either digs deeply into feelings or uses just as much energy avoiding them . . . because once he starts digging into them, there's no stopping until we have scorched earth." Full-on Scorpios, whether they're crawling scorpions or rising eagles, can be scary folks. I bet we've all been stung or lifted into the heavens once or twice in our lives.

The year is getting darker and colder. We're looking at shadows and the secrets of life and death. On the one hand, I think we all recognize the power of emotions when they erupt in negative ways. We've seen wounded feelings and their consequences. Dealing with consequences is one way circles, covens, and traditions change and reform and re-form.

On the other hand, let's consider the power of emotions in their multitudinous manifestations—for example, the love of partners, of parents and children, of priestesses and teachers and saints. When you stand, or kneel or dance, in the presence of such emotional power, you can do effective magic.

Tonight is a good night to devise a ritual that will use beneficial emotion to help and heal. Gather your circle or coven and join hands. Talk only long enough to find a beneficial intention you all feel strongly about. Cast your circle silently from heart to heart, feeling the emotional energy pour out of your hearts and flow around your circle through the bridge of your linked hands. Create your emotional magic and use it well.

In 1570, Bishop James Ussher added up all the ages of all the Old Testament patriarchs and determined that the world was created on October 23, 4004 B.C. Creationism is an issue I think pagans should stay well away from.

The French Revolutionary Calendar

Even though the goddess Reason stood in triumph upon Mt. Parnassus, when the French Revolution began in May, 1789, Louis XVI was still on his throne and the nobles were safe on their estates. The Reign of Terror and the guillotine were yet to come, and Napoleon was only a corporal in the army. In an elegant, civilized, reasonable world, mankind was facing a glorious future. We can see Reason's face in paintings by Jacques-Louis David. In literature, art, and music, it was the beginning of the Romantic Age.

The French revolutionary calendar was meant to purge every Christian influence out of French life. Adopted on October 24, 1793, and lasting until December 31, 1805, it was designed by a mathematician. As the monarchy was abolished, the new calendar opened the Republican Era. Those Revolutionaries were proposing a brave new world.

The new calendar began with the fall equinox and had twelve months of thirty days each:

- Autumn: Vendémaire, Brumaire, Firmaire
- Winter: Nivôse, Pluviôse, Ventôse
- Spring: Germinal, Floréal, Prairial
- Summer: Messidor, Thermidor, Fructidor

The descriptive names of the months were based on Latin and Greek words. Nivôse means "snowy," Floréal means "flowery," Thermidor means "hot" (Greek: *thermos*). Unlike the ecclesiastical calendar, where every day has a saint, in the revolutionary year every day had a plant, an animal, or a tool. The left-over days needed to make the year come out even became holidays from September 17 to 23: Virtue Day, Talent Day, Labor Day, Opinion Day, Rewards Day, and—in leap years—*La Fête de la Révolution.*

Air + Water = Mist

In our hearts and imaginations, our pagan religion arises through the mists of antiquity. We're revitalizing the classical deities of the Mediterranean world, Asia Minor, and Northern Europe. We're reviving the mysteries of the Celts and a hundred more tribes. From the mists and tides of the old faiths, we're weaving a new one.

We can learn the factual history of Wicca in Ronald Hutton's *Triumph of the Moon*, Grey Cat's *Deepening Witchcraft*, and Michael York's *Pagan Theology*, and even in a book hostile to the Goddess, Philip G. Davis's *Goddess Unmasked*.

Our roots, they tell us, are in the soil of Romanticism—the poetry of Wordsworth, Coleridge, Keats, and others—and *Le Sorcière* (1862), a novel by Jules Michelet. These men wanted to create a new world. The Romantics imagined woman to be a "natural Power," a "creature of Enchantment." They saw the witch as an archetypal figure symbolizing true spiritual freedom and the rights of the working class. They were writing to elevate spirit over materialism. It was thealogy and poetry as an anodyne to theology and reason.

But we know there are Truths and there are truths. Blaise Pascal wrote, "The heart has its reasons which reason knows nothing of," but Madame Blavatsky wrote, "Thoughts are things." We use language to create reality. When we promote myth as truth, people start to think it's historical truth. It happens in every religion. Just read the holy books.

We need to know what our historical antecedents are. We also need to recognize our foundational myths *as myths*. Other religions may accept faith over historical fact, but pagans have minds and hearts wide enough to encompass both myth and history. Reader, let's blow the smog out. Let's put our religion to work in the world to bless all and harm none.

Research

Here's a glimpse of the writer's life. While I was searching in books and online for goddesses, gods, and events of interest to pagans, for October 26 I found a Zoroastrian festival celebrating a divinity of water. Hymns were recited to the water goddess, and flowers and offerings were cast into streams. It sounded like well dressing. I added it to my list.

I've just searched again. No water festival. I went to the Zoroastrian archives. No water festival. Which reminds me of the day I picked up a pagan almanac at a local book store and found the "ancient Greek salamander festival."

This is not to put down other authors. My point is that perhaps we're trying too hard to make paganism . . . what? Relevant? Universal? Give us ancienter roots than we actually have?

Here's how I think ancient festivals are invented on modern Web sites. Old books are being copied on the Web. Perhaps while scrolling through an online copy of some nineteenth-century book someone finds an obscure reference to an event the Victorian scholar mistakenly identified as an "archaic fire sacrifice" because he (it was usually he) inadequately understood the culture or the language, or the women were making up things to tell him. "Eureka!" shouts our modern pagan. "I've found another fire festival." It's posted on a list. Someone comments that salamanders are elemental fire spirits. Someone writes that the elementals were "discovered" by the ancient Greeks. Someone posts "ancient Greek fire festival honoring elemental spirits" on his Web site. Someone visits that site and sees "fire festival" and "salamander" and—adding two and two and getting five—puts them together. Someone needs a nifty festival, or maybe we just need something to do tonight . . . and so we get an ancient Greek salamander festival.

A Hallows Altar

As we enter the season when the invisible ones are more accessible than at any other time of the year, it's time to honor them and build our Hallows altar. Mine is inspired by Samhain, the Day of the Dead, and All Saints' and All Souls' Days.

My dining room table is about four feet in diameter. Because the Mexican *ofrenda* is typically multi-layered, I stack my dictionaries toward the back to make hills and valleys. Over the books I lay a white tablecloth my mother crocheted. This is the altar's base.

Now I get my box of treasures out of the closet. Commercial Halloween candles. A sugar skull from a ritual I attended a decade ago. Glow-in-the-dark plastic skeletons. I gather the mementoes of my honored dead. A photo of my grandparents when they were twenty years younger than I am now. Old photos of my parents and brother. Photos and souvenirs of friends whose deaths left holes in my universe. Paper skulls upon which I've written the names of my AIDS buddies. My first cat's collar, the ashes of two beloved cats.

All of these things and more I set on my altar. I'm creating sacred art to honor the dark goddesses and my shining beloved dead. I move a candle an inch, set a chocolate coin or paper marigold here or there, add another *memento mori*.

Reader, I hope you're inspired to construct your own altar. If you have a tablecloth or quilt that is a family heirloom, use it and protect it with plastic wrap under the candles. Find beautiful frames for your family photos. If you don't have photos, write their names on paper skulls. Light the candles and sit with your altar an hour every night until November 2. Then carefully take it down.

Isis

Isis and Osiris civilize the land. Set murders Osiris. Isis sets forth and searches the world. In Phoenicia, she finds the body of Osiris in an acacia tree. She takes it home and hides it in the swamps of the Nile, but Set finds it again. He cuts it into fourteen pieces, which he scatters around Egypt. She finds thirteen of them, builds the fourteenth out of ivory, invents embalming, and pronounces magical words. From her labors of love, Isis creates life.

Reader, how many quests can you count? Demeter searches for her daughter, Theseus and Oedipus for fathers who disowned them. Ninshubur looks for her queen. The prince seeks the girl whose foot the shoe fits. Gilgamesh searches for immortality and the meaning of life. Cúchulainn seeks fame, Odin seeks the runes, and the steadfast tin soldier seeks true love. Arthur's knights set out in search of the Holy Grail, Frodo and his companions set out to destroy the One Ring. Dorothy and her companions set out to find a brain, a heart, courage, and a way home. Gautama sets out to find enlightenment, and Grandmother Spider sets out to bring the sun to the people. The Ugly Duckling and Harry Potter are looking for people like themselves. All around the world, from time out of mind, people have been telling stories about people who are searching for *something*.

What is our quest in "real life"? Are we looking to marry a girl like Mom or a boy like Dad? The perfect career that's both emotionally satisfying and significantly remunerative? The perfect priestess or ritual? A way through the Dark Night of the Soul?

A quest can be a dangerous journey through darkness, both inner and outer. Darkness is coming. Reader, where will you be during the year's longest night?

Fireless Altars and Crone Encounters

Ten or fifteen years ago, I led a group of students through the wheel of
the year. At Imbolc, we held a divination party. At Beltane, we painted our
faces and carried wreaths of flowers through the streets to the ocean. At
Lammas, we harvested our gardens and cooked a feast.

At Samhain, we met at Alice's house. Her back yard was a miniature
jungle of oaks and olive trees with a clearing near the center. It was a
windy night, and the fire season that year was ferocious. As we were laying herbs and flowers, skulls and bones, and a cauldron for scrying on the
altar, the wind came up again. That's when I decided it would be both prudent and meaningful to have a fireless altar. No candles. No incense. We
cast our circle, invoked the dark goddesses, and a dog howled nearby. It
was a most satisfactory ritual.

Think of the dark altar as a dark mirror. As you quietly sit in the darkness, look with the eyes of your imagination and see what the dark altar
shows you. Use the night vision of your soul and look for the crone or
sage you're growing up to be.

"Mirror, mirror on the wall, who's the fairest one of all?" Regard the
fair crone, the fair sage. Not fair as in "pretty," although you may see the
fairness of a face lined with the lessons of a lifetime. Fair as in "without
bias, distinct, pleasant and courteous in speech."

Reader, what do you want to know about your life in the coming season or year? Who knows more about you than you yourself? Who can
speak more truly for you? Sit in the darkness with the crone or sage you
will become and ask your question. Listen to your answer.

Mischief

Reader, do you remember the scene in the movie *Meet Me in St. Louis* where the kids are throwing furniture on the bonfire in the street on Halloween, and Tootie (Margaret O'Brien) approaches the door of the "evil neighbor" and throws flour on him?

For reasons having much to do, I suspect, with the Puritan foundation of the United States, an enormous amount of mischief is associated with the hallowed evening we call Samhain. In Detroit, for example, it's called Devil's Night. People commit acts of vandalism and set fires. Trying to fight the "devil," city officials have recently organized an Angel's Night, wherein volunteers monitor the streets to stop the vandalism.

Possibly the most interesting bit of Halloween mischief occurred on October 30, 1938, when Orson Welles and the Mercury Theatre broadcast a realistic adaptation of H. G. Wells's novel *The War of the Worlds* on CBS radio. Wells's novel was set in England in the 1890s, but in Welles's adaptation the fictitious invasion took place in New Jersey. The drama was a simulated news broadcast that interrupted a musical show, much like our Eyewitless News interrupts with breaking news—"This just in." Welles's listeners were captured by the drama. People rushed to New Jersey, there was a public panic, and eventually the police had to be brought in. Ever since, TV networks have broadcast disclaimers, especially during movies about atomic war, plague, and the late, great Y2K bug.

I've noticed a new mischief. I collect witches. From August through October, I shop for new ones. But you know what? I'm finding fewer and fewer witches. I find vampires and movie monsters, but there's almost no witches. Children are being "kept safe" from Halloween. Retailers are being pressured not to sell witches. Preachers are still preaching that *their* devil is behind *our* holiday.

Circle Sanctuary

Circle Sanctuary, near Mt. Horeb, Wisconsin, is one of our oldest pagan resource centers. Founded in 1974 by Selena Fox, it was incorporated as a nonprofit religious organization in 1978. *Circle Network News* started as a tabloid the same year and was transformed into a glossy magazine in 1998. I occasionally write for *Circle* magazine. *The Circle Guide to Pagan Groups* has been published since 1979. After Circle won its battle for religious freedom in 1988, all two hundred acres of the sanctuary were zoned as a church.

When you visit Circle's Web site, you learn that the group's purpose is to "promote dialogue, cooperation, and mutually beneficial networking among individuals, groups, and organizations of a wide range of Pagan denominations and paths." Circle maintains its land as a nature preserve and works for songbird repopulation, wetland protection, and forest management. It sponsors religious-educational activities for adults and children. It engages in "academically sound and publishable research" and helps researchers in various academic fields get it right when they write about us. Circle engages in community services and is famous for its activist work carried out through the Lady Liberty League. Circle participates in the Nature Religions Scholars Network and has sent delegates to the Parliament of the World's Religions.

Of all that Circle does, I most admire its outreach work. If neopaganism is to be taken seriously and accepted as equal by the standard-brand religions, then our research needs to be respectable and accurate. We need to be talking to people in language they and we understand. We need to be demonstrating that we are friendly, that our intention is to cooperate for "greater planetary peace and wellness."

All Saints' Day

✳

During the persecutions of the Roman emperor Diocletian (245–313), the number of Christian martyrs became so great that separate days could not be assigned to honor them. They were given common memorial days. All Saints' Day, the *Catholic Encyclopedia* informs us, was instituted in the fourth century when dioceses began to divide up and exchange the relics of martyr-saints. At first, only martyrs and St. John the Baptist were recognized, but in 609 Pope Boniface IV consecrated the Pantheon in Rome to the Blessed Virgin and all martyr-saints. The vigil for All Saints is Hallows Eve, which was also first celebrated in the fourth century.

By the thirteenth century, All Saints' Day was solemnly celebrated to honor "all saints known and unknown" and to remedy any deficiencies by the faithful in remembering the saints on their proper days. In other words, it became a sacerdotal catch-up day. If a saint was neglected on his assigned day, he could be honored today.

Why do pagans need to know about All Saints' Day? We have records of our own martyrs, some of whom were actually witches, many of whom were women, most of whom were found to be disobedient to the Church. Today is the one day of the year, I think, when we should think about the mythical nine million and say, "Never again." More important, we can acknowledge people who have come out as witches and lost jobs or custody of their children or suffered mockery (or worse). We can send them healing energy from our circles and covens.

Pagans can celebrate All Saints' Day not by elevating anyone to sainthood but by remembering that *every single one of us is a holy being*. We're neither martyrs nor sinners, just ordinary people getting along in the world. Reader, if that's not cause for celebration, what is?

All Souls' Day

❄

To commemorate "the faithful departed," the *Catholic Encyclopedia* tells us, the priest recites the Office of the Dead and celebrates a Requiem Mass. The theological basis for All Souls' Day is the doctrine that "souls that have not been perfectly cleansed from venial sin are debarred from the Beatific Vision." With prayers, the living can help the dead pass through purgatory.

Pagans seem to think that the word soul is the private property of the standard-brand religions. For a thousand years, however, soul, which comes from the Teutonic sáwl and the Gothic saiwala, has meant "the spiritual part of man" (women were believed not to have souls), "the principle of life in man or animals." Linguists tell us that in English the most basic words are the Anglo-Saxon words; "soul" is thus an idea basic to our knowledge of ourselves.

Clarissa Pinkola Estés writes about the "unquestioned status quo, the 'behave yourself; don't make waves; don't think too hard'" value system of our modern society. The point of "running with wolves" is that women should reclaim their wild souls, their true selves, which have been polluted or stolen or subjugated.

Isn't this true for all people? We're reading all the time that our children's souls are being hijacked by video games or leached away by schools that don't teach them anything. We're seeing TV shows about women who subject themselves to "extreme makeovers" so they match some impossible (soulless?) image. We're hearing about men who sell their souls to corporations so they can build gazillion-dollar houses.

On All Souls' Day, let us talk about our souls and about soul itself. Let us examine our pagan values with renewed respect. I've heard it said that we're the wave of the future. What do you think?

Silence

November is a month of growing silence. The days are noticeably shorter and, at least where I grew up, gray, cloudy, and often rainy. It has always seemed to me that the month is closing in on itself, that people are turning inward. Even today in southern California, I feel that delicious melancholy of tiny silences, slender endings, secret closings.

In the novel *The Secret Life of Bees*, when the teenage protagonist encounters the face of the Black Virgin on a jar of honey, she thinks, "I realized it for the first time in my life: there is nothing but mystery in the world, how it hides behind the fabric of our poor, browbeat days, shining brightly, and we don't even know it."[23]

A major component of mystery is silence. True mystery is that which cannot be spoken. Mystery is the silence that whispers or shines if we have ears to hear it, but it makes no audible sound. Notice—I can't even write about mystery without using paradoxical language. We need silence, the silence that seeps into us and, yes, enlightens our darkness.

For two millennia, women in the standard-brand churches have been admonished to be silent. The silence surrounding the Black Virgins is, as they say, deafening. We know that many of the Black Virgins are remnants of pagan goddesses. What is the mystery of the official silence concerning them? Is silence perhaps not only golden but also black?

Reader, what do you see as the value of silence? Think about rituals you've been to where silence rises, sometimes spontaneously, and authentic magic happens. Think about the silence of meditation, of inner prayer. Have you ever spent a day in which you did not utter a word to another living being? Let silence be present in your life this month.

King Tut's Tomb

✻

> Creator uncreated.
> Sole one, unique one, who traverses eternity,
> Remote one, with millions under his care;
> Your splendor is like heaven's splendor.
> —Suti and Hor, *First Hymn to the Sun God*

Suti and Hor were architects to Amenhotep III (r. 1411–1375 B.C.E.), the grandfather of Tutankhamun, who became pharaoh at age nine. King Tut was entirely unimportant. Why did they bury him in such awesome splendor?

Immanuel Velikovsky (1895–1979) was a controversial Russian author whose historical and cosmological theories were scorned by the academic establishment. Influenced by Freud's Moses and Monotheism, Velikovsky asserted that the Greek Oedipus, king of Thebes, was the same person as Amenhotep IV, the pharaoh who, according to Freud and others, invented monotheism. Amenhotep changed his name to Akhnaton. Before he moved to his sun city, Akhet-Aten, he was the king of Thebes. Amenhotep III died very suddenly; Oedipus killed his father, Laius. Akhnaton's sons, Tutankhamen and Semenchkare, were killed in battle at the same time; so were Eteocles and Polynices, the sons of Oedipus. Queen Tiy, mother of Akhnaton, was Jocasta; Meritaten, Akhnaton's daughter, was Antigone. Read Velikovsky's ideas for yourself in *Oedipus and Akhnaton*.

English archaeologist and Egyptologist Howard Carter began working in Egypt at age seventeen. He worked with Flinders Petrie and in 1907 was introduced to George Herbert, the fifth Earl of Carnarvon. Carnarvon financed Carter's search for the tomb of the previously unknown minor pharaoh, Tutankhamun. Carter found the two anterooms of Tutankhamun's tomb on November 4, 1922, and opened the sealed door of the tomb itself on February 16, 1923.

Catastrophic Illness

❋

I'm a few years past menopause, so when I noticed some spotting, I was curious. I finally went in for a biopsy. On May 23, 2003, Dr. Jennifer told me that I had endometrial cancer.

Cancer. People used to be afraid to utter the word. Cancer was a disease of silence. Nice people didn't talk about cancer. In the olden days, they didn't even tell you that you had cancer. They put you in a cone of silence and watched you die.

The first thing I did was put the word out for healing energy. One friend told me about Essiac. Other women told me they were survivors (one for thirty years). Within the month, the Iseum of Isis Paedusis and the Raven's Haven ritual group put me in the middle of healing circles.

In addition to finding a good surgeon, I also put myself into the care of Dr. Mark, a naturopathic physician who gave me supplements to stimulate my immune system.

And I began doing a nightly healing visualization. Every night without fail, I would visualize rubbing "Goddess goo" all over my uterus. The Goddess goo's job was to find every little cancer cell and dry it up. The cells fell like dead, dry leaves. Not wanting to be untidy "down there," I also visualized a tiny Goddess vacuum cleaner to suck up the dead cells.

Early one morning, I had the following vision. I watched the tumor slide over a cliff and crash into rubble. The tumor left a bright red, slimy path like a snail trail, and the rubble where it crashed looked like twigs and gravel.

I had surgery a month later. I'm still getting regular blood work and CT scans because cancer is kind of like alcoholism: it never quite goes away. Nevertheless, I am healthy.

Tiamat: Chaos and Creation

Once upon a time, the primeval waters mingled together, and from these waters emerged the earliest gods. They were so noisy that old Apsu decided to destroy them. His plan was thwarted by Ea, whose consort gave birth to Marduk. Marduk's vigor disturbed Tiamat, the consort of Apsu. She became angry. Marduk raised a storm, captured her, and split open her body, from which he created the stars, the planets, and the earth.

Once upon a time, the Goddess rested alone in a place where nothing else existed. She sang and danced, she dreamed and touched herself, or the winds touched her, or a snake touched her, and after a time she gave birth to seas and lands and stars and her multitude of children.

Once upon a time, a god created the heaven and the earth. "And the earth was without form and void; and darkness was upon the face of the deep. And the Spirit of God moved upon the face of the waters. And God said, Let there be light: and there was light." This god worked for six more days. He created the firmament above the water, plus the earth, grass, herbs, fruit trees, the sun, the moon, the stars, moving creatures, and finally, Adam and Eve.

Once upon a time, a goddess had a cauldron in which bubbled everything that ever was. She stirred it, added ingredients, stirred again. All things went into that roiling, boiling cauldron, and all things came out again, newborn and transformed.

Once upon a time, Atun sat alone beside the Nile. When he realized that he needed other gods to assist him in the creation of everything, he masturbated and from his semen emerged Shu and Tefnut. Their children were Geb and Nut, whose children were Isis and Osiris.

Wonder Woman

Wonder Woman, Diana Prince—Princess Diana—is a modern American Amazon. Her stories were first written by William Moulton Marston in the December-January, 1941, issue of All Star Comics. Six months later, she had her own comic.

She was born on Paradise Island and trained in Amazonian martial arts. She wore bulletproof bracelets. Her magic lasso was forged by Hephaestus from links removed from Aphrodite's Girdle. Her mother was Queen Hippolyta, whom we remember from the story of Theseus.

The Wonder Woman Web site quotes Marston as saying in 1943, "Not even girls want to be girls so long as our feminine archetype lacks force, strength, and power. Not wanting to be girls, they don't want to be tender, submissive, peace-loving as good women are. Women's strong qualities have become despised because of their weakness. The obvious remedy is to create a feminine character with all the strength of Superman plus all the allure of a good and beautiful woman."

The New Original Wonder Woman first aired on ABC on November 7, 1975, starring Lynda Carter. Lyle Waggoner costarred as Steve Trevor, Chloris Leachman as the queen, and Debra Winger as Wonder Girl. American war hero Trevor is shot down over the Bermuda Triangle and winds up on Paradise Island, where the Amazons hold a contest to determine who will return with him to America and fight the Nazis. Princess Diana wins. She hides her red, white, and blue bustier and shorts under a Navy uniform, and the story continues. The first season, set during World War II, remained faithful to Marston's original.

Today there are other female superheroes, but Wonder Woman was the first and the best. She didn't kill the villains, and she was honorable in all of her dealings in our flawed modern world.

Election Day, Pagan Unity Campaign

✳

> ... [A] men's House of Representatives, a women's House. ...
> Instead of gingriching issues affecting primarily women and
> children, like ... abortion, welfare, [and] childhood educa-
> tion, ... men would leave them to women to decide. Men
> could then pay full attention to issues of preeminent concern
> to men, like restructuring professional baseball.
> —Sheri S. Tepper, *Gibbon's Decline and Fall*

The first Tuesday of November is election day. This is an appropriate
time to consider the Pagan Unity Campaign (PUC), which was founded
by Storm Bear Williams on the day after the election of 2000, when we
didn't know who'd won or that an unelected president would be appointed.

The PUC's mission is "to unify the many diverse branches of paganism
in America." The PUC is not, Williams says, trying to unify pagans in a
single religion or tradition. Their ten-point Pagan Bill of Rights begins,
"Pagans shall have the same freedom to worship that is granted to followers of other religions."

The PUC is best known for its postcard campaigns. First held on the
summer solstice, 2001, it's simplicity itself. PUC provides postcards and
the addresses for government officials, plus a short, inoffensive note for
pagans to write in their own handwriting. The message? "We're pagans
and we vote." The PUC even mails the post cards for us. Other campaigns
have been birthday-card drives for certain officials and protests of policies
that may be unfriendly to pagans.

On November 8, 392, the Roman emperor Theodosius banned pagan
worship and shut down the Olympic Games. This gave Christians permission to loot temples, destroy relics, attack pagan worshipers, and—within
a few years—start declaring each other heretics.

Kristallnacht

❋

The "Night of Broken Glass" was the beginning of the Nazi persecution of the Jews in Germany and Austria. On this night in 1938, Jewish homes and synagogues were vandalized and destroyed, and thirty thousand human beings were sent to Buchenwald, Dachau, and Sachsenhausen. The word Kristallnacht refers to the broken glass that carpeted city streets that night. This atrocity was carried out not only by the SS, but also by the general population, for anti-Semitism has a long history in Europe. Protests from Allied countries had no effect on Nazi policy.

It's said that the twentieth century was the bloodiest in history. Millions of people—most of them innocent civilians—were killed in World War I (the "war to end all wars"), World War II (the "good war" against the Axis powers), the Korean War, the Vietnam War, the numerous wars between Israel and Arab states, an illegal war in Iraq. People were killed at Guernica, in the Soviet gulags, during Chairman Mao's Great Leap Forward. People were killed in the Turkish genocide of the Armenians; in apartheit, which was government policy for thirty years in South Africa; by Pol Pot in his war against his own people in Cambodia; by the generals in Burma (now Myanmar); in atrocities of ethnic cleansing in Yugoslavia; throughout Africa. Add to this list suicide bombers, lynchings and burnings, gang warfare, and drunk driving and drug addiction.

Reader, every single person who murdered or was murdered was a living human being. Every single person had a life and ideas about the way the world should work. Every single person felt hunger and thirst and happiness and misery. They were all real, live people. They had mothers who cried for them.

La Liberté et La Raison

✳

The French revolutionary goddesses embodied the political ideals of the revolution—La Liberté, L'Egalité, La Raison, La République. Because these are feminine nouns in French, the revolutionaries decided they had to be portrayed as goddesses (not gods) to make them concrete to the citizens of the new republic. The revolutionaries, who were all male, put pictures of the goddesses on everything from public notices to coins to playing cards.

La Liberté became their paramount goddess. Dressed in her Phrygian cap and Roman toga and carrying the French flag or a pike, she represented the people taking their freedom back from the noble oppressors. The noble oppressors called her Marianne, implying that she was nothing but a common woman, perhaps even a prostitute. (During World War II, however, Marianne became the symbol of the Free French and the Resistance.)

On November 10, 1793, a festival was held in Notre Dame de Paris to honor La Liberté et La Raison, both of whom were represented by actresses in costume and wearing wreaths of oak leaves and red, white, and blue ribbons. A "temple of philosophy" was erected in the cathedral, and soon churches throughout France were transformed into temples of reason.

Although women participated in the storming of the Bastille, which kick-started the French Revolution, and the French adopted revolutionary goddesses, women gained no more rights in France than they had in the American Revolution. Our Declaration of Independence states that all men are created equal; in France, although women demanded the right to vote, "liberty, equality, and fraternity" were for men only until 1944. On November 3, 1793, in fact, Olympe de Gouges, author of the Declaration of the Rights of Woman, was executed for being a counterrevolutionary. Marie Antoinette, a true counterrevolutionary, had been guillotined a month earlier.

The treaty that ended World War I was signed at the eleventh hour of the eleventh day of the eleventh month of 1918. In November, 1919, President Woodrow Wilson issued his Armistice Day proclamation, which concludes:

> To us in America, the reflections of Armistice Day will be filled with solemn pride in the heroism of those who died in the country's service and with gratitude for the victory . . . because of the opportunity it has given America to show her sympathy with peace and justice in the councils of the nation.

I remember the Armistice Day assemblies we had in grade school. We gathered in the gym at eleven o'clock for two minutes of silence, after which we sang the national anthem, recited the Pledge of Allegiance, and listened to a patriotic speech. The name of the holiday was changed to Veterans Day in 1954 to acknowledge the dead of World War II and Korea. Today, the holiday honors the dead of all of America's wars.

It is worth noting that the terms of the 1918 treaty were so harsh that Germany never repaid its war debts and Germany fell into destitution. This is one reason Adolf Hitler was voted into office by the Germans.

In Norse mythology, the einheriar is the army of men who have fallen in battle. These are the fellows picked up by the Valkyries. Half of them are adopted as sons by Odin, who houses them in Valhalla. The other half live with Freya in Vingólf, a hall of goddesses. The duty of the fallen warriors is to prepare for Ragnarok, when they will fight beside the gods against the giants. While they're waiting for the war to end all wars (and the world), they spend most of their time fighting, feasting, and drinking (and, no doubt, chasing Valkyries).

The Prophet and the Little Prince

✳

The Prophet Mohammed's revelations, which were written down by his followers after his death, began in 610 C.E., when he was praying and meditating in a cave at the foot of Mt. Hira, near Mecca. He fell asleep. As he slept, the Angel Gabriel appeared with a book in his hands. When Gabriel told him to read the book, Mohammed protested that he was unable to read, whereupon the angel pressed his weight on him so heavily that Mohammed thought he might die. When the weight was lifted, he was able to read. He declared that the words of the angelic book were written on his heart.

Le Petit Prince, by Antoine de Saint-Exupéry, is supposed to be a children's story. Le renard, the fox, asks the little prince to "tame" (make friends with) him. When the fox learns that there are no hunters on the little prince's home asteroid, he cheers, but when he learns that there are no chickens either, he simply sighs and says, Rien n'est parfait. "Nothing is perfect." Later, the fox gives the little prince (and us) another life lesson when he says, On ne voit bien qu'avec le coeur. L'essentiel est invisible pour yes yeux— "It is only with our hearts that we can truly see. What is essential is invisible to the eyes."

The Koran reveals the words the Prophet saw with his heart. It often happens that we're reading and all of a sudden the words from the page seem to fly up into our hearts and minds and lodge there forever. Reader, what books have impressed their words into your heart? I know you read books for and about pagans. Do you also read good fiction? Good nonfiction? Drama? Poetry? What literature nourishes your heart?

Plebeian Games, Feronia, Pietas

❊

The plebeians (the first syllable rhymes with web; it's not "pleebian") were Roman citizens who were not patricians. Like the merchant class of the Renaissance and the wealthy Victorian middle class, the plebs bought themselves patrician entitlements. They also invented the nobilis, the man who ennobled his family by becoming consul, which gives us our word noble. The Plebeian Games, held in the Circus Maximus, probably grew out of Etruscan funerary games. Prominent in the games, or ludi, were the athletic contests we call track and field.

The games began with a solemn procession in which wagons carried images of the twelve Olympians, Saturn, Ops, and other deities and Roman heroes. Next were held religious rites, then theatrical presentations, both tragic and comic. The purpose of the whole event was to honor gods and deceased civic heroes. In the classical world, athletic skill was thought to be a gift from the gods equal to intellectual skill. Mens sana in corpore sano, as Juvenal wrote: "You should pray for a sound mind in a sound body."

Feronia, the patroness of freed slaves, is an ancient goddess associated with agriculture. She received the first fruits of the harvest and had a sacred grove and temple in Rome. As the goddess of freedom, she had a temple in Terracina, where a feast was held every November. Slaves were freed there and given their freedom caps (this is the same cap we see on La Liberté). An inscription at the temple says, "Let the deserving sit down as slaves and rise as free men."

Pietas, "Holiness," is another of the Roman civic deities. She embodies their devotion to their gods and goddesses, Rome, and their parents. This is the same sentiment expressed in the Fourth Commandment, "Honor thy father and thy mother."

Harry Potter

✳

The first Harry Potter book was released in the United States on November 1, 1998, the first movie, on November 14, 2001. As a former English teacher, I'm pleased that J. K. Rowling's books have inspired children to read real novels—thick ones, at that. The books are enormous fun, and the movies are entertaining, too, especially when we get to watch actors like Maggie Smith and John Cleese having fun at work.

I'm not convinced that pagans should take Harry and Hogwarts totally to heart. Hogwarts is an English public school, which in the United States would be an expensive private school. The racism (Muggles and "mudbloods") expressed by Draco Malfoy and others derives from nineteenth-century imperialism, of which many white people were guilty.

Any pagan who has ever sat in a ritual circle recognizes that Rowling knows nothing about authentic magic. We don't need Latinificated "magic words," we don't carry wands in our jeans, and when we study herbs we study real ones. Though her allusions to mythology and legend are obvious—the three-headed dog, Professor Dumbledore's phoenix, the magic mirror, the philosopher's stone—her magic is mere trickery and illusion. I wonder if she's met any real witches (like us).

Like J. R. R. Tolkien and George Lucas, Rowling is constructing a modern mythos. Especially in the later books, we see that Harry = Frodo = Luke Skywalker, Dumbledore = Gandalf = Obi-Wan Kenobi, and Voldemort = Saruman = Darth Vader. Like every archetypal hero, Harry rises through adventure and pain from a state of peonage to achieve his true identity. I wouldn't be surprised to see him on the tenure track at Hogwarts by the time he turns eighteen.

There was a Muggle Street in London in Shakespeare's day; its real name was Monkwell Street.

Albertus Magnus and Donna Henes

✳

Albert the Great (1200–1280) was a German philosopher, scientist, theologian, Dominican friar, saint, and the teacher of Thomas Aquinas. He was so wise he was called Doctor Universalis. It's possible that only Roger Bacon (1214–1294), a Franciscan monk and creator of an artificial man, was wiser. Both men mastered medieval knowledge: astrology, astronomy, chemistry (alchemy), economics, ethics, geography, logic, metaphysics, mineralogy, the natural sciences, phrenology, physics, physiology, politics, rhetoric, and zoology.

Donna Henes, an urban shaman who lives in Exotic Brooklyn, New York, is the author of a number of good books. I "met" her via e-mail about the time she and I had the same idea. The old threefold goddess and threefold division of a woman's life are inadequate to describe the lives of modern women. Women are living too long past menopause these days to be crones, so Donna and I propose a stage between Mother and Crone. We call this stage Queen, and Donna teaches that we should become *queens of ourselves.*

In 1982, Donna composed the first (and to this date, only) satellite peace message in space, *Chants for peace*Chance for peace*:

> Chant for peace. There's a chance for peace, for peace
> on earth, for peace on earth, for peace of mind. There's a
> chance for peace, there's a chance for earth, for peace on
> earth, for peace of mind . . .

Reader, Albertus Magnus caught the zeitgeist of the Middle Ages. Donna and I seem to have caught a new idea. What other ideas are floating around in the pagan ethers?

Night of Hecate

✳

Older than the Olympians, Hecate comes from Thrace. Hesiod says she's the daughter of the Titans Perses and Asteria, both representatives of shining light, which tells us that she was not originally Shakespeare's dark and midnight hag. In early Greek art, in fact, she's Hecate Phorphoros, "the Light Bringer," a beautiful maiden holding two torches.

Another of Hecate's titles is Propylaia, "the One Before the Gate," guardian of our space, whether at home or where three roads meet. She's also Hecate Propolos, "She Who Leads" us through the darkness of the underworld and the mysteries. Denise Dumars and Lori Nyx write, "When you access darkness, you access power, and it is up to you what you do with it. It can consume you, like a black hole in space, or it can set you free."[24]

It's half-past November, and we're sitting in the dark. Pagans aren't supposed to be afraid of the dark . . . but what if there's a monster under the bed? From time out of mind, we've built fires—or turned on the lights—to protect ourselves from things that go bump in the night.

Maurice Sendak knows how to deal with the dark. In *Where the Wild Things Are*, young Max hears mysterious midnight noises. He dresses up in his wolf suit and sets out to discover the Wild Things. He dances with them and learns that he can be a Wild Thing, too.

Reader, tonight is a good night to dance with Hecate and roar with the Wild Things. Here's an exercise from Denise and Lori (which they got from H. P. Lovecraft). Walk across your room with the lights on. As you walk, study your path and note where the obstacles are. Turn off the lights. Walk the path again. Meet the darkness. Meet the Wild Things. How's your witchy night vision?

Drumming

✳

How on earth do drumming and silence go together? Reader, we've been to drum jams, a room full of people with djembes, ashikos, doumbeks, tambourines, frame drums, and rattles, all going at once, making a joyous and mighty noise.

Joyous, yes. Mighty, yes. Noise? No. I've studied with Layne Redmond and once took a lesson from Arthur Hull. They both teach that we don't need to be what Hull calls "hippie thunder drummers," guys who drum louder than everyone else. When I went to a full moon drum jam the other night, the leader said it in another way: "We drum to express not to impress." Drumming can be loud, especially with a community drum in the room, but if you're attentive to the patterns of the rhythms, you'll hear the silences.

It's those silences in the rhythms that we drum to. Not to fill them. To decorate them. As when we're chanting the MA chant, the magic happens when we can't hear ourselves. That's when we're "in the groove." We can't hear our own drum, but we feel the groove. Our muscle memory is over-riding our left brain, which keeps wanting to count. Our souls are in our drumming fingers.

I used to drum every full moon with a group of New Agers. Most of them played frame drums with mallets. *ONE, two, three, four* was all they could produce with their mallets. So I took my doumbek and played *beledi* rhythms in the silences of their *ONE, two, three, four: DOUM, DOUM, tek-a-tek-a, DOUM tek-a-tek, tek-a*. It got our hearts beating together. It entrained us with each other. It silenced our monkey-chattery minds. Drumming together brought us to the edge of ecstasy and into the groove. We were in resonance with the rhythms of the drums and the dancing of the universe.

First Printed Book in English, 1477

✳

William Caxton (1422–1491) was the first English printer. He was apprenticed to a textile merchant, but when his master died he went to the Low Countries, where he began translating French romances into English. He probably learned printing in Cologne, Germany. When he returned to England in 1476, he found favor with King Edward IV, Richard III (who was not the villain Shakespeare's Tudor propaganda play makes him), and Henry VII. In 1477, Caxton established his print shop in Westminster, near the center of London. The first book printed in English was his translation of *The Dictes and Sayings of the Philosophers*.

Reader, where would we be without our books? What would we know if everything we learned had to be passed from mouth to ear? How many people did Gerald Gardner teach in person, and how many people have his initiates taught in person? How many people have read books on Gardnerian Wicca? Starhawk gets around, but she hasn't come close to meeting all the people who have read the original edition, or the tenth and twentieth anniversary editions, of *The Spiral Dance*. We've been to talks and classes and rituals led by big-time pagans, but can they reach out and personally touch the thousands of us who sit home and read their books?

We learn many things from books, both what an author knows . . . and, alas, doesn't know but writes anyway. Half the publishers I know are jumping on the Goddess bandwagon. I wish (she says crankily) that they knew anything about pagans or the Goddess. I've edited two books by New Age authors that instruct the reader to close the circle at the end of a ritual and one that says the witches in *The Wizard of Oz* are real witches. Books are entertaining and useful, but should we believe everything we read?

The Silences in Our Minds

When I walk, I always walk the same route so I don't have to think about where I'm going and I often see two homeless people at various points along the way. For several months, I tried greeting them—a smile, a good morning—but they never responded. One of my neighbors who knows them says they never talk to anyone, so now we just keep walking our separate ways.

I wonder about the people I see. When I go anywhere, I take a book along, but I've seldom seen anyone sitting on a bus bench or church steps and reading. When I walk, even though I'm listening to music through my earphones, I'm thinking. I have, in fact, composed at least half the pages of this book while walking.

Which leads me to wonder . . . what's in the spaces of our minds? What's in our inner silences? What kinds of silent signals do we send out? It's said that everybody is psychic, but that only some people are able to reach a silent state where they can hear what cannot be heard with our physical ears. Reader, does this explain psychism?

We know that thoughts are things and that energy embraces us and walks around with us. With the eyes of your imagination, see yourself standing on a yellow brick road that winds and wanders through your world. It has little paths leading to the people you know. The paths that lead to people you know well are wide and well paved, and maybe there are flowers growing beside them. The paths that lead to people you recognize but don't know—like my two homeless people—may be narrow and broken. Bricks are probably missing and weeds are growing in the empty spaces. What can we do to plant more flowers?

Bahá'u'llah

The Baha'i faith is said by some—who apparently don't know about Wicca—to be the youngest religion on earth. It's a monotheistic religion that stands on the shoulders of Islam, as Islam stands, through Ishmael, on the shoulders of Judaism. It teaches that the "one god" progressively reveals his will to humanity through his messengers: Moses, Krishna, Buddha, Zoroaster, Jesus, Muhammad, and the Báb.

In 1844, a Persian named Siyyid Ali-Muhammad adopted the title Báb, "the Gate." He and his followers were persecuted, and he was executed. One of his followers, another Persian nobleman named Mírzá Husayn 'Ali, adopted the title Bahá'u'llah, "the Glory of God." He, too, was arrested. In 1852, while he was in prison in Tehran, he received the message that he was the chosen one anticipated by the Báb. A year later in Baghdad, he revealed his mission to his followers.

Islamic authorities in Persia and the Ottoman Empire (modern Turkey) drove Bahá'u'llah into exile, and he died in 1892 in the penal colony of Acre (in modern Israel). The Baha'i believe that his resting place outside the city is the holiest spot on earth; as Moslems face Mecca, they face Acre in their daily prayers. The other Baha'i holy place is the Shrine of the Báb on the slope of Mt. Carmel. Bahá'u'llah revealed one hundred volumes of divinely inspired writings, the *Kitáb-i-Aqdas*, "Most Holy Book." Bahá'u'llah's successor and the sole interpreter of his teachings was his oldest son, 'Abdu'l-Bahá, the "Center of the Covenant." In the 1920s, when Kemal Ataturk became Turkey's first president, 'Abdu'l-Bahá was freed from prison.

The major teachings of Bahá'u'llah say there is one supreme god who is unknowable to man and that all of the world's great religions arise through progressive revelation from the same divine source.

Sun Enters Sagittarius

❋

The symbol for Sagittarius is the arrow. An arrow, once released from the bow, cannot change its course in midflight. Once having set his course, Sagittarius seldom changes it.

Reader, even as I was typing that paragraph, my mind went, "That needs a reality check." So I phoned another astrologer and asked her. She replied that the Sagittarian is the arrow. He is always looking for new experiences or ideas, she is always expanding her awareness. Physically or mentally, Sagittarians are always on the move.

Here's my take on the arrow. We are all outward bound. We have paths in our lives that we follow or don't follow, but the essential business of life is being outward bound. It's moving from our mother's womb toward whatever there is in the universe.

The journey can be interesting. Some people take so many detours they lose the main path, which can be troublesome if you believe in pre-destination . . . unless, of course, you believe you're predestined to take all those detours. Some people go around in circles. Maybe their arrows are really boomerangs? Some people are straight arrows and proceed right to their goal. They don't pass "Go," and they collect whatever they want to collect. Some people wander through the woods and get caught by the wolf.

It's often good to stay the course and stay on course. Think about this in terms of our religion. Some of us find a teacher, take our year and a day, and get initiated. We're Gardnerians or Dianics or whatever, and that's totally what we are. Some of us take every class in the pagan catalog and end up as eclectics, open to every new spiritual experience that comes along. Reader, which path is yours? Is it possible that you might take flight along another path?

St. Cecilia's Day

✳

According to *The Golden Legend*, when Cecilia was given in marriage, she heard the church organ playing and sang for her virginity to be preserved. An angel promptly appeared and granted her wish. Her singing makes her the patroness of music. There's no historical truth to this legend, but it's such a nice story that the Church has used it ever since. When guilds were established in the Middle Ages, musicians adopted Cecilia as their patron saint.

In 1683, the London Musical Society met annually at St. Brigit's church to "keep [Cecilia's] day in a worthy manner." John Dryden and other poets composed odes to honor the day; Henry Purcell and George Frederic Handel wrote songs. Cecilia also became popular in literature and art and is still celebrated wherever people love music.

In his ode to St. Cecilia, Dryden refers to Orpheus, another sort of musical patron saint. Orpheus was a musician of such boundless talent that when he played the lyre the wild beasts of the Thracian forests sat at his feet and listened. Even the trees followed him as he sang. When he sailed on the Argo, his music tamed the Sirens and Symplegades, and when the ship was beached, his singing made it move itself back into the water.

When his wife, Eurydice, was bitten by a snake and died, Orpheus followed her into the underworld. His singing charmed Hades and Persephone, who gave him permission to take her home. Unfortunately, he disobeyed instructions to keep his eyes forward and looked back at Eurydice, at which point she was lost to him. He was later killed by maenads. His head and lyre were flung into the sea and floated—still singing—as far as Lesbos.

Wayland Smith

✻

In these days when everything is computerized and we're staring at nanotechnology, we don't remember blacksmiths, but 150 years ago when Henry Wadsworth Longfellow wrote his famous poem "The Village Blacksmith," technology employed iron, fire, and human muscle:

> Under the spreading chestnut tree
> The village smithy stands;
> The smith a mighty man is he
> With large and sinewy hands. . . .

The smith's work was as marvelous as the alchemist's. It was the smith who built our early machines and got us moving into the Industrial Age.

Wayland, also known as Weyland, Wieland, and Watlende, is a smith-god who came to Britain with the Saxons. Wayland's Smithy, a chambered-passage tomb of Sarsen stones and chalk (mentioned as early as 955, but probably constructed about 3700 to 3400 B.C.E.), lies in southern England near the Uffington White Horse. A grove of beech trees surrounds the site. Legend says that Wayland still lives and maintains his magical forge there. He reshoes horses and fashions armor, magical swords, and other implements for those who leave him silver coins.

Wayland appears in Norse sagas as Völund. In one story, King Nidud of Sweden is so impressed with Völund's craftsmanship that he imprisons him. Before escaping to Asgard, Völund kills the king's sons. In one version, he encases the head of one son in fine metalwork. In another, he fashions goblets from the princes' skulls and sends them to the king. In another story, he marries a swan maiden (or Valkyrie). Völund may be the prince of elves or related to the mountain dwarves.

In *Beowulf*, Wayland Smith forges the hero's sword and the armor. Wayland also appears in Sir Walter Scott's *Kenilworth* and in Rudyard Kipling's *Puck of Pook's Hill*.

Adar Jashan

❊

Adar Jashan is a Zoroastrian celebration of fire deities in which prayers and offerings are made, incense is burned, and no cooking is done at domestic hearths. The author of a Zoroastrian Web site explains that the prophet Zarathushtra (Zoroaster) told his followers not to worship fire, but to acknowledge it as a symbol of eternal light. "The zest for fire in Zoroastrianism," he writes, "became the quest for truth." The fires in our homes are as sacred as temple fires. "For almost a thousand years after the advent of Zarathushtra," he adds, "only the hearth fire . . . was venerated." Permanent fire altars in temples came later and symbolized victory, on the physical level, over darkness and cold and, on the spiritual level, over the forces of vice and ignorance.

Pagans worship as well at home as in any temple. Yesterday was the first day of winter in the Julian calendar. It's cold outside and the nights are long and dark, so let's cozy up to the fire tonight, not worshipping it, but appreciating its warmth and light.

Let's do some domestic fire magic. One kind of fire magic is brewing and cooking. As you heat the water for your tea, bless the elements—the fire that heats the water, the "earth" of your cup and the tea itself, the warmth and fragrance in the air. Another domestic fire magic is cooking, the magical transformation of raw grains and meats our bodies cannot digest into something tasty and nourishing. Cook something to go with your tea, and bless both the cook and the cooking.

If you've heard of anyone who is in need of help, light a healing candle or a green candle for prosperity and let it burn and send its magic through the night.

St. Catherine

❋

St. Catherine of Alexandria is another virgin martyr, a scholar (or queen) who is said to have lived in the fourth century. One day, so the story goes, she demanded an audience with the emperor and upbraided him for persecuting Christians. When the emperor sent fifty pagan scholars to debate with her, her arguments converted them. He had all fifty burned. After he arrested Catherine, his mother visited her in prison and was also converted (along with the jailers). One of the instruments of Catherine's torture was a spiked iron wheel, but when she touched it, the spikes flew off, leaving her unharmed. So the emperor had her beheaded. Angels carried her body to Mt. Sinai, where there is still a St. Catherine's monastery. Although the *Catholic Encyclopedia* says that Catherine ranks with St. Margaret and St. Barbara as "one of the fourteen most helpful saints in heaven," it does not mention the fate of her head, which bled milk instead of blood.

In the Middle Ages, the spiked wheel became known as the Catherine Wheel, and workers who used wheels—spinners, millers, wheelwrights, mechanics—adopted her as their patron saint. She is also the patron saint of young girls and students. Looking at the Web sites of schools named after Catherine, we find that the torture instrument has been transformed into networks of students.

Out of the hands of the medieval fabulists, the wheel is a symbol of cosmic order and the cycles of time. We see the solar hoop, the wheel of dharma, Fortuna's Wheel, the wheel of the year, the Celtic cross, mandalas, and rose windows. Author Nigel Pennick connects St. Catherine with the wheel goddesses of the underworld, known variously as Persephone, Proserpina, Kore, and Arianrod. These goddesses represent the cycle of life and death.

Paracelsus

❋

Theophrastus Phillippus Aureolus Bombastus von Hohenheim (1493–1541) was the most famous physician and alchemist of the Middle Ages. He took the name Paracelsus ("above Celsus") to show his low opinion of a Roman physician much admired by medieval doctors.

Paracelsus was born in Einsiedeln, Switzerland, where a Black Madonna, Our Lady of the Dark Forest, was found in the ninth century by a Benedictine hermit named St. Meinrad. Paracelsus spent most of his life wandering the world and doing research in medicine, alchemy, astrology, and occult topics. He traveled to Egypt, Arabia, Jerusalem, and Constantinople. At one point, in Russia, he was captured by Tartars and brought before the "Great Cham," who took him to China.

Not only did Paracelsus coin the word "alcohol," but he is also said to have learned the secret of the Philosopher's Stone. He became a surgeon and taught that wounds could heal themselves if drained and kept clean. (The usual procedure was to pour boiling oil on a wound to cauterize it or let a limb become gangrenous and amputate it.) He believed that the body must be in balance to be healthy. Paracelsus actually healed people. He also attacked the greed of medieval apothecaries, investigated the causes of contagious diseases, and espoused the "doctrine of signatures" later used in homeopathy. He is known as the founder of the modern materia medica and father of scientific chemistry.

Reader, are you attending to your health? No matter whether we're using establishment or alternative medical modalities (or both), we need to ask questions, do our own research, become informed, get third and fourth opinions, and make educated decisions. The physician isn't god anymore. Today, many physicians stay on top of new research and—if you're assertive enough—will explain things to you and listen to your opinions.

The Crusades

❋

A century after Sylvester II (the "alchemical pope"), the Fatimid caliph Al-Hakim ibn Aziz, and Holy Roman Emperor Otto III tried and failed to unite the medieval world, Pope Urban II responded to a plea from the Byzantine emperor, Alexius I, to defend Constantinople against the Seljuk Turks. The Seljuks were part of an aggressive tribe of Asian refugees called Kazars, some of whom would become the Ashkenazi Jews of Eastern Europe. They had already conquered Palestine. Now they were headed for Constantinople.

On November 27, 1095, Urban called the Council of Clermont and appealed to the assembled nobles of Europe to come to the aid of their Christian brethren in the east. His address must have been stirring, for a roar of *Dius li volt* ("God wills it") swept through the crowd.

There were eight Crusades between 1097 and 1272. The only successful one was the First, in which the Christian army led by Godfroi de Bouillon captured Jerusalem. Godfroi let himself be declared Defender of the Holy Sepulchre; in 1100, his brother, Baldwin, modestly accepted the title King of Jerusalem. The Second Crusade is famous because Eleanor of Aquitaine, wife of Louis of France, went along. She and her court ladies dressed themselves as amazons. The Third Crusade was Richard Lionheart's. (Richard was a masterful warrior but a lousy king; we love him only because he's the *deus ex machina* of the Robin Hood story.) The Fourth Crusade's only accomplishment was the sack of Constantinople, the Fifth and Seventh Crusades were unsuccessful invasions of Egypt, and the Sixth and Eighth ended in truce. Acre, the last Christian outpost in the Holy Land, was retaken by the Muslim armies in 1291.

Some modern Muslim terrorists say they are seeking to avenge the horrors of the medieval crusades.

Thanksgiving

❊

Back in the olden days, we had a Thanksgiving assembly each year with a harvest pageant and speeches telling us exactly what we should be thankful for. As I recall, we kids were thankful for a couple days of freedom from homework, our mothers were thankful for modern appliances, and our fathers were thankful that they were participating in the fabled American Dream. I grew up in a white, working-class neighborhood and was totally unaware that people who lived in a black ghetto just five miles away went to segregated schools, had no modern appliances, and were generally barred from having any dreams of social progress at all.

Reader, we all have Thanksgiving stories. My family gathered at my grandparents' house, where Gramma got out the good china. I can still remember the year I got old enough to sit at the big table. My uncles used to tease Gramma; one year she "accidentally" got Uncle Don right between the eyes with the Reddi-Wip. Whether we're eating turkey or tofurky, and whether we're sitting around a table with our birth family or our extended family of friends, Thanksgiving is a good day to share our stories. As you eat, go around the table and tell your stories. Some of them are hoary with decades of telling, but the family still laughs.

We can make up new stories, too. Perhaps pagans at a Thanksgiving potluck have stories about earlier holidays. Perhaps you've spent a Thanksgiving serving dinner at a homeless shelter to people who don't remember what Thanksgiving's about anymore. Perhaps you've spent Thanksgiving alone, reading a cheap novel or doing art while you ate your hot dog from the 7-Eleven.

Reader, what are you thankful for? Look at where you live. Look at your coven or circle, at your partner and children. Make a list of things you are thankful for. Recite your list aloud.

Sons of Saturn

❈

The sons of Saturn are Jupiter, Neptune, and Pluto, the soon-to-be Olympians who came to southern Europe with the Ionians, Achaeans, and other tribes. They castrated their father, conquered the elder gods, then divided up the territory.

There are at least fourteen saints named Saturnius or Saturninus, most of them early martyrs about whom little is known. One was dragged to death behind a bull (today is this one's feast day), and another was martyred when, it is said, he refused to hand over a letter of Paul to the Emperor Julian.

In the Christian art and literature of the Middle Ages and Renaissance, Saturn was shown as a gloomy, gray-bearded man, often wearing a crown and carrying a sickle, which represented not his agricultural genesis but his persona as old Father Time. He was generally identified with God the Father. After about 1100, miniature illustrations begin to appear in the margins of manuscripts—Saturn, Cybele, Apollo, Jupiter, or Juno drawn to illustrate the lesson of the text at hand. But they don't look like Greek and Roman statues. At first, they look like medieval ecclesiastics; later, they're dressed like French and Italian courtiers. Saturn becomes an Old Testament prophet and is later shown as the Holy Roman Emperor and giver of wisdom (*donum sapientiae*), associated with prudence, memory, intelligence, foresight, virtue, heaven, time, fertility, and syphilis.

Reader, today is a good day to celebrate the cycle of generations. What do you know about your ancestors? Do you have mementoes or photos? Get them out of boxes and set them on an altar with Saturn. Do something nice for your parents today. Do something significant with your children, something they'll remember and tell their children about. Pass along wisdom you received from your parents.

Comparative Religion

✳

It's useful to know about other people's faiths so that we can talk to each other and practice freedom of speech and religion. Two of the best Web sites for learning about the world's religions and finding accurate, unbiased information are *Beliefnet.com* and *Adherents.com*.

Beliefnet.com presents discussions, quizzes, meditations, and prayers, plus opportunities to sign up for free newsletters with "angel wisdom"; a Bible reading, horoscope, or prayer for the day; notes on "spiritual weight loss"; and Buddhist, Hindu, Muslim, and Jewish wisdom.

When I'm in One Of Those Moods, I go to Beliefnet and read the jokes. Q. How many Jewish mothers does it take to screw in a lightbulb? A. None. "It's all right; I'll sit in the dark." Q. How many pagans . . . ? A. "One to change it, and five to sit around complaining that lightbulbs never burned out before Christians came along." The Unitarian answer (a hilarious essay) is too long to reprint here; go to *Beliefnet.com* and read it yourself.

Adherents.com is "a growing collection of over 41,000 adherent statistics and religious geography citations." It references statistics for "over 4,200 religions, churches, denominations, religious bodies, faith groups, tribes, cultures, movements, ultimate concerns, etc." We can read the Federal Guidelines for Religious Expression in Public Schools.

As of 2002, the largest religion in the world is Christianity, which includes not only Catholics, Protestants, and Eastern Orthodox, but also Pentecostals, Latter-Day Saints, Jehovah's Witnesses, and "nominals." Next in size is Islam, then Hinduism. The fourth category is Secular/Nonreligious/ Agnostic/Atheist (850 million people around the world). Buddhism completes the top five. There are one million neopagans worldwide.

The Voice of the Witch

❖

Fritz Jung and Wren Walker are my heroes. At the same time they're
holding down regular jobs, they're serving you and me—and the whole
pagan community—by maintaining the hottest pagan Web site in the
known or unknown universe. They have delivered more than 100 million
pages to people who want to find out what witches have to say. I send
e-mails to Fritz asking all sorts of strange questions, and he not only
replies, but his replies are also courteous and helpful. Yeah, he's my hero.

Fritz and Wren got into the Web site business in 1996 when they put
up a site for the Witches League for Public Awareness (WLPA). On
January 28, 1997, they launched the Witches' Voice, *Witchvox.com*, with
fifty-six pages. In 1998, they moved to Florida. In December, 1998, their
site had its millionth hit. In 2002, Witchvox won the Webby Award for
the Best Spirituality Site on the Internet, based on write-in votes. Reader,
I'm sure our votes were part of that campaign.

The Witches' Voice front page sets forth its mission statement.

> The Witches' Voice is a proactive educational network
> providing news, information services and resources for
> and about Pagans, Heathens, Witches and Wiccans. [It]
> is a neutral forum open to all adherents of the various
> Heathen religions, Pagan, Witch, Wiccan traditions and
> to Solitary Practitioners who/that follow a positive code
> of ethics. . . . Witchvox is a truly free community
> resource.

Every day, we can read new articles from periodicals around the world
reprinted in the Wren's Nest, surf the site's historical files, and go to the
area listings to find pagans around the world (except in Antarctica, where,
Fritz reports, there are no pagans).

Shiva

We know the familiar figure of the Lord of the Dance, standing on one foot inside a rayed circle, dancing his cosmic dance of life-death-rebirth. Shiva, whose name means "benevolent" or "favorable," is a pre-Aryan god who, like Vishnu, was too popular for the Aryan conquerors of India to ignore. The Aryans first settled in the Punjab (northern India) around 1500 B.C.E., later overran the Indus Valley, and then moved south, bringing Vedism and the caste system with them.

The Brahmanic trinity is Brahma, Vishnu, and Shiva, three indivisible gods of continuous creation, life, and destruction. Shiva became the "prince of demons" who goes into battle against the asuras, or demons. His consort is Parvati, who is also Sita, Uma, and Durga, who becomes Kali standing over the supine Shiva, doing her own dance of victory.

Our Western minds want to see gods and goddesses as separate beings on opposing ends of a continuum of deity, as the two pans of the balance of polarity. In *The Witches' God*, Janet and Stewart Farrar say that when they showed their Shiva ritual to their friend, Dr. Ashok Singh, he said, "'Our Yoga, our Tantra, just do not gel with the Western way of thinking.' Far too many Westerners [the Farrars add] try to use the outer forms of these systems without even beginning to understand their inner meaning."[25]

We know that every Hindu god has a *shakti*, a feminine vitalizing force, but we Westerners don't fully understand the Hindu concept. That's one reason I'm wary of WASP men or women teaching tantra (or some Buddhist practices). Reader, what do you think? Can such teachings be shared by people who don't share cultures? Or does true understanding require some unknown genetic component that people raised in different cultures just don't have?

Divination

Before Gerald Gardner came home to England and found (or was found by) the coven in the New Forest, there were already practitioners of hedge and kitchen magic, which is different from the high magic of the Golden Dawn and the Rosicrucians. These "cunning folk" were the neighborhood's informal healers and diviners. They laid and removed curses, used herbs for healing, told fortunes, sold charms and talismans, cast horoscopes, and "devised spells and rites according to their own whims and creative talents, and the needs of their customers." They were good, solid, Christian men and women. Except for that last adjective, that description sounds just like us. Reader, perhaps they are among our spiritual ancestors.

As long as people have been conscious of a reality larger than their own bodies, they have wanted to manipulate reality and know the future. I know of a number of traditions that teach that divination is the proper occupation of pagans and that we should do it whenever a decision is needed. Let divination be our subject for December, when the invisibles are walking about in the land.

In *To Know*, Jade devotes a chapter to divination. "[If] life is not a series of random accidents," she writes, "but, instead, a series of synchronistic occurrences, then information about these patterns should be accessible. "[26] That's divination. We can use aeromancy (observing clouds and the air), alectryomancy (watching the actions of birds), apantomancy (meeting animals), cartomancy (using tarot or ordinary playing cards), and hydromancy (observing water). We can divine with runes or a pendulum; read someone's face, the soles of their feet (cartopedy), the lines in their hands.

How does divination work? I agree with Jade that it's largely a matter of training in using our psychic skills. Pagans are not required to be diviners, but I think it helps.

St. Barbara, Lady of Amboto

❖

> [T]he Wiccan view of Deity can totally incorporate the
> vision of God presented by Christianity or Judaism. . . .
> Instead of attempting to belittle or invalidate the main-
> stream beliefs of the society around us, we should seek
> to find truth and revelation. . . .
> —Amber Laine Fisher, *Philosophy of Wicca*

St. Barbara, it is said, was the daughter of a rich man who locked her
in a tower to preserve her from the corrupt outside world. She received
and rejected an offer of marriage, then told her father she'd become a
Christian. He had her tortured, but as he was getting ready to put her to
death, he was struck by a lightning bolt. Because of this lightning bolt,
Barbara became the patron saint of artillerymen. Because she was locked
in a tower, she's been compared to Rapunzel; the Renaissance artist
Ghirlandaio painted her holding the tower in her hands and standing on
her dead father's body. Barbara is popular throughout the world. There is
a fifth-century church of Saint Barbara in Cairo; in the Basque area of
Spain and France, where the Goddess is called Mari, Barbara is Our Lady
of Amboto; and in the Caribbean, she becomes the *orisha* Chango (Shango),
husband/lover of Oya and Oshun.

Reader, I hope you've noticed by now that Christian mythology, with
its *Golden Legend* of martyrology and hagiography, is as full and interesting
as any of our pagan mythologies. People have always liked stories, and the
fuller they are with noble heroes, graceful heroines, dastardly villains, and
fantastically gory events, the better. With medieval Christian mythology,
we get all of those elements, plus stories based on history—like the Trojan
War, the kings of Athens, the transition of the Roman Empire into the
Holy Roman Empire, the Crusades, and stories of popes and scholars.

Pandemonium, Faunalia

❖

John Milton (1608–1674) invented the word *pandemonium* for *Paradise Lost* to describe Lucifer's palace in hell, which was built by the fallen angels who joined Lucifer's rebellion against God: "Far to th'inland retir'd, about the walls / Of Pandaemonium, City and proud seat / Of Lucifer . . . ." From the Greek words *panikon deima*, *pandemonium* today means "general chaos and wild uproar."

We pagans are fans of Pan, whose name means "all" (as in *pan*theon). His archetype is the hypermasculine, horny forest god we recognize in all those nice ithyphallic statues. Originally an Arcadian god of unknown parentage (though Zeus is suspected), Pan is older than the Olympians and is said to have given Artemis her dogs and taught the secret of prophecy to Apollo. The citified Greeks thought Pan was a raucous, lecherous, intoxicated, musical, hillbilly god of wild things. (Does this make him a rock-and-roll god?)

The staid and solid Roman Republicans, who loathed the idea of pandemonium, worshipped a kindlier spirit of the wild. Their hillbilly god was Faunus, who is invoked by Horace in one of his odes as a frisky agricultural fellow. Faunus, who protects lambs (he is also called Lupercus, "protection from wolves"), is the father of Bona Dea and Latinus. At the Faunalia, the Romans asked him to walk the boundaries of their farms to separate the tame from the wild. "In your honor, Faunus," Horace writes, "the forest sheds its foliage [and] the valley resonates with the beat of music and dancing feet. . . ."

Reader, celebrate your own Faunalia today. If there's a good band in town, attend a concert. Find a wild place where you won't bother civilized people, offer wine to the god, and celebrate the good life. Rock on!

Dion Fortune

❖

Dion Fortune (1890–1946) was a British occultist and author of occult fiction and nonfiction. In her writing, she distinguishes between occultism and mysticism and Eastern and Western metaphysics, but she doesn't mention witches or Wicca (which hadn't been invented when she was writing). Her novels, including *The Sea Priestess* and *Moon Magic*, show ordinary Englishmen and women discovering Isis, Pan, and the mysteries of Atlantis. Although her work may inspire and influence us, Fortune was never associated with any Wiccan coven; she worked in a thoroughly Judeo-Christian stream of occultism that used pagan imagery and ideas, but generally clung to the One God.

Dion Fortune is the magical name of Violet Firth, who was born into a family of Christian Scientists and grew up to be a psychiatrist. In 1911, she experienced a psychic attack that left her a "mental and physical wreck" for several years. (The attack allegedly came from Moina Mathers, who was jealous of her.) Fortune turned to Freudian and Jungian psychology, but finding them both inadequate turned to occultism. In 1930, she wrote *Psychic Self-Defense*, which is the original of today's feebler attempts to address the issue.

Fortune joined the Alpha and Omega Lodge of the Stella Matutina, an outer lodge of the Hermetic Order of the Golden Dawn, in 1919 but left in 1929 and later founded the Fraternity of the Inner Light, which is still in business. Her name comes from her magical motto, *Deo Non Fortuna* ("By God, not chance"). Her nonfiction includes *The Mystical Qabalah* (1936), which is a thorough and lucid study of that metaphysical system, and *The Cosmic Doctrine* (1923–1924), which she said she channeled from the inner planes and which is so profound as to be nearly incomprehensible.

Scholars of Mythology

❖

The primary sources of the mythologies we know are written in dead languages. Linguists can read these languages, but you and I depend on secondary sources, which are the translations, interpretations, and commentaries. The great age of scholarship in mythology lasted from about 1850 until about 1950.

Thomas Bulfinch (1796–1867) was an American writer whose *Age of Fable* (1855) retells the myths, legends, and stories of Charlemagne, King Arthur, and the Greco-Roman gods and heroes. It is the first significant American book of mythology.

Sir James Frazer (1854–1941) was a Scottish social anthropologist who traveled widely in Greece and Rome. His most famous work is *The Golden Bough*, originally written in 1890. The third edition (completed in 1936) runs to thirteen volumes.

Edith Hamilton (1867–1963) was a classicist whose most famous books, *The Greek Way* (1930) and *Mythology* (1942), are still in print. Hamilton was born in Germany and grew up in Indiana; she and her sister were the first female students accepted at German universities. Her books are based not on archaeology, but on a love of the classics and the daily life of olden times.

Robert Graves (1895–1985) was a prolific scholar and novelist. He is best known to pagans as the author of *The White Goddess* (1948)—neither history nor herstory, neither theology nor thealogy—in which he invents the "capricious and all-powerful Threefold Goddess." His book *The Greek Myths* was published in 1955.

Joseph Campbell (1904–1987) is best known for *The Hero With a Thousand Faces* (1949) and his interpretations of mythology, as given in the PBS series, *The Power of Myth* (first broadcast in 1988).

Ix Chel

❖

Ix Chel, "Lady Rainbow," is a Mayan goddess of the moon, water, healing, childbirth, and weaving. She may be married to Voltan, an earth god,
or to Itzamna, lord of all gods, founder of Mayan culture, and inventor of
writing. Their children are the Bacabs, wind or jaguar gods who hold up
the sky in the four directions. Ix Chel is frequently shown as an old
woman, sometimes holding a serpent, sometimes a water jug.

One story about Ix Chel tells that when she falls in love with the sun,
her jealous grandfather hurls lightning at her and kills her. Thirteen drag-
onflies grieve over her for thirteen days, at which time she is reborn. She
follows her lover, the sun, up to his palace in the sky. But now he becomes
jealous and accuses her of taking a new lover, the morning star, who is the
sun's brother. Stalked and chased out of heaven by the jealous sun, Ix Chel
finds sanctuary on earth among vultures, but the sun finds her again and
lures her home. Wearying of this persistent domestic violence, she leaves
him and wanders through the skies, making herself invisible whenever he
comes near.

Reader, think about the stories about goddesses and gods and saints
and heroes you've been reading in this book. Some stories are allegorical—
vegetation gods and goddesses like Attis and Persephone, or Jupiter and
Saturn, who are used to represent Christian virtues. Other stories are
quasi-historical—the founding of Athens and Rome, the Trojan War, the
Arthurian mythos, St. Margaret. Some are miraculous—various metamorphoses, Leda's egg, Catherine's wheel. When we tell such stories, are we
recreating their worlds? Are we bringing the stories into our world and
learning lessons to apply to our own lives? When we retell the old stories,
are we creating new worlds?

The Virgin of Guadalupe

❖

History tells us that the *conquistadores* brought monks with them. The monks proclaimed the Incan, Mayan, and Aztec deities to be devils. As fanatics always do, they converted the people and destroyed as much of their civilization as they could.

In 1531, Tonan, or Tonantzin, an Aztec goddess whose name means "mother" and who was honored at the winter solstice, appeared on the summit of Tepeyac Hill in Mexico. As was customary among Indian woman, she wore a black belt to show that she was pregnant. She encountered Juan Diego, an Indian. Speaking in Nahuatl, she told him that she was the mother of god and instructed him to gather roses. Diego knew that nothing could grow on that hill but cactus, but when he looked, he found roses. Tonantzin directed him to gather them in his *tilma* (cloak) and take them to the bishop. When he finally met the bishop, roses spilled out on the floor, and the *tilma* held the goddess's image.

The bishop, Zumarraga, declared the apparition to be Guadalupe, the Dark Madonna of Estremadura, Spain. This same Zumarraga burned the Aztec codices, destroyed their "idols," and tore down their temples. He was the keeper of the branding iron used to stamp the Indians' faces with the names of their new owners.

In 1737, "the Most Holy Mary of Guadalupe" became the patroness of Mexico City, and, in 1746, of New Spain from California to El Salvador. In 1945–1946, Pope Pius XI pronounced her queen of Mexico and the patroness of the Americas. In 1976, a new Mexico City basilica was dedicated to her. Diego's *tilma* hangs there, looking as fresh as it did five hundred years ago. In July 2002, Juan Diego was declared a saint. What I find curious is how European he looks in the pictures.

U.N. Declaration of Human Rights, Lux Mundi

❧

Coming to the longest night of the year, we need light to see where we're going. That's why we have festivals of light, both literal and metaphorical. I think it's significant that when the newly formed United Nations presented its Universal Declaration of Human Rights in 1948, it did so at the darkest time of the year. People were just starting to recover from the blackouts and darkness of World War II.

> All human beings are born free and equal in dignity and rights. They are endowed with reason and conscience and should act towards one another in a spirit of brotherhood [*sic*].

Lux is the Roman goddess of light, and *lux mundi* means "light of the world." Surfing the Web, I found Lux Mundi candlemakers and hotels, churches and ecumenical centers, artists, a university cinema connection, and a hymn by Sir Arthur Sullivan. In their ways, all who use the name Lux Mundi are bringing some kind of light to the world. In his Sermon on the Mount, Jesus of Nazareth says, "You are the light of the world; a city that is built upon a mountain cannot be hidden. . . . Let your light so shine before men that they may see your good works. . . ."

In 1793, the French Revolutionaries were still celebrating the light of reason. On December 10, a Mademoiselle Maillard was selected to personify *La Liberté* in a ceremony in Notre Dame. She was brought into the cathedral and seated on the altar, where she lit a large candle. Liberty was thus seen to be the Light of the World.

Reader, perhaps as we bring the elder gods and goddesses back into the light *we* are the new light of the world, inspiring the world to see the varieties of religious experience more clearly.

Hanukah

❖

Though we're familiar with the story of Hanukah, the eight-day
Festival of Lights, we may not know its historical context. As Alexander
the so-called Great built his vast Hellenistic empire in the eastern
Mediterranean and Asia Minor, among his conquests were Palestine and
Judea. Following his death in 324 B.C.E., his empire was divided up by his
generals. Seleucus grabbed the Near East, and for two hundred years the
Seleucid dynasty forced Hellenistic values, including the worship of a multitude of gods, on the Jews. Jerusalem was surrounded by Greek settle-
ments, including Samaria, Gaza, Haifa, Acre, and Damascus. Meanwhile,
Greece had been overcome by Rome. By 165 B.C.E., therefore, the culture
in Asia Minor was Hellenistic Greek, the law was Roman, and the Jews
were not happy.

The Maccabees rose up in revolt. Their leader, Judah, was a rigorist.
Rigorists believe in One True God and try to force their belief on everyone else. They never compromise. After Judah defeated the Seleucids, he
cleansed the temple by removing the pagan altars and ornaments and
restoring its ancient furnishings and service. He invited the orthodox to
return. But when the temple was to be rededicated, they had enough oil
for only one lamp. That lamp burned miraculously for eight full days. This
is why a Hanukah menorah properly holds nine lights: one for each day
and one from which to light the others.

According to *The Jewish Catalog*, long before the time of the Maccabees
there was already "some kind of established winter festival" associated with
the solstice. Another "ancient Jewish custom" was the kindling of fire, which
is why it was necessary to light a lamp at the dedication of the temple. The
only "special mitzvah" related to the winter holiday is to light the lights
each night.

The Business of Oracles

❖

I am Sir Oracle,
And when I ope my lips let no dog bark!
—William Shakespeare, *The Merchant of Venice*

The folly of mistaking a paradox for a discovery, a
metaphor for a proof, a torrent of verbiage for a spring
of capital truth, and oneself for an oracle, is inborn in us.
—Paul Valéry, *Introduction to the Method of Leonardo da Vinci*

From the *I Ching* and the tarot to runes, Angel Cards, and Goddess
Amulets, we love our oracular tools. We scry and dowse. We look at the
flights of birds, converse with bees, and listen to the whispers of the leaves
on the trees. Though the Muggles want to know the future as fervently as
anyone else, they scoff at our "superstitions." Then—just like everyone
else—they plunk down their silver and get a reading. Some readers
believe that it's best to be prudent when reading at a psychic fair. Others
tell it like it is, letting the cards (or stalks or coins or runes or bones) fall
where they may.

I quit doing readings because I became weary of questions about people's love lives and jobs. When I said, "Trust the oracle but do your homework," my querents didn't understand. I had to explain that magic arises
out of hard work and adjustments in consciousness that put us in the right
place, physically, emotionally, or mentally, for change to happen.

Reader, what precautions do you take when you do a reading? We know
it's easy to read someone's mind or ask careful questions and then tell that
person what she wants to hear. How do we avoid creating self-fulfilling
prophecies or fantasies? How do we deal with a possible or potential
future that may contain death or disaster? What makes an *honest* reader?

St. Lucy

❖

> early morning light
> fills the empty glass:
> rainbow
> —Patricia Kelly

Lucina is an early Italian goddess of light, who merges with or becomes an aspect of Juno or Diana. St. Lucy was a fourth-century Sicilian girl who consecrated her virginity to God and vowed to distribute the family wealth to the poor. "Her largesse," says the *Catholic Encyclopedia*, "stirred the greed of an unworthy youth." He arranged their betrothal, then denounced her to the Roman governor. When they tried to burn her—here's the light connection—God put the fire out. So they beheaded her. She came to symbolize the light of faith that shines in the darkness.

Somehow Lucy brought her sacred light, and possibly the custom of lighting sacred midwinter candles, to Norway and Sweden, where they have long winter nights. One story is that there was a terrible winter famine in Sweden, and St. Lucy brought a shipload of food. She was so radiant that the whole ship glowed. What may have really happened is that the Vikings heard stories about Lucy as they were conquering Sicily and northern Italy and took them home. Before the calendar was reformed, her feast day was the longest night of the year. People lit Lucy candles and Lucy fires, which guided the sun back to the sky. Children wrote the word *Lussi* on fences, walls, and doors to inform the demons of winter and darkness that their reign was ended. Young men, called star boys, paraded around town in her honor.

Reader, you've seen pictures of the little girls wearing garlands of Lucy candles. Gather your circle or coven tonight, crown your own Lucy and your own star boys, and sing in the sacred light.

Publication of the Smith-Waite Tarot

Mary Greer probably knows more about the history and interpretation of the tarot than anyone else on the planet. In Appendix F of *Women of the Golden Dawn*, she tells how Pamela Colman Smith (1878–1951) created the deck that bears A.E. Waite's name. Smith's only recorded comment about her work on the deck, Mary writes, is in a letter to her friend and mentor, photographer Alfred Stieglitz: "I just finished a big job for very little cash." Mary says the deck should properly be called the Smith-Waite deck.

Smith, who claimed to be the goddaughter of a witch and sister to a fairy, was a set designer at W. B. Yeats's Abbey Theatre. When she joined the Golden Dawn, she took the magical motto *Quod Tibi id Aliis* ("to yourself as to others"). Although she attained initiation in the order, her first love was not magic but art. She was able to "see" music, and when she went to Ireland, she tuned in to Celtic visionary traditions.

Although Waite conceptualized the Major Arcana of the deck, which was published in 1910, the images on the Minor Arcana number cards were most likely Smith's original work. Her deck was the first in history to have illustrated number cards. Previously, the Marseilles deck had been the model, and decks without pictures are referred to as the "French stream." When I was a student of the tarot, I read that Waite had a vision that cards VIII (Justice) and XI (Strength) should switch places, though he apparently never said why. The deck he commissioned became the first deck of the "English stream" and the model for most modern decks. As we know, neither stream flows from an ancient spring; the tarot was most likely invented during the Italian Renaissance as a card game.

What's Your Divination I.Q.?

1. The tarot was created by:
   a. The Nommo of Sirius B
   b. Priests of Thoth in ancient Egypt
   c. Artists of Renaissance Italy
   d. The Inner Chiefs of the Golden Dawn

2. When you pass a sheet of paper through a candle flames you are creating:
   a. A smoke billet
   b. A billet-doux
   c. A tussie-mussie
   d. A pile of ashes

3. Bibliomancy is:
   a. Dancing oneself into a trance
   b. Opening a book at random
   c. Prophesying after imbibing strong drink
   d. Writing small books of prophetic verse

4. Which does not use psychokinesis?
   a. Scrying
   b. Tarot
   c. Ouija board
   d. I Ching

5. We can use a pendulum or dowsing rod to:
   a. Find water
   b. Analyze handwriting
   c. Irrigate our inner organs
   d. Light a need fire

6. If you want to find out about your etheric body, you should consult:
   a. A fiscal reader
   b. A telepath
   c. An auric reader
   d. An autodidact

7. Getting vibrations from an object is done by means of:
   a. Psychiatry
   b. Psychosynthesis
   c. Psychopannychy
   d. Psychometry

8. Numerology is based on the teachings of
   a. Machiavelli
   b. Wittgenstein
   c. Pythagoras
   d. Euripides

9. The Yoruban oracular system is:
   a. Obol
   b. Ifa
   c. Runes
   d. Mah Jongg

10. Which divinatory system reveals the mysteries of the earth?
    a. Pyromancy
    b. Aeromancy
    c. Geomancy
    d. Hydromancy

Answers: 1-c, 2-a, 3-b, 4-a, 5-a, 6-c, 7-d, 8-c, 9-b, 10-c

Sophia

❖

Sophia is huge these days. I have a dozen books about her. Her name is Greek; *philosophia* means "love of wisdom." To the Gnostics, she is the revealer of *gnosis* to humankind, the youngest aeon, or offspring, of God. Though I have heard people who should know better equate Sophia and Mary Magdalen, they are not the same person, nor are they goddesses per se. Whereas Athena, Voluspa, Ma'at, and Danu are goddesses *of* wisdom, Sophia *embodies* wisdom. She *is* holy wisdom. She is sometimes identified with Chokmah (also spelled Hokkma), "Wisdom," the head of the right pillar of the Qabalistic Tree of Life. Dion Fortune calls Chokmah the "active male potency." If, as some modern scholars say, Chokmah is a suppressed goddess, then is feminine "illuminating intelligence" the hidden head of masculine wisdom?

Sophia is also identified as the author of the Book of Proverbs. Although Lady Wisdom is a shadow figure in the Judeo-Christian Bible, a close reading of the books of Proverbs, Ecclesiastes, and Job finds her hiding behind and inspiring the male god. In Proverbs 8:12, Sophia says, "I am Wisdom. I bestow shrewdness/and show the way to knowledge and prudence." To the early Hebrews, she is God's "darling" and "delight." You can see this relationship on the Sistine ceiling, where Michelangelo painted Yahweh holding a woman in his left arm. To Martin Luther, however, she is merely the *Werkmeister* ("master mechanic").

In her book *Sophia: Aspects of the Divine Feminine*, Susanne Schaup traces Wisdom's history and relates her to Hildegard of Bingen (who addressed hymns to her), Jacob Boehme, and the Russian sophiologists. Sophia holds a special place in Russia, where the oldest churches in Kiev and Novgorod are named for her. Unlike the Western churches, the Orthodox Church never marginalized Lady Wisdom.

Saturnalia

Saturn, who was conflated with the Greek Titan, Cronus, was an ancient Latin agricultural god whose name may derive from *satur*, "stuffed," or *sator*, "a sower"; in either case he stands for abundance. A working god who oversaw viniculture and farming, he was the king of Italy during the golden age. When Jupiter conquered him, he hid (*latuit*) in the region that came to be called Latium. The Romans said Saturn's body lay beneath the Capitol in Rome. Because his reign brought prosperity to the city, the state treasury and the standards of the Roman legions were kept in his temple when the army was at home. Saturn's statue was bound in woolen strips to keep him from leaving Rome.

The Saturnalia was originally a series of rural festivals—including the *sementivae feriae, consualia larentalia, paganalia*, and *dies juvenalis*—that gained civic importance when a military defeat in 217 B.C.E. inspired a religious revival. After the religious ceremonies of the Saturnalia came celebration, feasting, and merriment. Civic work was suspended, courts and schools closed, and commerce and warfare stopped.

We can find useful information on the Roman winter solstice celebrations on Circle's Web site. In addition to Saturn, the Romans honored Ops, Sol Invicta, Mithra, Consus, Juventas, and Janus. Saturnalia is echoed in today's holiday celebrations, religious rituals, honored figures (Santa Claus, Father Time), sacred flames (candles and bonfires), greens (the decorated tree, wreaths, garlands), time off from work, gift giving, feasting, helping the less fortunate, and exuberant play.

Reader, organize your own Saturnalia this year. Sing pagan versions of Christmas carols and have a lovely feast. More important, think of people who are living in the dark—homeless people, battered women and children, people in nursing homes and hospitals. How can we bring cheer to these people?

Saturnalia: A Christmas Carol

❖

> [Scrooge asked], "But why do spirits walk the earth, and
> why do they come to me?"
>
> "It is required of every man," [Marley's] Ghost
> returned, "that the spirit within him should walk abroad
> among his fellowmen, and travel far and wide; and if that
> spirit goes not forth in life, it is condemned to do so
> after death. It is doomed to wander through the world . . .
> and witness what it cannot share, but might have shared
> on earth, and turned to happiness!"
> —Charles Dickens, *A Christmas Carol*

There's no way *A Christmas Carol* (1843) can be considered a pagan
classic, but if we read it closely we can see that the muscular Victorian
Christianity of the book foreshadows our modern pagan belief in spiritual
awakening. If we're willing to indulge in personal and literary excavation,
in fact, and to connect ideas that don't appear to have any connection, we
can find pagan applications in nearly anything we read. It just takes some
knowledge of metaphysics and a nimble imagination.

In his book *Transforming Scrooge*, psychotherapist Joseph D. Cusamano
writes, "There is no doubt that the three . . . ghosts were performing inten-
sive, brief, experiential psychospiritual therapy to free [Scrooge] from
the bonds of the past." Scrooge's experience is like a kundalini opening. It
shatters the chains of his miserable, lonely childhood and his miserly, solitary adulthood and leads him into "a new-found spiritual attitude about his
own life and a caring concern for the general welfare of the planet."[27]

What lessons can the Ghosts of Christmas Past, Present, and Future
teach us? Although we don't celebrate Christmas as Christians do, we celebrate the winter holiday. We know that spirits walk upon the earth at the
solstice. Just because we're pagans, should we abandon the old, familiar
holidays?

Saturnalia: Ops

❖

We get our word *opulence* from the name of Saturn's consort, the grain, fruit, and harvest goddess who is also associated, Patricia Monaghan says, with the god Consus, "'ruler of conservation of the grain that Ops brought to her people."

It's possible that worship of Ops has been misconstrued. One of the books I'm editing is about "affluenza." Advertising teaches us, the author says, that shopping is not only a major pastime, but also an almost religious rite/right. Except now it's a disease that has metastasized throughout the body of society. Affluenza isn't a new idea, however. The Roman Senate passed sumptuary laws, setting limits to what Romans could own (and show off). The laws didn't work. Medieval monarchs, including popes, tried passing similar laws, and we know that one motivation for the Protestant Reformation was to protest against the Vatican's wealth and greed. The robber barons of late nineteenth century were great *opulists*, and we see how their descendants—The Donald, Gordon Gecko—live today.

Reader, wealth is not bad, but we need to spend our money wisely. I don't know about you, but I don't live on trust funds or stock dividends. I earn my money and live thriftily. I think all pagans do. We share and recycle and have give-aways.

This holiday season let's be Opulists. We can do magical work. When I walk I pick up any coin I see lying on the sidewalk. When I get home, I lay the coin on my Fortuna altar and say, "For those in need." (Which can include me.) One penny isn't much, but pennies add up. What other Opulistic work can we do? We can also donate things we don't need to shelters for people who do need them. Ops was a goddess of grain and fruit; we can also make donations to feed people.

Saturnalia:
The Yule Tree, the World Tree

❈

Our familiar decorated Christmas tree comes to us from Germany by
way of Victorian England. When Prince Albert came to England in 1840
to marry young Queen Victoria, he brought a number of holiday customs
with him.

When I wrote a women-only party back in March, I promised I'd give
men a night for their own party. I've never been to a boys' night out and
don't want to suggest macho activities, so how about decorating the holiday tree? The AEGSA Roman calendar Web site tells us that the Romans
exchanged gifts at the Saturnalia, including candles, clay doll-like figures,
and *strenae*, boughs of trees to which cakes and candies were tied.

In *The Rites of Odin*, Ed Fitch says, "It is often rewarding to decorate the
Yule tree so that it reflects Yggdrasill, the mythic World Tree." We can trim
the tree "as normal," but add a bright star (the North Star) and an eagle for
Odin, giver of victory and wisdom, at the top. In the upper branches,
place Valkyries and swan maidens and lots of stars and lights. At the base
of the tree should be a cave with the earth dragon, images of the Three
Norns, a pool (use a mirror), and a cauldron. Reindeer can stand in the
snow around the base of the tree and squirrels can sit in the branches. A
manger is also appropriate for Mother Frigga and her newborn son, "the
promise of the new year." A pair of wolves can guard them, and the "three
male wanderers" can be Odin, Thor, and Loki bringing gifts to Frigga's
Sacred Child.[28]

I know other pagans who decorate their holiday trees with multitudes
of glass fruits and vegetables, tiny animals and birds, runes and sigils, and
bells and lights, and tiny wrapped gifts.

Temple of Diana

❖

The Temple of Diana was founded on the winter solstice, 2000, in Madison, Wisconsin, by Ruth Barrett, high priestess emerita of Los Angeles's Circle of Aradia. Ruth, who is famous for her music and beautiful rituals, travels around the United States with her partner to teach classes in women's mysteries and lead Dianic rituals.

The Temple of Diana is a national feminist, Dianic Wiccan organization dedicated to celebrating women's magic and mysteries. It provides religious services and classes that nurture women's spiritual needs in the Dianic tradition, as revived by Z. Budapest (who ordained Ruth) in the early 1970s.

The Dianic tradition is named after the Roman goddess of the moon and guardian of women and nature. Diana was originally an Italian sky goddess and part of a trinity that included Egeria (a minor water goddess) and Virbius (an otherwise unknown woodland god). This trinity lived in the Wood of Nemi, where runaway slaves fought to secure the Golden Bough (mistletoe) and become Diana's priests. She has been conflated with the Greek goddess, Artemis, twin sister and midwife to Apollo. Artemis is older and more complex than Diana. In one aspect, she was the familiar moon goddess, in another, the guardian of the woodlands and mistress of the animals. In a third aspect, she was the many-breasted Artemis of Ephesus. Finally, Artemis was a goddess of the Amazons. Dianics capitalize on all aspects of the Diana-Artemis combination, working to heal (overthrow) the patriarchy and preserve and revive feminist mysteries.

I once met a woman who told me that the only "real Dianics" were those in her tradition, which dates back to the fifth century B.C.E. and split in the first century, some going along one multi-god path, others henceforward worshipping only Diana.

Sun in Capricorn

❖

Capricorn, Lilith the astrologer says, likes a sense of order. Web sites I visited say Capricorn is the most stable of the zodiacal types. They're people who are strong willed, serious, good in business. Like mountain goats, they climb across rocky terrain to reach the heights of achievement. Capricorn is ruled by Saturn, whom astrologers see as a karmic lord of discipline and limitations, a teacher of difficult lessons.

This Saturn doesn't seem to be the same as the god of an agricultural golden age who rules the Saturnalia. Not being an astrologer, all I can figure out is that astrologers must see Saturn in his aspect as Cronus, the Greek Titan who swallowed his children. *Cronus*, "crow," is not, however, cognate to *chronos*, "time." The "time" words begin with *ch* (the Greek letter *chi*). "Crone" isn't a time word either; it comes from the Dutch *kronje*, "carrion." "Xmas," by the way, is not just a way to secularize the word *Christmas*, "Christ's Mass." The *X* is *chi*, also the first letter in the word *Christos*, making *Xmas* an abbreviation. The etymology of *Capricorn* is clearer. *Capra* is the genus name for goats, and *cornus* means "horn," as in *cornucopia*, "horn of plenty." Some Web sites write vaguely about sea-goats and the fish tail, saying Capricorn is half dolphin.

Hey, it's the sixth day of Saturnalia. Let's not worry about discipline or limits. We can start building a new golden age. Let's send holiday greetings to friends, former friends, and, if we can find them, lost friends. The AEGSA Roman Calendar reminds us that temples provided feasts to the poor. Let's make a symbolic cornucopia and fill it with gifts. Let's go around committing random acts of kindness. I like the idea of playing kindness forward.

Blank Day in the Celtic Tree Calendar

❁

Our earliest hominid ancestors were born in East Africa about seven million years ago and evolved to become *homo sapiens* during the Pleistocene epoch, about one million years ago. The hominid "mitochondrial Eve" from whom everyone living on the planet today is descended, lived about one hundred fifty thousand years ago.

The true Garden of Eden, Lucia Chiavola Birnbaum writes in *dark mother: african origins and godmothers*, was Africa's Rift Valley. About fifty thousand years ago, humans began walking out of Africa. They walked north, turned right, and walked across Asia. They walked north, turned left, and walked across Europe. Their travels took a long, long time.

They carried their goddess with them. Because they came from Africa, their goddess was black. As the peoples' skins became lighter, so did their goddesses, but we still find Black Virgins, not only in the deepest layers of our consciousness but also deep down under our cathedrals. The eldest goddess was black. She was black, as the Song of Solomon says, and she was comely, and the sun looked down upon her. Her children loved and worshipped her for as long as they lived. Birnbaum writes that we need to find our dark mother again. "The next step toward religious understanding, and a just world, [is] to bring her to public knowledge and public evidence that verifies that all of us descend from an african dark mother."[29]

The goddess figures we buy today are white. It's time to reclaim the black goddess. Buy a goddess or select one from your collection. Buy a dollar bottle of black model paint and a small brush. Paint your goddess black. As you're painting, think about how you feel about painting a goddess. How do you feel about making what once was white, black? Now paint another goddess black.

Modraniht

If we have Mother's Day in the springtime, it seems only fair that we should celebrate Mother's Night in the winter.

We get Mothers' Night from the English monk, Bede, who said that the Angles began their year on the night of December 24–25. We don't know if he was reporting on a custom that honored three goddesses called the Mothers or referring to Christmas, newly arrived in Germanic lands. In 706, the Church forbade believers to follow the old Roman ceremonies honoring the confinement of the Mother of God, which included the distribution of cakes called *placentae* (the Divine Mother's afterbirth). Christmas Eve became the night of the Virgin Mother.

Tonight is probably the night we go home to our own mothers. (If I were cynical, I'd add, ". . . at least if we want our Christmas presents.") Reader, I'm guessing that your birth family is not pagan. I'm guessing they don't understand what you're up to with your talk of solar gods and solstices. I'm further guessing that Mom and Dad still invite you to go to the midnight service with them.

Go to church with them. Your mother has cooked for you. She's shopped for you. We pagans are pantheists and panentheists. We see deity everywhere. Why not in a Christian church on the night their god was born? Go to church and enjoy the ritual and the singing. Don't argue theology. Don't announce that Jesus may be mythological and if he was a real person, he was probably born in the spring or in the fall between 7 and 4 B.C.E. If we can agree that other pagans can celebrate their gods in their ways, why can't we extend that privilege to Mom and Dad? Keep peace in the family. Go to church with them.

Merry Christmas to one and all.

Solar Gods

❖

Today is near enough to the winter solstice to mark the birth of a whole crew of solar and grain gods: Adonis, Amon-Ra, Apollo, Attis, Baal, Horus, Jesus, Lugh, Marduk, Mithra, Shamash, Sol Invictus. These are gods who live for a season in great honor. They are sacrificed, spend a season underground, and are reborn.

Sol Invictus, the Unconquered Sun, was the chosen god of Constantine, whose famous vision told him to "conquer in the sign of the cross." Constantine prayed to Sol Invictus and his battle cry was an ambiguous *Deus summus salvator* ("God the highest, Savior"). People were supposed to think Sol Invictus was just the Latin name for the Christ, and Christians in his army thus called themselves "soldiers of Christ." Sol, a Latin sun god often identified with Helios, had been worshipped by an earlier emperor, Aurelian, who established a cult and a feast to be celebrated on the Campus Agrippa on the winter solstice. Aurelian's Sol Invictus was probably the Syrian solar god, El Gabel. Early in the third century, one of Rome's emperors was a Syrian sun-worshipper who renamed himself Heliogabalus.

Mithra (also spelled Mithras) is an Indo-Iranian solar god, partly derived from the Hindu pantheon. He is the god of the airy light between heaven and earth, one of the Persian *yazatas* ruled by Ahura-Mazda. Belgian scholar Franz Cumont wrote that the Roman Mithras was the same as the Zoroastrian Mithra. The Roman mystery cult of Mithras arose in the first century C.E. among legionnaires stationed in Asia Minor and spread throughout the empire.

By the fourth century, the Roman Brumalia (winter solstice festival), Sol Invictus, and Mithra had come to be associated with the birth of Jesus. In 354, Bishop Liberius of Rome moved the birthdate of Jesus to match the date of Mithra's birth.

Haloa, Horus, Yule, Kwanzaa

❖

The Haloa was an Attic harvest festival named for the *halos*, or thresh-ing floor. This festival, originally sacred to Poseidon, involved a ritual pro-cession from Athens to Eleusis in honor of Demeter and Dionysus. Vines were pruned, the magistrates at Eleusis prepared a feast for the female cele-brants—married women, no men allowed—and the day was spent in ritual obscenity and fun. Z. Budapest has recreated the Haloa for modern women.

Horus (Hor), the Egyptian falcon-headed son of Isis and Osiris, is a solar god identified by the Greeks and Romans with Apollo and born on the winter solstice. The *Larousse Encyclopedia of Mythology* identifies twenty Horuses, all in some way identified with the sky in which the falcon flies.

In northern Europe, Yule originally meant the two-month period of December and January, and according to some sources, there was a "first yule" in November. By about 800, Yule was coming to be a feast held around the time of the solstice, and a century later, King Hakon the Good of Norway (940–963) declared that Yule, sometimes called Winter Nights, should be held at the same time that Christians celebrate their holiday. By 1000, Yule had become a major feast. Our modern pagan holiday is in many ways modeled on Germanic customs.

Kwanzaa is a modern seven-day African-American festival established by Dr. Maulana Karenga, who wanted to affirm the community and values of the African diaspora by teaching African cultural values: *Umoja* (Unity), *Kuji-chagulia* (Self-determination), *Ujima* (Collective Work and Responsibility), *Ujamaa* (Cooperative Economics), *Nia* (Purpose), *Kuumba* (Creativity), and *Imani* (Faith). As we know, this is not a religious festival, but the official Kwanzaa Web site says that Kwanzaa has a universal message of goodwill for all people.

Circle of Aradia

❖

Diana moves with strength and will / To bend the arrow's bow.
Sending it true into the heart, / Of all we see and do.
For She is every woman born, / The Mother of All Life.
We must remember who we are, / We must take back the night!
—Ruth Barrett, *Every Woman Born*

The Circle of Aradia (COA), consecrated on this date in 1993 by the
Re-Formed Congregation of the Goddess, was founded in Los Angeles in
April, 1988, by Dianic High Priestess Ruth Barrett and members of Ruth's
first coven, Moon Birch Grove (which still meets in Pasadena). COA is a
nonprofit religious-educational organization that is "Goddess-focused, with
rituals focusing on the celebration of women's mysteries." Its magical practices are "aligned with feminist visions of an egalitarian and healed world,
free of patriarchal violence toward women, animals, and the earth."
Because Dianic Witchcraft is a teaching tradition, Ruth chose the name of
her new group to honor Aradia, said to be the first female avatar, sent to
earth during the Middle Ages to teach witchcraft to the oppressed. By
1993, Ruth was leading six public rituals a year, teaching classes in Dianic
Witchcraft, and giving concerts.

I attended my first COA ritual at the 1996 winter solstice. The women
looked like goddesses in their long gowns of silver and white and red. As
part of the ritual, the lights were turned out to symbolize the darkness of
the long winter's night. Then a priestess danced, holding a glowing globe
over her head. Two hundred women were present that night, and every
eye was on the dancer and her dance and the light bobbing and weaving
around the circle as Ruth sang to welcome the rebirth of the light.

The Horae

❖

The Horae, "hours" or "seasons," were at first a group of weather goddesses responsible for rain. Sometimes there were two Horae, Thallo and Carpo (spring and autumn), though Hesiod says there were three— Eunomia ("lawful order"), Dike ("justice"), and Eirene or Irene ("peace"). Sometimes they personified the natural order and the yearly cycle. Daughters of Themis, they were Hera's stepmothers. They also greeted Aphrodite when she came ashore at Cythera (as shown in Botticelli's famous painting) and danced with the Graces.

Thornton Wilder, author of *Our Town* and *The Matchmaker*, wrote a Pulitzer Prize-winning play called *The Skin of Our Teeth* (1942), which is too seldom performed. (In 1983, it was the first stage play broadcast live on television.) It's a surrealistic, hilarious play that tells the story of Mr. and Mrs. Antrobus, their children, and their maid, Sabina. They're a typical American family living in New Jersey; at the same time, they are Adam, Eve, Lilith, and Cain. They invent things like the wheel and the apron.

There is a lovely scene in the third act. As the Antrobuses return from war, twelve Horae parade across the stage in disguise as philosophers. Their message is one of optimism and hope: even though we have to start all over again, we will survive. "We're learning," Mr. Antrobus says a bit later as he picks up a few books that have survived the devastation, "and the steps of our journey are marked for us here."

Reader, we're nearly at the end of our year together. We've seen goddesses and gods, philosophers and poets and playwrights march across the pages of this book. Like Janus, let's look back and ahead. What has been our pagan path to the present? Where will pagans stand in the world in the twenty-first century?

Australian Goddess Temple

❖

Here I am, nearly at the end of this book—and I've just found another Goddess temple. This one is in Australia. On the temple's Web site (*www.herwill.net*), Anique Radiant Heart, the priestess, tells us that she was born in Egypt of French/Lebanese/Jewish parents. When her family was forced to emigrate in 1956, they settled in Australia. She discovered feminism in the 1970s, went to her first Goddess workshop in the 1980s, and—like many of us—has never looked back. What has Anique learned about the Goddess? "That her message was simple: honour the Earth and all that lives upon her, honour the sky and all that lives within her, honour the oceans and all that lives within her, and honour the feminine, from which all life flows."

After visiting the Sekhmet Temple in Nevada, Anique understood that Australia needed "at least one temple," a place of power where people can connect with the divine. The Australian Goddess Temple is still a work in progress. It is currently housed in a shed decorated with a banner of an enormous Willendorf Mother behind the main altar. Anique is raising money to buy land for a permanent building. As you explore the Web site, you see the photos and read the story of how this temple is being built on faith, donations, and the goodwill of men and women, plus proceeds from the sale of Anique's goddess art.

Reader, we need to support our modern temples. The standard-brand churches appeal to believers and rake in millions of dollars. Why shouldn't the Goddess temples receive just as many "green blessings"?

Perchta

❖

Perchta is a Slavonic Bride of the Sun and a mother goddess in Germany, Switzerland, and Austria. Her favorite time of the year is the "twelve days of Christmas," which end on her day. On Perchta's Day, everyone eats pancakes and drinks milk. Smart people leave bits of pancake and milk for the goddess, who comes at night to enjoy her own private feast. If you spy on her, though, she'll blind you. The rest of the year, she floats on a soft mist across the fields to make them fertile.

We've come nearly to the end of the year, to its midnight, its eldest days. Everything seems old, old, old. This is the season of the crone, the hag. *Hag* comes from *hagia* and means "holy." The hag is the Holy One. In Northern Europe, hags, called Volvas, were sibyls; an important Icelandic text is the *Voluspa*, "Sibyl's Vision." In the Netherlands, Dutch wise women were called the *Hagadissae*, and they gave their name to the capital of the country, *Den Haag* (today The Hague). Fancy that—a capital city named for old women!

Reader, isn't it splendid that our culture is starting to acknowledge elderly women as wise, beautiful, and beneficial? Consider Jessica Tandy, who earned her Oscar at age eighty-one, and Julia Child, who was cooking until the end of her life. Thanks, of course, to the aging of the baby-boom generation, crones and sages (some of whom are, alas, not wise) are a big market nowadays.

Ten years ago, I took a "croning class" in which there were women in their twenties and thirties. They said, "Crone is a state of mind." That wouldn't happen today. I have perhaps twenty-five books on crones on my shelf. Aging writers are producing books of new and useful wisdom.

...DECEMBER 31...
New Years Eve

❖

In Japan, the last day of the year is called *Omisoka*. People clean their houses. On each side of the front door, they place a decoration called a *kadomatsu* made of pine branches, bamboo, and straw; it's said to attract good fortune to the house. To bring happiness and chase away bad spirits, they also hang a decoration called a *shimekazari* above the door. On New Year's Eve, they eat buckwheat noodles (as people in the United States eat black-eyed peas) for prosperity and luck, then go to their temples and shrines to make offering to their Buddhist or Shinto deities. At midnight, the bell in every Buddhist temple rings 108 times to announce the turning of the year. The number 108 signifies the number of sins with which mankind is afflicted; the ringing of the bell liberates us from our baser instincts.

In Europe, people go wassailing on New Year's Eve. At midnight, the "first-footer" crosses the threshold, carrying a sprig of mistletoe or a gift of bread, salt, coal, or kindling. The first-footer is welcomed with a moment of silence, then everyone wishes each other a happy new year.

Reader, instead of watching football and getting ready for post-holiday shopping, let's combine the Japanese and European customs. I think starting the new year with a clean house is a splendid idea. It's good feng shui that also shows our house spirits our intention for the coming year. (Maybe it will inspire our family to neatness, too.) We can devise our own version of the *kadomatsu* and *shimekazari* to decorate the front door. When we have our ritual/party, we can designate a friend to be the first-footer. This person can bring a small symbolic gift—a bit of sacred salt, a candle, a sprig of fresh mistletoe—to everyone present.

... J A N U A R Y   1 ...

A Year and a Day

❖

> It is the individual readers who matter most, for in their
> eyes resides the worth of writing. Writing is not survival
> of the fittest but survival of the survivor.
> —Matthew Pearl, *The Dante Club*

Reader, we've just spent a year and a day together. We've come clear
around the wheel of the year. I've written about more feasts and festivals
than I ever knew existed and learned a great deal. I hope you did, too. I
had enormous fun writing this book. I hope you enjoyed reading it.

You can start the year over again with this book, or you can buy a new
book for a new year. Or *you can write your own book.* Maybe it can be a journal in disguise or your *Artist's Way* morning pages put together.

Begin by either buying a three-ring binder and lots of lined paper or
setting up a new file on your computer. Write "January 1." What's your
new year's inspiration?

Reading my book, you found out what interests me—literature, history,
music, movies. What interests you? Are you an artist? A sports fan? A scientist? A technowizard? You're probably already familiar with significant
events in your areas of interest, but it's always possible to learn more.

You can find useful resources in my list of sources to get you started.
Do searches on Google and Wikipedia, where you'll get long lists of
events, births, deaths, and holidays. If you want to open your days with
words of wisdom, consult *Bartlett's Quotations*. There's no good reason why
you can't create your own book. With on-demand publishing, you can
publish it, too.

NOTES

1 Bernstein, *Classical Living*, 29.

2 Monaghan, *The Red-Haired Girl from the Bog*, 154–155.

3 Monaghan, *O Mother Sun*, 3.

4 See *www.iranchamber.com/religions*.

5 Graves, "Greek Mythology," *Larousse Encyclopedia of Mythology*, 133.

6 Lord, *Forever Barbie*, 6.

7 Chicago, *The Dinner Party*, 58–59.

8 Goodall, *Reason for Hope*, 242.

9 Jade, *To Know*, 18–19.

10 Dawson and Brechin, *Farewell, Promised Land*, xi.

11 Campbell, *The Hero With a Thousand Faces*, 3.

12 McIntyre, *Flower Power*, 265.

13 Welch, *Goddess of the North*, 102–104.

14 Fortune, *Glastonbury*, *passim*.

15 Hall, *Secret Teachings of All Ages*, cvii.

16 Cameron, *The Artist's Way*, 3.

17 Graves, trans. *The Golder Age*, 264.

18 Leland, *Aradia*, *passim*.

19 Graves, *The Greek Myths*, section 36a, 134.

20 Siegel, et al., *The Jewish Catalog*, 123–124.

21 Miss Piggy, *Miss Piggy's Guide to Life*, 24.

22 Budapest, *The Grandmother of Time*, 206–207.

23 Kidd, *The Secret Life of Bees*, 63

24 Dumars and Nyx, *The Dark Archetype*, 14.

25 Farrar, *The Witches' God*, 105.

26 Jade, *To Know*, 102–103.

27 Cusamano, *Transforming Scrooge*, 2.

28 Fitch, *The Rites of Odin*, 178–179.

29 Birnbaum, *dark mother*, 26.

LISTS OF SOURCES
Useful Books (and One Article)

Ardinger, Barbara. *Finding New Goddesses: Reclaiming Playfulness in Our Spiritual Lives*. Toronto: ECW Press, 2003.

Artress, Lauren. *Walking a Sacred Path: Rediscovering the Labyrinth as a Spiritual Tool*. New York: Riverhead Books, 1995.

Awiatka, Marilou. *Selu: Seeking the Corn-Mother's Wisdom*. Golden, CO: Fulcrum Publishing, 1993.

Ballou, Robert O., ed. *The Viking Portable Library World Bible*. New York: Viking Press, 1966.

Bates, Brian. *The Real Middle Earth: Exploring the Magic and Mystery of the Middle Ages, J.R.R. Tolkien, and "The Lord of the Rings."* New York: Palgrave Macmillan, 2002.

Bernal, Martin. *Black Athena: The Afroasiatic Roots of Classical Literature.* Volume I: *The Fabrication of Ancient Greece 1785-1985*. New Brunswick, NJ: Rutgers University Press, 1987.

Bernstein, Frances. *Classical Living: Reconnecting with the Rituals of Ancient Rome; Myths, Gods, Goddesses, Celebrations, and Rites for Every Month of the Year*. San Francisco: Harper San Francisco, 2000.

Biedermann, Hans. *Dictionary of Symbolism: Cultural Icons and the Meanings Behind Them*. Translated by James Hulbert. New York: Facts on File, Inc., 1992.

Birnbaum, Lucia Chiavola. *dark mother: african origins and godmothers*. San Jose, CA: Authors Choice Press, 2001.

Bogdanovich, Peter, ed. *A Year and a Day Engagement Calendar: Adapted from the Works of Robert Graves*. Woodstock, NY: Overlook Press, 1993.

Brewer, Ebenezer Cobham. *The Wordsworth Dictionary of Phrase & Fable*. 1870. Revised by Ivor H. Evans. London: Cassell & Co., Ltd., 1994.

Budapest, Zsuzsanna E. *The Grandmother of Time: A Women's Book of Celebrations, Spells, and Sacred Objects for Every Month of the Year*. New York: Harper & Row, 1989.

Cameron, Julia. *The Artist's Way: A Spiritual Path to Higher Creativity*. New York: Jeremy P. Tarcher/Putnam, 1992.

Campbell, Joseph. *The Hero With a Thousand Faces*. Bollingen Series XVII. Princeton, NJ: Princeton University Press, 1968.

Chicago, Judy. *The Dinner Party: A Commemorative Volume Celebrating a Major Monument of Twentieth-Century Art.* Photography by Donald Woodman. New York: Penguin Books, 1996.

Churton, Tobias. *Gnostic Philosophy: From Ancient Persia to Modern Times.* Rochester, VT: Inner Traditions, 2005.

Christ, Carol P. *She Who Changes: Re-Imaging the Divine in the World.* New York: Palgrave Macmillan, 2003.

Cirlot, J. E. *A Dictionary of Symbols.* Translated by Jack Sage. New York: Philosophical Library, 1962.

Conn, Eileen, and James Stewart, eds. *Visions of Creation.* Aylesford, Hants., U.K.: Godsfield Press, 1995.

Cooper, J. C. *The Aquarian Dictionary of Festivals.* London: Aquarian Press, 1990.

Cotterell, Arthur, ed. *World Mythology.* Bath, U.K.: Paragon Publishing, 2003.

Cunningham, Elizabeth. *The Passion of Mary Magdalen.* Rhinebeck, NY: Monkfish Book Publishing Co., 2006.

Cusamano, Joseph D. *Transforming Scrooge: Dickens' Blueprint for a Spiritual Awakening.* St. Paul, MN: Llewellyn Publications, 1996.

Daly, Mary, and Jane Caputi. *Websters' First New Intergalactic Wickedary of the English Language.* Boston: Beacon Press, 1987.

Davis, Philip G. *Goddess Unmasked: The Rise of Neopagan Feminist Spirituality.* Dallas: Spence Publishing Co., 1998.

Dawson, Robert, and Gray Brechin. *Farewell, Promised Land: Waking from the California Dream.* Berkeley, University of California Press, 1999.

Dexter, Miriam Robbins. *Whence the Goddesses: A Source Book.* Athene Series. New York: Pergamon Press, 1990.

Dreher, Diane. *Inner Gardening: Four Seasons of Cultivating the Soil and the Spirit.* New York: William Morrow, 2001.

Dumars, Denise, and Lori Nyx. *The Dark Archetype: Exploring the Shadow Side of the Divine.* Franklin Lakes, NJ: New Page Books, 2003.

Durant, Will. *Our Oriental Heritage. The Story of Civilization.* Vol. 1. New York: Simon and Schuster, 1954.

———. *The Life of Greece. The Story of Civilization.* Vol. 2. New York: Simon and Schuster, 1966.

————. *Caesar and Christ. The Story of Civilization.* Vol. 3. New York: Simon and Schuster, 1972.

Durdin-Robertson, Lawrence. *The Year of the Goddess: A Perpetual Calender* [sic.] *of Festivals.* London: Aquarian Press, 1990.

Eilers, Dana D. *Pagans and the Law: Understand Your Rights.* Franklin Lakes, NJ: New Page, 2003.

Ely, Richard. "The Nine Layers of Gaia." *PanGaia*, No. 13 (Autumn, 1997).(Richard says we can find the article online at *www.enlightenment.com.*)

Farrar, Janet and Stewart. *The Witches' God.* Custer, WA: Phoenix Publishing House, 1989.

————. *The Witches' Goddess.* Custer, WA: Phoenix Publishing House, 1987.

Feder, Lillian, ed. *Crowell's Handbook of Classical Literature.* New York: Thomas Y. Crowell Co., 1964.

Ferguson, Diane. *The Magickal Year: A Pagan Perspective on the Natural World.* York Beach, ME: Samuel Weiser, 1996.

Fitch, Ed. *The Rites of Odin.* St. Paul, MN: Llewellyn Publications, 1996.

Fortune, Dion. *Avalon of the Heart.* 1934. Reprinted as *Glastonbury.* Wellingborough, U.K.: Aquarian Press, 1989.

Gachot, Theodore. *Mermaids: Nymphs of the Sea.* Photography by Leah Demchick. San Francisco: HarperCollins, 1996.

Galland, China. *Longing for Darkness: Tara and the Black Madonna, a Ten-Year Journey.* New York: Viking, 1990.

Gedge, Pauline. *Child of the Morning.* The Hera Series. New York: Soho Press, 1977.

Gimbutas, Marija. *The Living Goddesses.* Edited and supplemented by Miriam Robbins Dexter. Berkeley: University of California Press, 1999.

Goodall, Jane. *Reason for Hope: A Spiritual Journey.* With Phillip Berman. New York: Warner Books, 1999.

Graves, Robert. *The Greek Myths: A Retelling of the Stories of the Greek Gods and Heroes, Embodying the Conclusions of Modern Anthropology and Archaeology.* New York: George Braziller, 1955.

Grey Cat. *Deepening Witchcraft: Advancing Skills & Knowledge.* Toronto: ECW Press, 2002.

————. *The Golden Ass: The Transformation of Lucius*. New York: Farrar, Strauss & Giroux, 1951.

Hall, Manly P. *The Secret Teachings of All Ages: An Encyclopedia Outline of Masonic, Hermetic, Qabbalistic and Rosicrucian Symbolical Philosophy*, golden anniversary edition. Los Angeles: Philosophical Research Society, 1977.

Hart, Jack, et al. *The Old Heathen's Almanac, 2003*. Berkeley, CA: The Troth, 2003.

Haskins, Susan. *Mary Magdalen: Myth and Metaphor*. New York: Riverhead Books, 1993.

Hutton, Ronald. *The Triumph of the Moon: A History of Modern Pagan Witchcraft*. Oxford: Oxford University Press, 1999.

Jade. *To Know: A Guide to Women's Magic and Spirituality*. Oak Park, IL: Delphi Press, 1991.

Jones, Prudence, and Nigel Pennick. *A History of Pagan Europe*. London: Routledge, 1995.

Kidd, Sue Monk. *The Secret Life of Bees*. New York: Penguin Books, 2002.

Kirsch, Jonathan. *God Against the Gods: The History of the War Between Monotheism and Polytheism*. New York: Viking Compass, 2004.

Larousse Encyclopedia of Mythology. Introduction by Robert Graves. Translated by Richard Aldington and Delano Ames. London: Paul Hamlyn, 1965.

Lauck, Joanne Elizabeth. *The Voice of the Infinite in the Small: Re-Visioning the Insect-Human Connection*, revised ed. Boston: Shambhala, 2002.

Leeming, David and Margaret. *A Dictionary of Creation Myths*. New York: Oxford University Press, 1994.

Leland, Charles Godfrey. *Aradia or the Gospel of the Witches*. Self-published pamphlet, 1899.

Lord, M. G. *Forever Barbie: The Unauthorized Biography of a Real Doll*. New York: Avon Books, 1994.

Markova, Dawna. *The Open Mind: Exploring the 6 Patterns of Natural Intelligence*, Berkeley, CA: Conari: 1996.

Marks, William E. *The Holy Order of Water: Healing Earth's Waters and Ourselves*. Great Barrington, MA: Bell Pond Books, 2001.

Matthews, John, ed. *The World Atlas of Divination: The Systems, Where They Originate, How They Work*. A Bullfinch Press Book. Boston: Little, Brown, 1992.

McIntyre, Anne. *Flower Power: Flower Remedies for Healing Body and Soul Through Herbalism, Homeopathy, Aromatherapy, and Flower Essences*. New York: Henry Holt, 1996.

———. *The Red-Haired Girl from the Bog: The Landscape of Celtic Myth and Spirit*. Novato, CA: New World Library, 2003.

Monaghan, Patricia. *The New Book of Goddesses and Heroines*. St. Paul, MN: Llewellyn Publications, 1997.

———. *O Mother Sun! A New View of the Cosmic Feminine*. Freedom, CA: Crossing Press, 1994.

Nabarz, Payam. *The Mysteries of Mithras: The Pagan Belief That Shaped the Christian World*. Rochester, VT: Inner Traditions, 2005.

Pagram, Beverly. *Heaven & Hearth: A Seasonal Compendium of Women's Spiritual and Domestic Lore*. London: Women's Press, 1997.

Pennick, Nigel. *The Pagan Book of Days: A Guide to the Festivals, Traditions, and Sacred Days of the Year*. Rochester, VT: Destiny Books, 1992.

Piggy, Miss. *Miss Piggy's Guide to Life*. As told to Henry Beard. New York: Muppet Press/Alfred A. Knopf, 1981.

Pratchett, Terry. *Equal Rites, A Novel of Discworld*. New York: Penguin/ROC, 1987.

———. *Small Gods, A Novel of Discworld*. New York: HarperCollins, 1992.

———. *Wyrd Sisters, A Novel of Discworld*. New York: Penguin/ROC, 1990.

Schaup, Susanne. *Sophia: Aspects of the Divine Feminine*. York Beach, ME: Nicolas-Hays, 1997.

Schneider, Michael S. *A Beginner's Guide to Constructing the Universe: The Mathematical Archetypes of Nature, Art, and Science*. New York: Harper Perennial Book, 1995.

Seznec, Jean. *The Survival of the Pagan Gods: The Mythological Tradition and Its Place in Renaissance Humanism and Art*. 1940. Bollingen Series XXXVIII. Translated by Barbara F. Sessions. Princeton, NJ: Princeton University Press, 1972.

Siegel, Richard, et al., eds. *The Jewish Catalog: A Do-It-Yourself Kit*. Philadelphia: The Jewish Publication Society of America, 1973.

Spretnak, Charlene. *Lost Goddesses of Early Greece: A Collection of Pre-Hellenic Myths*. Boston: Beacon Press, 1978.

Stewart, Louis. *Life Forces: A Contemporary Guide to the Cult and Occult.* Kansas City: Andrews and McMeel, 1980.

Vinci, Felice. *The Baltic Origin of Homer's Epic Tales: The Iliad, the Odyssey and the Migration of Myth.* Rochester, VT: Inner Traditions, 2006.

Welch, Lynda C. *Goddess of the North: A Comprehensive Study of the Norse Goddesses from Antiquity to the Modern Age.* York Beach, ME: Samuel Weiser, 2001.

Wetterau, Bruce. *The New York Public Library Book of Chronologies.* A Stonesong Press Book. New York: Prentice Hall, 1990.

York, Michael. *Pagan Theology: Paganism as a World Religion.* New York: New York University Press, 2003.

Useful Web Sites

Adherents of world religions *www.adherents.com*

Ancient history (Egypt, Greece, Rome) *http://ancienthistory.about.com/*

Ardinger, Barbara *www.barbaraardinger.com*

Australian Goddess Temple *www.herwill.net*

Baha'i faith *www.bahai.org*

Barrett, Ruth, chants and CDs *www.dancingtree.org*

Beliefnet *http://beliefnet.com*

Beltane Papers, The www.thebeltanepapers.net

Bewitched www.bewitched.net

Budapest, Zsuzsanna, Dianic University *www.zbudapest.com*

Catholic Encyclopedia www.newadvent.org

Cherry Hill Seminary *http://cherryhillseminary.org*

Chinese Historical and Cultural Project *www.chcp.org*

Chinese religion in the twentieth century *http://philtar.ucsm.ac.uk/encyclopedia/china/hsien*

Church of All Worlds (CAW) *www.caw.org*

Circle Sanctuary *www.circlesanctuary.org*

Colbert, Joanna Powell, artist *www.jpc-artworks.com*

Covenant of the Goddess (CoG) *www.cog.org*

Fellowship of Isis (FOI) *www.fellowshipofisis.com*

Gentile, Norma *www.healingchants.com*

Glastonbury Goddess Temple *www.goddesstemple.co.uk*

Goddess Temple of Orange County, California
 www.goddesstempleoforangecounty.com

Grey School of Wizardry, Oberon Zell-Ravenheart *www.GreySchool.com*

HaMakom, Rabbi Malka Drucker *www.hamakomtheplace.org*

Henes, Donna, urban shaman *www.donnahenes.net* and *www.thequeenofmyself.com*

Internet Movie Database *www.imdb.com*

Iran Chamber Society *www.iranchamber.com/religions*

Iseum of Isis Paedusis *http://mywebpage.netscape.com/isispaedusis/*

Isis Oasis Sanctuary *www.isisoasis.org*

Jane Goodall Institute for Wildlife Research, Education and Conservation,
 www.janegoodall.org

Johnny Appleseed Festival *www.johnnyappleseedfest.com*

Kelly, Patricia, poetry and dreaming *http://roswilla-dreampoetry.blogspot.com/*

Lady Liberty League *www.ladylibertyleague.org*

Language of flowers *www.thegardener.btinternet.co.uk* and *www.victorianbazaar.com*

Lord of the Rings official site *www.lordoftherings.net*

Matrifocus www.matrifocus.com

Michael Ball Fan Club *www.mbfc.co.uk*

Mithraism *http://eawc.evansville.edu/essays/mithraism.htm*

Motherpeace, Vicki Noble, Karen Vogel *www.motherpeace.com*

Muppets *www.muppetcentral.com*

National Public Lands Day *www.npld.com*

Nevada Test Site *www.atomictourist.com*

newWitch www.newwitch.com

Oedipus and Akhnaton *http://home.att.net/~a.a.major/oedakhoutline.html*

Officers of Avalon *www.officersofavalon.com*

Operation Migration *www.operationmigration.org*

Oxford English Dictionary www.oed.com

Pagan Unity Campaign *www.paganunitycampaign.org*

PanGaia www.pangaia.com

Pratchett, Terry, Discworld Library *www.lspace.org*

Public Broadcasting Service (PBS) *www.pbs.org*

Rachel Carson Council *http://members.aol.com/rccouncil/ourpage/*

Reclaiming Collective *www.reclaiming.org*

Re-Formed Congregation of the Goddess, International *www.rcgi.org*

Roman calendar *www.clubs.psu.edu/up/aegsa/rome/romec.html*

Sacred Source *www.sacredsource.com*

SageWoman www.sagewoman.com

Shakespeare on PBS *www.pbs.org/wgbh/pages/frontline/shows/muchado* and *www.pbs.org/shakespeare/theshow/mike.html*

Sierra Club *www.sierraclub.org*

Sikhs *www.sikhnet.com*

Simon Wiesenthal Center, Museum of Tolerance *http://motlc.wiesenthal.com*

Star Wars www.starwars.com and *www.filmsite.org*

Stone Pages, *Archaeo News www.stonepages.com*

Tara Dance, Prema Dasara and Anahata Iradah *www.taradhatu.org*

Teen Witch Newsletter www.teenwitchonline.org

Temple of Diana *www.templeofdiana.org*

Temple of Sekhmet *www.sekhmettemple.com*

Theosophical Society in America *www.theosophical.org*

Trail of Tears *http://ngeorgia.com/history/nghisttt.html*

Twelve-step program *www.alcoholics-anonymous.org*

United Nations Universal Declaration of Human Rights *www.un.org/rights*

Velikovsky, Immanuel *www.knowledge.co.uk/velikovsky/oedipus.htm*

Veriditas, Voice of the Labyrinth Movement *www.veriditas.net*

Voice of the Witch *www.witchvox.com*

Wikipedia *http://en.wikipedia.org/wiki/Main_Page*

Wilderness Society *http://earthday.wilderness.org*

Wonder Woman *www.wonderwoman-online.com*

World Wildlife Fund (WWF) *http://worldwildlifefund.org*

Zoroastrianism *www.avesta.org* and *www.parsicommunity.com*

Zundell, Kathleen, storyteller *www.KathleenZundell.com*

ACKNOWLEDGMENTS

My first task is to thank the women at RedWheel/Weiser. Jan Johnson phoned me and said, "I like the way you write. Will you write a book for us?" Caroline Pincus said in an early email that she would rather work with obsessive authors (moi?) than with authors who don't care about the quality of their writing. She's helped me unscrew the inscrutable several times. Bonni Hamilton has been courteous and helpful with PR and courtesy copies I want to send to people who are in the book. Thank you!

Although an author sits alone at her keyboard (well, except when the cat is sitting on her lap between her and the keyboard), she is always connected to a network of friends. Maybe it's cyberenergy, maybe it's metaphysical energy, maybe it's just good vibes; it's always there. Some of the people who are always there for me are Ava Park and the community at the Goddess Temple, especially Letecia Monteil and Darcelle Foster; my sisters on the GoddessCreative and GoddessScholars lists; Nancy Blair; Elizabeth Cunningham, Miriam Robbins Dexter, Cristina Eisenberg, Michelle Gandy, Rayna Hamre, Margaret and Jon Harwood, Patricia Kelly, Kelly King, Sandra and Ron Lange, Lilith Mageborn, Alexis Masters, Nanette McLlellen, Valerie Meyer, Anne Niven, Chuck Pennington, Tim Roderick, Leah Samul, Patrick Sweeney, Teddy Tapscott, Marsha Smith Tomlinson, and Suzan Walter.

TO OUR READERS

Weiser Books, an imprint of Red Wheel/Weiser, publishes books across the entire spectrum of occult and esoteric subjects. Our mission is to publish quality books that will make a difference in people's lives without advocating any one particular path or field of study. We value the integrity, originality, and depth of knowledge of our authors.

Our readers are our most important resource, and we appreciate your input, suggestions, and ideas about what you would like to see published. Please feel free to contact us, to request our latest book catalog, or to be added to our mailing list.

Red Wheel/Weiser, LLC
500 Third Street, Suite 230
San Francisco, CA 94107
www.redwheelweiser.com